Where the Grizzly Walks

Books by Bill Schneider

Where the Grizzly Walks, 1977

Hiking Montana, coauthor, 1979

The Dakota Image, 1980

The Yellowstone River, 1985

The Flight of the Nez Perce, 1988

The Tree Giants, 1988

Hiking the Beartooths, 1995

Bear Aware: Hiking and Camping in Bear Country, 1996

Hiking Carlsbad Caverns and Guadalupe Mountains National Parks, 1996

Best Easy Day Hikes Canyonlands and Arches National Parks, 1997

Best Easy Day Hikes Yellowstone, 1997

Exploring Canyonlands and Arches National Parks, 1997

Hiking Yellowstone National Park, 1997

Backpacking Tips, coauthor, 1998

Best Easy Day Hikes Beartooths, 1998

Best Hikes on the Continental Divide, coauthor, 1988

Best Easy Day Hikes Grand Teton, 1999

Hiking Grand Teton National Park, 1999

Bear Aware: The Quick Reference Bear Country Survival Guide, rev. ed., 2001

Best Backpacking Vacations Northern Rockies, 2002

Best Easy Day Hikes Absaroka-Beartooth Wilderness, rev. ed., 2003

Hiking the Absaroka-Beartooth Wilderness, 2003

Learn more about Bill Schneider's books at www.billschneider.net.

Where the Grizzly Walks
The Future of the Great Bear

Bill Schneider

FALCON®

GUILFORD, CONNECTICUT
HELENA, MONTANA

AN IMPRINT OF THE GLOBE PEQUOT PRESS

Falcon and FalconGuide are registered trademarks of The Globe Pequot Press.

Text design: Mary Ballachino
Maps by Stefanie Ward © The Globe Pequot Press

Library of Congress Cataloging-in-Publication Data
Schneider, Bill.
    Where the grizzly walks: the future of the great bear / Bill Schneider.
    —1st ed.
        p. cm.
    Includes bibliographical references and index.
    ISBN 0-7627-2602-4
      1. Grizzly bear. I. Title
    QL737.C27S28 2003
    599.784—dc21

                                                    2003049102

Manufactured in the United States of America
First Edition/First Printing

To my daughter Heidi,
who has not seen a wild grizzly, yet

Contents

Foreword

There are almost as many books about grizzly bears as there are opinions about how we should manage them. People write about grizzly bears because no other species in the United States or Canada has a reputation that ranges from wilderness God to beastly killer. Writers have shared their experiences of raising grizzly bear cubs and then reintroducing them into the wild, of studying and discovering the details of grizzly bear biology and ecology, of hunting grizzlies, and even of shooing (not shooting) them out of their gardens. Lewis and Clark's experiences with grizzly bears were the first to capture the fascination of the nation. Some writers, looking to titillate readers, turned a superficial reading of the Lewis and Clark Expedition journals into myths, primarily about how aggressive these turn-of-the-nineteenth-century grizzlies might have been. Lately, careful scholarly study has been used to try to better understand grizzly bears as Lewis and Clark experienced them.

Our seemingly insatiable interest in grizzly bears has fueled a North America-wide effort to recover and maintain existing populations. Classification as a "threatened species" in the United States south of Canada in 1975 led to a major and sustained effort to recover at least some of these populations. In the short term this effort has been successful within the Yellowstone ecosystem, one of the crown jewels of America. Perhaps as fascinating as the grizzly bear are the biologists, bureaucrats, and conservationists whose careers are intertwined with grizzly bear recovery. Few books even touch this interesting aspect of the grizzly bear story. The first to do so was *Where the Grizzly Walks* by Bill Schneider, published in 1977. Schneider's passion for this topic did not subside, and now, twenty-six years later, he presents us with a thoroughly updated version of what people are doing in relation to grizzly bear recovery in the lower 48 states. Read about conservation battles as fierce as Custer's last stand, intertwined with reports of the latest scientific methods, including the use of DNA fingerprinting to identify, and occasionally convict, individual problem (victimized) bears without the waffling of OJ's trial. Meet the "grizzly czar," Dr. Chris Servheen, the scientist who holds bear-size power and takes responsibility, at the national level, for grizzly bear recovery. Meet such conservation activists as Hank Fischer, whose work with Defenders of Wildlife led to compensation payments for ranchers who lose stock to grizzly bear predation, and Louisa Wilcox, whose sharp, aggressive, and insightful efforts keep government scientists wondering what holes she will poke in their research and conservation plans. The new *Where the Grizzly Walks* is about the lives of people trying to make a difference for grizzly bears. It is also about people trying to leave their mark on history.

The great bear is probably unaware of these efforts. The grizzly lives as the embodiment of several million years of biological evolution during which there were few other species that could kill a grizzly save its cubs. Now there is only one species, humankind, that kills adult grizzlies, and we do it with shocking ability. Eighty to over 90 percent of adult grizzly bear mortality in the lower 48 is caused by people. Once the repeating rifle was introduced, the game was no longer one between somewhat equal players—grizzlies paw-to-hand with men armed with muzzleloaders and knives—but became a contest between people trying to figure out how to not kill the last grizzly in the lower 48 and those who continued to blast away. The lack of biological resilience—a species' ability to bounce back from excessive mortality—is a primary reason grizzly bear recovery is difficult. The Yellowstone experience shows that short-term recovery is possible, at least when the force of the Endangered Species Act is used. There are a lot of Americans, however, who don't like to be told what to do on their or public lands. Economic growth, the foundation of our society, has typically resulted in ever more development of land for profit. Somewhere in this inexorable equation grizzly bears need habitat without much human use. The future of grizzlies in the lower 48, the endangered wild heritage of the United States, rests on applying what we know about their biology within the context of human institutions and aspirations. As Bill Schneider writes, "the grizzly will walk where we allow it."

—Stephen Herrero, Professor Emeritus of
Environmental Science at the University of
Calgary and Chair, the Eastern Slopes
Grizzly Bear Project Steering Committee

Preface

The Reason for This Book

Over a long career in book publishing, I have always been amazed at the number of bear books in the marketplace. This reflects the degree of interest in these big hairy animals. I have, in fact, been heard to say that there has never been an unsuccessful bear book, but that might not be completely true. There probably are a few financial flops among the many hundreds that have been published, but not many, I can assure you.

While studying the long list of bear books, I've noticed a few interesting facts. Black bears, polar bears, and other bear species are well covered, of course, but by far most of the books are on the grizzly bear. Many of these books thoroughly cover the subjects of bear biology and behavior, the colorful history of man's discovery of the grizzly bear, how to travel safely in bear country, and various recounts of bear incidents, both historical and modern day. There is only one book about preserving the grizzly bear, and you're reading it. That was as true back in 1977 when I published the first *Where the Grizzly Walks* as it is in 2003 when this book went to print. Many bear books have sections advocating the preservation of the grizzly, but no other book devotes all its pages to how we can save the great bear from modern civilization.

Giving a future to the grizzly bear is a huge challenge for us. As explained in the pages that follow, it's impossible to keep bears and people apart. As the bear's only enemy (except bigger bears, of course), we relentlessly continue to penetrate every corner of the last wild places. The traditional wilderness home of the grizzly is now at or near its carrying capacity, and the bear population is expanding into rural communities and nontraditional habitat where there have been no grizzlies for decades. It's a setup for conflict.

But there has always been conflict between civilization and the grizzly bear. Lewis and Clark started it, and it has not gone away. A desire to solve this conflict motivated me to write the original book, and it compels me to write this new book, which is a nearly complete rewrite of the 1977 edition. Only the historical chapter, "The Passing of Old Ephraim," comes from this first edition. Since 1977 the details and issues involved in saving the grizzly have changed so much that a new book was required.

When I wrote the original book in the late-1970s, the grizzly population, at least south of Canada, was plummeting. Some bear experts thought they were watching the process of extinction. Then in the early 1980s, the grizzly population bottomed out and started to slowly rebuild. Now the grizzly is expanding its range into habitat it hasn't used in fifty years or more.

It's hard to figure which situation—a declining or an expanding grizzly population—is more controversial. As you'll learn as you read on, an expanding grizzly population hardly means the battle has been won and the big bear saved.

One thing that hasn't changed, however, is the bear people. The same people I interviewed in the 1970s are still at it, working hard every day to save the grizzly. It was fascinating to re-visit them and discuss how things have evolved.

Read on. You'll agree.

Acknowledgments

When I wrote the original book, I started out the acknowledgments by writing, "It's with some reservations that I list my name as author of *Where the Grizzly Walks* because so many people helped this book become reality." As I write this, twenty-five years later, that statement is doubly true.

I certainly couldn't have done it without the sincere cooperation of the "Bear People," the champions of the grizzly bear, a dedicated group of scientists, agency managers, and environmentalists. Without them the grizzly would be in big trouble—and this book would have been, too. They are Colleen Campbell, Dan Carney, John Craighead, Hank Fischer, Kevin Frey, Kerry Gunther, Caesar Hernandez, Steve Herrero, Chuck Jonkel, Jamie Jonkel, Kate Kendall, Mike Madel, Tim Manley, Gary Moses, Brian Peck, Andy Russell, Beth Russell-Towe, Bob Sandford, Chuck Schwartz, Chris Servheen, Chris Smith, John Varley, and Louisa Willcox.

Also helping me with the research were Pat Bigelow, Ken Britton, Jim Caswell, Dick Clark, Dusty Crary, Dan Crockett, Stacie DeWolf, Tom France, Steve Gale, Doug Honnold, Dirk Kempthorne, Heather Marstall, Ralph Maugan, Bob Peart, Jack Rich, Greg Schildwachter, Heidi Skaggs, Clarence Tabor, Bill Thomas, and Steve Wagner.

Special thanks to my eldest son, Russ, who has become quite the bear expert himself, and my wife, Marnie, for helping me in a thousand ways to get to the finish line.

Finally, many thanks to the people at The Globe Pequot Press—Jeff Serena, Gillian Belnap, and Melissa Evarts—for doing a great job editing, producing, and marketing the book.

Writing these acknowledgments after two years of work on this book brings back pleasant memories of all the people I met along the way. I sincerely hope I didn't forget anybody.

Prologue:
The Grizzly Landscape

This can't be only a book about bears. It must also be about people—their lifestyles, their government, their land, and their dreams.

—from *Where the Grizzly Walks* (1977)

The grizzly's problems started back in 1804 when Lewis and Clark began their amazing expedition from St. Louis, Missouri, to the Pacific Ocean. One of their great discoveries was the "white bear." They described the grizzly as a "monster bear and a most terrible enemy," and for no apparent reason killed about forty grizzlies along the way. Soon after the expedition the public became infatuated with the "terrible bear," and after two centuries of controversy, that fascination continues.

Ten years after the Lewis and Clark Expedition, taxonomist George Ord named the grizzly *Ursus horribilis,* or "horrible bear." Ord had never seen a grizzly bear dead or alive. Instead he based his nomenclature on information provided by Lewis and Clark. Ord magnified the bear's image with his "scientific" description of the grizzly. "He is an enemy of man," Ord wrote, "and literally thirsts for human blood." Later that taxonomic name was changed to *Ursus arctos horribilis* (northern horrible bear), but the reputation didn't change.

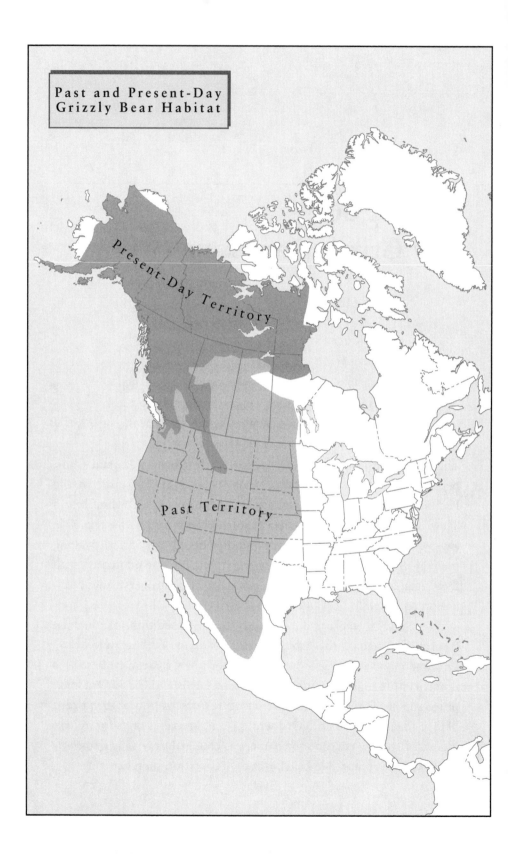

Past and Present-Day
Grizzly Bear Habitat

Present-Day Territory

Past Territory

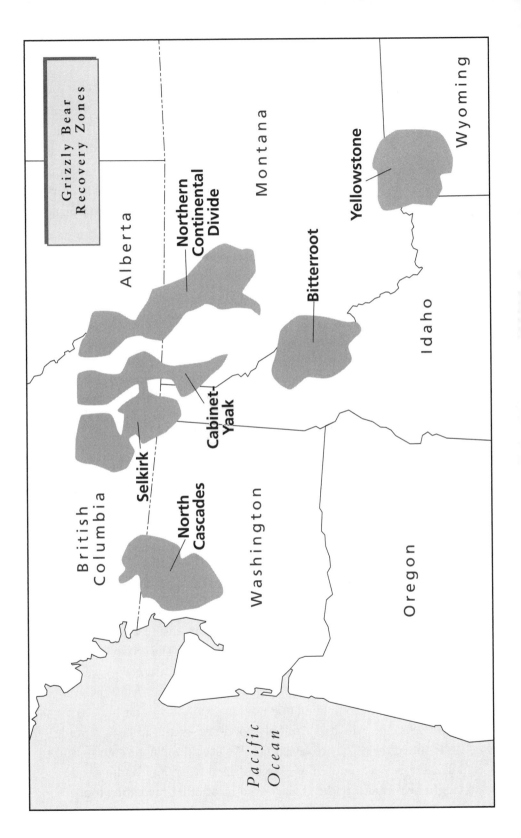

That's how the grizzly entered the public consciousness of the nonnative world. Throughout the 1800s and in the early 1900s, writers and hunter-naturalists continued to build on the grizzly's ferocious image, and in the twentieth century Hollywood and the modern media kept piling it on, over and over, to make sure we would never forget that the grizzly bear was a bloodthirsty beast, a threat to man and livestock alike.

Along the way the grizzly struggled to survive the advance of civilization. At first it was outright hatred and ruthless intent to exterminate the horrible bear. Then it turned to insensitivity of the big bear's needs, favoring instead the shrine of progress and the conquering of the great wilderness. Finally it came down to the bear's last stand in the remnants of a once-vast habitat: the northern Rockies, western Canada, and Alaska. In the continental United States, the grizzly's range shrunk to a pittance of its former vastness.

This book focuses on this final fight of the great bear and addresses these questions: Will the grizzly bear survive? If so, how? And where?

The answers to these questions can get complicated, so before diving into them, I've outlined some basic information about the geographic, social, political, and legal situations affecting the grizzly bear both today and in the future. These facts form the foundation for the rest of the book.

A Perspective of Time

This book is about what's happening today to ensure a viable population of grizzly bears a hundred years from now. The grizzly is a long-lived species. There's no immediate threat to its existence—unless, of course, we consciously decide to eliminate the species from the western landscape. Keep in mind that not long ago, only as far back as the mid-1900s, we still had the only-good-bear-is-a-dead-bear attitude and wanted the grizzly to be extinct. We used the slimmest excuses to kill every bear we could find. We budgeted federal and state tax dollars to help eradicate the grizzly—and most other predators, too.

Fortunately we barely fell short of our goal, and then, even more fortunately, our attitude toward grizzlies changed. Now most of us accept the grizzly where it is, how it is, and most bear experts and environmentalists have a high degree of confidence that the grizzly will be with us for two or three decades at least, but not all of them think the grizzly will be with us when our children and grandchildren enter the twenty-second century.

A Perspective of Space

Where will the grizzly walk? That's one question I plan to answer in this book.

When Lewis and Clark made their epic journey, the grizzly bear ranged throughout the western United States and Canada. Today the grizzly only walks in 2 percent of its original range south of Canada: in Glacier, Grand Teton, and Yellowstone National Parks and some roadless country between the parks. The same is true in the Canadian Rockies. Here the grizzly haunts the national parks (Jasper, Banff, Yoho, Kootenay, and Waterton Lakes) and the wild land in between. Other wild land in the northern Rockies on both sides of the border could provide excellent habitat for the grizzly, but the bear hasn't yet been able to establish viable populations there.

This book focuses on this geography, the remaining habitat (occupied or unoccupied) in the northern Rockies on both sides of the border, but not on the vast reaches of Alaska and northern Canada that support many thousands of grizzlies. Most habitat in the northern Rockies and most of the remaining grizzlies are in Montana, so the majority of this book covers what's happening to the grizzly in the Big Sky state.

A Perspective of Numbers

There were, of course, no scientific population estimates done in the early 1800s when we started our war on the grizzly bear. The best estimates we have, however, indicate there were more than 50,000 and perhaps up to 100,000 grizzly bears walking throughout the territory soon to become the western states.

Then we started shooting, trapping, and poisoning every grizzly we could find. By the early 1900s we had reduced grizzly numbers down to somewhere between 1,000 and 1,500 bears south of Canada. From the mid-1900s to the low point in the late 1970s and early 1980s, continued killing (some legal hunting, some sanctioned predator control) coupled with rapid habitat loss further shrunk the population to probably around 800 animals. Grizzlies north of the border experienced similar declines.

Although we don't know for sure, most bear experts believe that around 1980 the big bear started a gradual rebound. Ever so slowly the population climbed to around 1,000 grizzlies (with a few optimistic estimates as high as 1,500) south of Canada, which is about where it was when this book was written.

A Perspective of People

Part of the story of saving the grizzly is the people doing it—and what a crew! The grizzly has some very good friends, a team of dedicated professionals working together on the bear's behalf. They've been doing it for decades, and they definitely aren't in it for the money. After reading this book, you may wonder why they do it, but in any case, you'd want them on your side if you were in trouble. (See The Bear People.)

The Legal Landscape

In 1975 the U.S. Fish and Wildlife Service (FWS), the federal agency charged with enforcing the Endangered Species Act (ESA), designated the grizzly as a threatened species (not quite as jeopardized as an endangered species) as defined by the ESA. Prior to that designation Idaho, Montana, and Wyoming considered the grizzly a big-game animal, but the designation and subsequent lawsuits closed down hunting seasons.

This designation covered all areas south of Canada, including the Selway-Bitterroot Wilderness and the rest of the Bitterroot Ecosystem even though there had been no documented grizzly sightings since the early 1940s. Some conservationists debate this point and believe a few stealthy grizzlies still survive in the area, but officially wildlife agencies haven't been able to verify this and consider the grizzly extinct in the Bitterroots.

The ESA requires the publication of a recovery plan for each threatened and endangered species. The plan for the grizzly bear came out in 1982 and listed the Bitterroot Ecosystem as a prime candidate for reintroduction. The Bitterroot Ecosystem is a whopping fifteen million acres of mostly wild country, mainly in Idaho, and about a third of it is designated wilderness areas (Selway-Bitterroot, Gospel Hump, and Frank Church River of No Return), which means two-thirds of it isn't protected from resource development.

The Bitterroot Ecosystem is, in fact, twice the size of the Greater Yellowstone Ecosystem (GYE) and also the Northern Continental Divide Ecosystem (NCDE), the two other major recovery areas designated in the recovery plan. The recovery plan also designated three smaller ecosystems important to recovering the grizzly population— Cabinet-Yaak in western Montana; Selkirks, mostly in northern Idaho; and North Cascades in Washington.

Many environmentalists believe recovery can't be achieved without restoring a self-sustaining grizzly population in the Bitterroot Ecosystem. However, the FWS considers recovery possible—but more difficult—without having grizzlies in the Bitterroots.

Currently state wildlife agencies and the FWS and its Interagency Grizzly Bear Committee and Interagency Grizzly Bear Study Team (both multiagency efforts managed by the FWS) believe the grizzly in the GYE has sufficiently recovered to allow what's called "delisting." This means removing the protective security blanket of the ESA. Environmentalists strongly disagree with this conclusion and insist the Yellowstone grizzly, the world's most famous population of bears, is still threatened with extinction.

The Grizzly Bearacracy

A plethora of government agencies work in concert, usually, to save the grizzly bear, but who's in charge? When asked that question, Chris Servheen, the FWS employee who coordinates the Interagency Grizzly Bear Committee (IGBC), answers "me."

Legally the FWS is charged with the task of recovering threatened and endangered species. To involve other state and federal agencies, the FWS created the IGBC, which has members from federal land management and state wildlife agencies.

Servheen has been called "the grizzly czar." The IGBC sets policy at their meetings, but between meetings Servheen makes essentially every major decision affecting the future of the grizzly bear as a species and sometimes even individual bears involved in conflicts.

"Technically I'm an advisor to a committee of suits," Servheen says as he starts to explain the so-called "bearacracy." He then sort of gives up and admits that it involves "lots of people, lots of agencies, lots of interests. It's very complex, but I think all these players have enhanced the process. We couldn't have done it without all the agencies being involved."

Suffice it to say grizzly bear management is intertwined into the fabric of wildlife and resource agencies at all levels. This provides access to the process for lots of people, but it also makes it nearly impossible to understand who is doing what for whom and why.

Servheen is probably as proficient at sorting this out as any person on Earth—and he definitely has staying power. Not many people stay in the same job for twenty-one years, let alone in a high-stress, thankless position like Servheen's, but, nonetheless, he has been there since the position was created in 1981. "I have a great institutional memory," he notes.

To address scientific issues, the FWS created the Interagency Grizzly Bear Study Team (IGBST), which includes the same agencies as the IGBC; its leader is Chuck Schwartz, who reports to Servheen. The IGBC/IGBST members are:

British Columbia Fish and Wildlife Branch
Bureau of Land Management
Idaho Department of Fish and Game
Montana Department of Fish, Wildlife & Parks
National Park Service
USDA Forest Service
U.S. Fish and Wildlife Service
U.S. Geological Survey, Biological Resources Division
Washington Department of Fish and Wildlife
Wyoming Game and Fish Department

State agencies lust for control of grizzly bear management and resent the "feds" being in charge. Governors and congressional delegations support the state's right to manage resident wildlife. This puts pressure on Servheen and the IGBC to speed up efforts to delist the grizzly bear and return management to state wildlife agencies. However, most environmentalists want management to stay with the federal government because they fear state control will favor resource extradition and destruction of remaining habitat, and they know the state wildlife departments want to resume grizzly hunting seasons. "The state's right issue was big at first when the bear was listed," Servheen admits, "but it has cooled off."

People on all sides of the issues complain about things Servheen did or didn't do, but most of them concede that he's done an admirable job of addressing the difficult political and scientific issues. And almost all of them say, "I wouldn't want his job."

So what does the grizzly czar think about the future of the grizzly bear? "I think the bear is doing fine," Servheen says proudly. "We've made huge progress, especially in Yellowstone where the grizzly is doing better than anywhere else. It might be doing well in the NCDE, too, but we don't have the data to prove it."

As you'll see as you read this book, though, not everybody agrees with the grizzly czar on this point.

Generalizations Galore

Even though people do it all the time, it's risky to generalize about grizzly bears. As soon as you do it, a bear comes along and proves you wrong. However, I believe there is one generalization you can make about the grizzly and never be wrong: Wherever the grizzly walks, controversy follows.

The Bear People

These are the main wildlife professionals and environmentalists I interviewed, sometimes several times, in writing this book. They are some of the "bear people" who spend their careers working on and for the grizzly bear.

Colleen Campbell, Naturalist, Banff National Park

Dan Carney, Director of Wildlife Research, Blackfeet Reservation

John Craighead, Chairman, Wildlife-Wildlands Institute

Hank Fischer, former Northern Rockies Representative, Defenders of Wildlife

Kevin Frey, Grizzly Bear Management Specialist, Montana Department of Fish, Wildlife & Parks

Kerry Gunther, Bear Management Specialist, Yellowstone National Park

Caesar Hernandez, Northwest Montana Representative, Montana Wilderness Association

Steve Herrero, Professor Emeritus of Environmental Science at the University of Calgary and Chair of the Eastern Slopes Grizzly Bear Steering Committee

Chuck Jonkel, Bear Scientist and President, Great Bear Foundation

Jamie Jonkel, Grizzly Bear Management Specialist, Montana Department of Fish, Wildlife & Parks

Kate Kendall, Project Leader, Northern Continental Divide DNA Monitoring Project

Mike Madel, Grizzly Bear Management Specialist, Montana Department of Fish, Wildlife & Parks

Tim Manley, Grizzly Bear Management Specialist, Montana Department of Fish, Wildlife & Parks

Gary Moses, Chair, Wildlife Management Committee, Glacier National Park

Brian Peck, Consultant, Sierra Club Grizzly Bear Ecosystems Project

Andy Russell, author and filmmaker

Beth Russell-Towe, Founder and Executive Director, Trail of the Great Bear

Bob Sandford, Coordinator, Heritage Tourism Strategy

Chuck Schwartz, Leader, Interagency Grizzly Bear Study Team

Chris Servheen, Coordinator, Interagency Grizzly Bear Committee

Chris Smith, Chief of Staff, Montana Department of Fish, Wildlife & Parks

John Varley, Director, Yellowstone Center for Resources

Louisa Willcox, former Project Coordinator, Sierra Club Grizzly Bear Ecosystems Project, now with the National Resources Defense Council

Acronyms for Dummies

The grizzly bear is sort of a government thing. A plethora of state and federal agencies, even local county commissions, get into the game, and if you don't work for one of them, you probably don't recognize the acronyms of the agencies, the laws they enforce, and the geographic areas they manage. So, for easy reference, here are the acronyms used repeatedly throughout this book.

CYE. Cabinet-Yaak Ecosystem

ESA. Endangered Species Act

FWS. U.S. Fish and Wildlife Service, Department of the Interior

GYE. Greater Yellowstone Ecosystem

IGBC. Interagency Grizzly Bear Committee, a multiagency committee created by the FWS to coordinate grizzly recovery efforts

IGBST. Interagency Grizzly Bear Study Team, a multiagency team created by the FWS to monitor grizzly research

MDFWP. Montana Department of Fish, Wildlife & Parks

NCDE. Northern Continental Divide Ecosystem

NPS. National Park Service

FS. USDA Forest Service

1

The Passing of Old Ephraim

Americans are often influenced by what psychologists call "negative conditioning." And the grizzly is an excellent example. Since the days of Lewis and Clark, we have been encouraged to view the grizzly as a bloodthirsty man-eater. We've been repeatedly told the grizzly is a huge, fierce, vicious beast. Now, we involuntarily believe it.

—from *Where the Grizzly Walks* (1977)

After Lewis and Clark discovered it, we had to conquer it—the great wilderness and the great bear living there. Once the white man started winning the West, the grizzly—or Old Ephraim, as the grizzly bear was commonly referred to following the rampage of an infamous Utah grizzly—steadily gave ground.

The plains grizzly went first—its primary food source, the bison, destroyed, and its habitat, the native sod, turned upside down by plows. Soon mountain range after mountain range became bearless. State after state saw the last specimen of this most magnificent mammal nailed on a barn door. Some states even failed to document the loss. Historical records are spotty and at times suspect, but diligent research has revealed the following details on the passing of Old Ephraim.

Strangely, Nevada has no record of the big bear, even though surrounding states supported large populations. The Nevada Division of Wildlife claims that the grizzly never existed in the state. Likewise, no other source verifies the past existence of the grizzly in Nevada, although it's likely that the grizzly at least occasionally walked there, especially on the western edge of Nevada next to California.

Kansas, Oklahoma, and Nebraska have sorely insufficient records of the grizzly, although the plains grizzly most likely frequented these states along with the "infinite" bison herds.

E. L. Cockrum, in his book *Mammals of Kansas*, notes, "Although few records remain, the grizzly bear probably formerly roamed over most of the western two-thirds of the state. Almost nothing of the occurrence and habits of this bear in Kansas has been recorded in literature."

Oklahoma and Nebraska have even less to offer history, but it's almost certain that Old Ephraim lived there. Regretfully the grizzly's presence passed into oblivion undocumented.

Texas, however, actually has an official record of the state's last grizzly. One October day in 1890, C. O. Finley and John Z. Means were riding the range in the Davis Mountains in western Texas. In a gulch near the head of Limpia Creek, they found where a bear had killed a cow and eaten most of it. Shortly thereafter they returned with a pack of fifty-two hounds to track down and finish the stock killer. Out of the large pack, only a few of the hounds would follow the trail even though all the dogs were accustomed to hunting black bears, and even those few followed the trail reluctantly.

After a 5-mile run through rough country, the dogs brought the bear to bay. The bear killed one hound before the rifles of Finley and Means quieted Texas's last recorded grizzly. It took four men to hoist the skin (with head and feet attached) onto a horse for the return to camp. Finley estimated the weight of the bear at about 1,100 pounds—"if it had been fat." Vernon Bailey noted in his book *Biological Survey of Texas* that this bear was indeed a very old male grizzly.

Most likely both North Dakota and South Dakota entered the twentieth century without grizzlies, but again documentation is sparse. Several early authors mentioned grizzlies in the Black Hills of western South Dakota; however, no official record of the last South Dakota grizzly can be found.

Early naturalists also observed grizzlies in North Dakota, particularly along the Little Missouri River in the southwestern part of the state, near where Theodore Roosevelt ranched, and in the Devil's Lakes/Sheyenne River country in eastern North Dakota. The last official report recorded two grizzlies killed by Dave Warren near Oakdale in 1897.

Of all the states where the grizzly once walked, California left the best testimony of its passing. Judging from the many historical accounts, California had a very large grizzly population, probably more bears than any other state. Now the "golden bear" lives only on the state's flag. Most sources claimed that Jesse B. Agnew shot the last grizzly near his cattle ranch at Horse Corral Meadow, Tulane County, in 1922. There are some historical hints that the golden bear haunted California for a few more years. For example, several qualified observers reported seeing a grizzly in the Sequoia National Park vicinity until 1924. Nonetheless, California repeated the story of other states—extermination.

The actual Old Ephraim really died in Utah. The life and death of Old Ephraim, the infamous stock-killing grizzly, has been immortalized in northern Utah. Because Frank Clark, the sheepherder responsible for the old bear's undoing, was dissatisfied with the publicity the incident received, he published the following article in the September 1952 *Utah Fish and Game Bulletin,* the former publication of the Utah Division of Wildlife Resources:

> I was transferred to the Cache National Forest from Idaho in 1911. This country was infested with bears at that time. They were of two varieties: the brown and the grizzly bear. Many of them were sheep killers. I know of them killing as many as 150 head of sheep in one summer from one herd.
>
> The men were not used to these killer bears, and I had some trouble trying to get men to stay on the job. After we

had killed and trapped one or two, however, their feelings toward them changed. I killed 13 in 1912 alone.

One bear had become known as Old Ephraim. He was a grizzly bear. The bear's name was given to him, I think, because of an outlaw bear found in California that had been written up by P. S. Barnham. Old Ephraim was well known, mainly because everyone who saw his tracks recognized him. He had one deformed toe. Many weird tales were told about him. He was supposed to have ranged all the way from northern Utah to the Snake River section in Idaho, but I never found his tracks more than two miles from the range that I was using.

I began in 1914 to trap for him, but it was not until 1923 that I caught him. He had a large pool scooped out in a little canyon, and at least once a week, he would come to wallow in the pool he had made. I set my trap in this pool thinking I would catch him, but every time I set it and the bear visited the pool, he would "pertly" pick it up and set it on the side of the pool. It was not until 1923 that he changed his plan of enjoying himself in this wallow. I thought of moving the trap each time. One time I came back and found the bear had dug another pool just below the old one. I set my trap in the new location and this proved Old Ephraim's undoing.

Old Ephraim was not the greedy killer that some bears seem to be. He usually would kill one sheep, pick it up and carry it into the more remote sections of the mountains and devour it. This is in strict contrast to the actions of some killer bears who may kill as many as 100 sheep in one night. It had become a legend that Old Ephraim never seemed to pick the same herd twice in succession, but roamed around for several miles in the proximity of the spring where he bathed and would take only one or two sheep from each separate camp.

I remember well the night of Old Ephraim's undoing. I had set the trap in his new pool, stirred up the mud so that it would set well on the trap. My camp was about one mile down stream from the site. April 23 was a beautiful cool night, and after supper I lighted my pipe and set my gaze at the stars that seemed to be trying to get a message of some kind to the people down here. My nearest company were other herders about four miles away and my horses on a meadow some distance below my camp.

After being down for the night and sleeping for some time, I was suddenly awakened by the most unearthly sound I have ever heard. Ordinarily my dog would bark at anything unusual, this time he did not. After the first cry I noticed that the grumbling of this bear stopped and then after a short time, a roar heard again, echoed from canyon wall to canyon wall. I quickly slipped on my shoes, didn't bother to put on pants, grabbed my rifle, and started along the trail. Expecting to go only a few yards from camp was why I did not fully dress. As the sounds kept up, I could tell they were in the bottom of the canyon nearing me. I skirted the mountainside above. I finally realized that I had caught either Old Ephraim or another bear and soon heard the noise in the willows along the creek bed below me. After it had passed I slipped down and along the trail in the bright moon light, and I could see the tracks of the big bear as he went down the stream. I followed the noise slowly down the creek until I got near the point where my camp was, and there came crashing out of the creek bottom the giant form of Old Ephraim walking on his hind feet. He was carrying on his front foot the large trap that weighed 27 pounds and the 15 feet of log chain nearly wrapped around his right forearm. As he came towards me, it chilled me to the bone, and for several paces I didn't even attempt to shoot. Finally, more out of fear than any other passion, I opened up with my small 25–35 caliber rifle and pumped six shots into him. He fell at my feet dead, and as I looked at the giant form of Old Ephraim, I suddenly became sorry that I had killed this giant bear. Retracing the bear's trail from the place where he had been caught, I found that for over one mile he had walked on his hind feet holding the trap and chain on his front foot. Also, that he had cut the large 15-foot log that I had the chain tied to in 2- and 3-foot lengths. All the trees as far as the length of the chain would let him go had been cut down. It looked as if the quaking aspen up to six inches in diameter had been cut with a single blow.

Old Ephraim's body was buried near my camp site and remained there until it was unearthed and his skull sent to the Smithsonian Institute, where it remains today. A monument has been erected by the Boy Scouts of America of Cache County to the memory of Old Ephraim, and hundreds of Boy Scouts have visited my camp and been thrilled to the story I have told hundreds of times of the killing of Old Ephraim.

In 1917 an official survey estimated the New Mexico grizzly population at forty-eight. In 1927 the same surveyors reported the species had reached the point of "almost total extermination." An article published in the July 1961 issue of *Arizona Wildlife Sportsman* stated that the "last kill" came in 1933. Hunting in the Jemez Mountains, Tom Campbell shot New Mexico's last grizzly in the stomach, but it ran away. Campbell found it dead three days later at the head of Santa Clara Canyon, evidence of the slow, agonizing end of Old Ephraim in New Mexico.

The U.S. Fish and Wildlife Service (FWS) claims Richard R. Miller was responsible for the last recorded grizzly kill in Arizona—in Greenlee County—in 1935. The same issue of *Arizona Wildlife Sportsman* carried this account of the bear:

The day the last grizzly reported to be killed in Arizona was no different than any other on the Joe Fillerman spread near Red Mountain northeast of Clifton. Dick had his 30–30 in the scabbard under his left leg and was riding his pet hunting horse. His seven hounds were along as Dick went out that day looking for a calf kill. He was in the bottom of Stray Horse Canyon, east of Rose Peak, when the dogs lit out on a bear scent. In a matter of minutes, they doubled back and came in under him. Dick fired from the saddle and killed the bear running in front of the pack. It was a two-year-old, and Miller estimated it to weigh about 200 pounds. He looked around the area and found evidence that the two-year-old had a twin and a mother in the area. It was late, so Dick skinned the bear and headed for the ranch.

A couple of days later, Kit Casto and Mr. Black rode in. Dick mentioned the kill and showed the men the skin nailed on a log. Both men immediately identified the bear as a grizzly.

Dick Miller told this writer that he would have never killed the bear had he known it was a grizzly. The other two grizzlies were never seen again. The date of the last recorded grizzly kill in Arizona was September 13, 1935.

In his classic book *A Sand County Almanac,* Aldo Leopold described one of Arizona's greatest grizzlies and how it passed away. This bear wasn't the last, but rather one of the last. Certainly the plight of Old Bigfoot symbolizes the frontier spirit and sentiment toward the grizzly bear.

Old Bigfoot lived on Escudilla, a famous mountain in the Apache National Forest. "There was, in fact, only one place from which you did not see Escudilla on the skyline; that was the top of Escudilla itself," Leopold wrote. "Up there you could not see the mountain, but you could feel it. The reason was the big bear."

Old Bigfoot crawled out of its den each spring, descended the mountain, and bashed in the head of a cow. After eating its fill the bear climbed back into the crags and stayed there all summer, no longer bothering the cattle herds. "I once saw one of his kills," Leopold noted. "The cow's skull and neck were pulp, as if she had collided head-on with a fast freight."

The aged grizzly killed only one cow per year, but that was too many. Leopold went on to write how progress—automobiles, telephones, electric power, and other "necessities" of modern man—began arriving in cow country. "One spring, progress sent still another emissary, a government trapper, a sort of St. George in overalls, seeking dragons to slay at government expense. Were there, he asked, any destructive animals in need of slaying? Yes, there was a big bear."

The government trapper tried everything—traps, poison, and all his usual wiles—but Old Bigfoot was too wise. Then the trapper erected a set-gun, and as Leopold put it, "The last grizzly walked into the string and shot himself."

"Escudilla still hangs on the horizon," Leopold remorsefully wrote, "but when you see it, you no longer think of the bear. It's only a mountain now."

The mind-set so eloquently chronicled by Leopold continued to spread. Oregon was next. According to the Oregon Fish and Wildlife Commission, Evans Stoneman, also a government trapper, killed the last Oregon grizzly on Chesnimnus Creek in Wallowa County on September 14, 1931. Reports of grizzlies continued until 1940, but none have been verified.

Colorado may have been the last in the long procession of states and provinces to wipe out the big bear. But this is still an active debate.

In a letter Ernest Wilkinson, a retired government trapper, claimed he killed the last Colorado grizzly. "As far as I know," Wilkinson wrote, "I took the last grizzly bear in Colorado in September 1951 on Starvation Gulch in the Upper Rio Grande River Country."

Later another retired government trapper, Floyd Anderson, said he killed the last one in 1952. Adding credence to this later record, the Colorado Division of Wildlife listed Anderson's bear as the last grizzly killed in the state.

Anderson, however, felt there were still a few grizzlies in the Continental Divide area between the Rio Grande and San Juan drainages in south-central Colorado. "We know they're there," Anderson assured, "but it's difficult to prove." The retired trapper recalled tracking a grizzly for several miles in 1957, and his hunting dogs chased another one for twelve hours in 1964. He also told of watching a female with two cubs for twenty minutes in 1967.

Richard Denny of the Division of Wildlife sided with Anderson, noting the sighting of a female with cubs in 1967. "Later unverified, or less credible, observations have been made through the 1960s and as late as 1973," Denny claimed.

Smokey Till, also speaking for the Division of Wildlife, was less optimistic. "I don't think so," he said. "As many hunters as we have in there each fall, we'd know (if there were any grizzlies left)."

After the original edition of this book came out in 1977, a bow hunter named Ed Wiseman came along and proved Anderson's theory. On September 23, 1979, Wiseman killed a female grizzly in a remote section of the San Juan Mountains.

Was this, finally, Colorado's "last" grizzly, or does a remnant population still exist in the remote reaches of the San Juans? This debate rages on today, but even if Colorado still has a few grizzlies, this population has likely slipped below the point of no return. The number of bears may be too low to constitute a viable population. Therefore, the passing of the Colorado grizzly, if not already a reality, is most likely assured.

Approximately 175 years of progress have been just about all Old Ephraim could take. When the twenty-first century rolled around, the grizzly's remaining habitat had shrunk to a small fraction of its original vastness. In the lower forty-eight states, the grizzly still walks only small portions of Idaho, Montana, Washington, and Wyoming.

The grizzly also clings to most of its original range in British Columbia, reports D. R. Halladay of the British Columbia Fish and Wildlife Branch, "but its numbers are greatly reduced near human settlements, particularly in southern valleys."

Manitoba lost its grizzlies along with the bison, but the Canadian Wildlife Service doesn't have a date for the bear's demise. The best estimate Manitoba wildlife officials can offer is about 1825.

Alberta, like Manitoba, lost its plains grizzlies early. However, the big bear hangs on in the western mountains along the Continental Divide and in the Swan Hills south of Lesser Slave Lake.

The grizzly also inhabits all of the Yukon Territory and the mountains west of the Mackenzie River in the Northwest Territory. The barren ground grizzly, a distinct subspecies, still exists in low numbers east of Hudson Bay.

Mexico did have a few grizzlies in the rugged Baranca country along the Sonora-Chihuahua border at the head of Yaqui Basin, according to Dr. A. Starker Leopold, a noted bear authority formerly with the University of California, Berkeley: "The small remnant that I found in the 1950s . . . has apparently been poisoned out of the Sierra del Nido Chihuahua. A local rancher had trouble with a bear killing livestock and got a hold of a batch of 1080 poison, which he used rather generously. We have no recent reports of grizzlies in that area." Gary Brown in his book *Great Bear Almanac,* lists 1969 as the last confirmed report of a grizzly bear in Mexico, in the Sierra del Nido Chihuahua area.

Of all the states and provinces, Alaska has the brightest news. "No one knows how many brown and grizzly bears Alaska has," Jim Rearden of the Alaska Board of Game reports. "There is, however, substantial agreement that the population is the highest it has been in years, and it is still increasing in the interior, on the Kenai Peninsula, and in some other areas. Some estimate 15,000 or more."

The last reported grizzly kill in Washington was in 1964, but the big bear still survives in the state near the Canadian border. "Each year our personnel receive reports of grizzly tracks or grizzly sightings in northern Pend Oreille County," J. Burton Lauckhart, former game division chief with the Washington Department of Fish and Wildlife, notes. "This is a small extension of the Selkirk Mountains (which lie mostly in British Columbia) that provides good grizzly habitat. The other area that still supports a small nucleus of grizzlies is the North Cascades area that is now in the national park."

"We carry an estimate of ten grizzlies in Washington, but this is only a guess to cover two or three family groups," Lauckhart admits. Grizzly management in Washington now includes total protection from hunting. However, the game department notes, "If a stray animal does move into farming areas, it would have to be eliminated."

Jim Humbird, formerly of the Idaho Department of Fish and Game, believes Idaho has more grizzly habitat than any other state, excluding Alaska. Yet Idaho's grizzly population has steadily declined, even though hunting was banned in 1946. In the million-acre Selway-

Bitterroot Wilderness on the Idaho-Montana border, for example, the last grizzly bear may have recently disappeared. The FWS still lists the grizzly as "threatened" in the Selway-Bitterroot; however, reports have been so sparse and suspect lately that many authorities fear the bear has disappeared from the area. Maurice Homocker, leader of the Idaho Cooperative Wildlife Research Unit, suspects this, as does John Craighead, chairman of the Wildlife-Wildlands Institute. But there is no firm proof, or as Homocker notes, "There may still be a few stragglers left."

In the late 1990s a major effort was launched to reintroduce the grizzly into the Selway-Bitterroot. To date, however, politicians have been able to prevent this reintroduction. (See Strange Bedfellows.)

Idaho still has grizzlies, most of which range in the Targhee National Forest on the west edge of Yellowstone National Park. The northernmost part of the panhandle also has a few. However, one of the largest expanses of primitive land remaining intact south of Canada, the 2.3 million-acre proposed River of No Return Wilderness in central Idaho, is without the big bear.

That leaves Montana and Wyoming. These two states shelter the vast majority of grizzlies still surviving south of Canada. Most authorities think the two states harbor about 1,000 to 1,500 grizzlies but admit this is merely an educated guess.

Most of Wyoming's share of this remaining population inhabits the Shoshone and Bridger-Teton National Forests, east and south of Yellowstone Park, and the park itself.

Montana has the largest grizzly population in the lower forty-eight states. The Gallatin, Beaverhead-Deerlodge, and Custer National Forests, west and north of Yellowstone Park, support a growing population. And northwestern Montana—Glacier National Park, the Blackfeet and Flathead Indian Reservations, and the Flathead, Lewis and Clark, Kootenai, Helena, and Lolo National Forests—probably hold more grizzlies than any other area south of the Canadian border.

It's in these few enclaves scattered around the northern Rockies, particularly Montana and Wyoming, where Old Ephraim is making its last stand.

Chronology of the Grizzly Bear

1,500,000 B.C.	Earliest archaeological evidence of the grizzly bear.
50,000 B.C.	Brown bears cross the Bering Land Bridge.
1602	Sebastian Vizcaino sees grizzly bears feeding on a beached whale in Monterey Bay, California; possibly the first European to see a grizzly bear.
1666	Claude Jean Allouez observes grizzly bears along the Assimiborne River in what is now Manitoba, Canada.
1758	Carolus Linnaeus, founder of the binomial nomenclature for species still used today, names the grizzly *Ursus arctos*.
1804	Lewis and Clark "discover" the grizzly bear and describe it as the "white bear" and "a most terrible enemy."
1815	Based on information from the Lewis and Clark Expedition, taxonomist George Ord gives the grizzly bear a new scientific name, *Ursus horribilis*, or "horrible bear."
ca. 1825	Last grizzly killed in Manitoba.
1851	Russian biologist Alexander Theodor von Middendorff recognizes the grizzly as the same species as the European brown bear and again renames the species *Ursus arctos horribilis*.
1890	Last grizzly killed in Texas.
1897	Last grizzly killed in North Dakota.
1922	Last grizzly killed in California.

1923	Last grizzly killed in Utah.
1931	Last grizzly killed in Oregon.
1933	Last grizzly killed in New Mexico.
1935	Last grizzly killed in Arizona.
ca. 1940	Last grizzly killed in the Bitterroot Mountains.
ca. 1969	Last grizzly killed in Mexico.
1969–1973	Yellowstone National Park garbage dumps closed.
1973	Endangered Species Act passed.
1975	Grizzly bear listed as a threatened species south of Canada under the Endangered Species Act.
1979	Last grizzly killed in Colorado.
1981	Low point for the Yellowstone Park grizzly population.
1982	Grizzly bear recovery plan published by the FWS.
1991	Last grizzly hunting season south of Canada, in Montana, ends after the state is sued.
1993	Grizzly bear revised recovery plan published by the FWS.
1999	Interagency Grizzly Bear Committee sets 2005 as goal for delisting the grizzly bear in the Greater Yellowstone Ecosystem.

For ages Old Ephraim walked where it pleased with a healthy defiance of other animals, fearing nothing except bigger grizzlies—not even the native tribes. Then the bear's nemesis, the white man, spread over the West, striking quickly, efficiently, and unemotionally. Even with the grizzly exterminated from most of its original range, the West's early residents searched every remote mountain cirque for the last bears. Apparently they felt little remorse when skinning each state's last grizzly, only a sense of pride for relieving the livestock industry of a serious menace.

Considering the warlike campaign to rid the West of Old Ephraim, it's remarkable that the bear survived at all. Indeed, a lesser animal may have disappeared. But apparently the king of the wilderness never lost its fierce tenacity for life. For centuries the big bear had ruled unchallenged—until it met its match. Then it was forced to retreat to the remotest corners of the wilderness. Here it adapted and somehow survived to carry its majestic race into the twenty-first century.

In his article "Vanished Monarch of the Sierra," published in the May/June 1976 issue of *The American West,* Ted M. Taylor came up with an appropriate closing for his detailed description of the disappearance of the big bear:

"In 1868, Bret Harte, editor of the *Overland Monthly,* explained the meaning of the publication's symbol, a grizzly crossing railroad tracks. After noting that the railroad, representing civilization, foretold the bear's doom, Harte wrote of the California grizzly: 'Look at him well, for he is passing away. Fifty years and he will be as extinct as the dodo . . .'

"Today, grizzlies still may be found in considerable numbers in Alaska and Canada, and a few are even said to survive in portions of Sonora, Mexico. But in the western United States, once home of some 100,000 such animals, a dwindling remnant of fewer than 1,000 grizzlies remains, most in remote sections of the Rocky Mountain region. Look at them well . . ."

A Few Bears I've Met
and What I Learned from Them

Date: July 12, 1966
Place: Starvation Creek, Glacier National Park
Lesson: The grizzly is more than a bear.

Everyone has experiences that last a lifetime—precious moments, often recalled and becoming more meaningful as the years hurry by. I have had several, and one definitely left a permanent mark on my psyche. For me, it helped clearly define the grizzly's place in modern America.

While attending college in 1966, I had the ideal summer job, working on the trail crew in Glacier National Park. My job was clearing trails in the North Fork region of the park, which meant I got paid to hike—definitely a dream job for me. One particular July morning seemed routine, but it hardly turned out that way.

I had been in Glacier the preceding summer, too, stuck in a spike camp 12 miles up Park Creek in the Middle Fork area with four other trail crew workers and a cook. We stayed in the shadow of Church Butte all summer reconstructing the trail to Lake Isabel, destroyed the previous year by a flood. The only other person we saw all summer was our crusty old packer, Omar Julian, a throwback to the Wild West, who brought a pack train in once a week with food and mail. Omar really knew how to talk to those mules, and he could roll a cigarette with one hand while riding his horse, even on a windy day. That really impressed a farm boy from South Dakota.

At camp and on the trail, we talked about bears, and Omar told us many wild stories about grizzlies—a few of them might have even been true. But I went all summer without seeing a grizzly. I saw the tracks of the great bear, and I imagined one behind every bush and outside my tent every night, but in September I went back to college in South Dakota without having seen one.

The next summer, in 1966, the National Park Service assigned me to the North Fork, a much more civilized existence. I stayed in the dorm at park headquarters on weekends and in patrol cabins during the week while working on the North Fork trails.

My foreman was nicknamed Jerky, but I never knew why. His real name was Gary Martin, and we got on just fine. That July day Jerky and I were clearing the Starvation Creek Trail near the Kintla Lake Campground. After hiking several miles we came to the ford of Starvation Creek, truly a wild mountain stream. It was fairly early in the season so the streambed was still choked with snowmelt.

We stopped for a cold drink, and Jerky made jokes as I almost fell while crossing the stream on a fallen lodgepole pine conveniently extending from bank to bank. Once across, I filled my hard hat with ice-cold water, downed it, and leaned back to drift into one of those momentary daydreams that come so easily in pristine places. Jerky stayed on the other side of the stream, eating a snack. After a few seconds I was rudely brought back to reality by Jerky frantically waving his arms and pointing upstream. The roar of the rushing water stole his words, but he was obviously startled. Upon peeking over the thick mass of branches from the lodgepole, I saw why, and the movie camera of my mind registered a few seconds for future daydreams.

There, knee-deep in the wild water, was a large female grizzly helping a small cub across the treacherous torrent. Her other cub had already crossed. Carefully the female monarch half carried, half pushed her offspring through the icy rapids. Probably only about 100 feet away, the bears seemed uncomfortably close.

Then, just as she nearly had the cub across, in a movement almost too fast to follow, the mother was on guard: Her nose went up, probably trying to identify the foreign scent some tattletale breeze had brought her.

That moment is frozen in time for me. The grizzly seemed to be exactly in the right place, her huge hulk silhouetted against the blue sky and the snowy crags of the northern Livingston Range. Here was the wilderness hallmark—a silvertip amid unspoiled scenery, ready to defend her cubs, a scene any wildlife artist would want to paint. Although the roaring waterway made so much noise we couldn't hear each other 20 feet apart, the scene was strangely silent.

Again the breeze brought her the suspicious scent, and all three bears bolted back across the stream, quickly melting into the forest from which they had just emerged. Since their speed blurred the details, I have always wondered how the cubs forded the stream so rapidly when a few seconds earlier they had needed help.

During the few seconds we watched the bears, I was frozen—not with fear but in awe. But after the bears burst back into the woods, fear took over. Jerky ran across the stream, not worried about getting his boots wet, and we hurried down the trail, constantly scanning the woods to the left and behind for any sign of the bears. Thankfully, I think, we saw none.

Later, when my fear subsided, I realized how fortunate I had been. Very few people will ever see a wild grizzly. Although every day many people gawk at grizzlies in zoos, only a handful will ever view the big bear in such a wild setting.

That day I saw America's strength, courage, and lifeblood embodied in a magnificent animal. I saw the wild world working the way it is supposed to work, in matchless harmony. If I were ever asked to describe a scene of total beauty, serenity, and peace, I would recount those few seconds on Starvation Creek. Ever since that day, I knew a grizzly was more than a bear.

Not many people will ever view a grizzly in a comparable setting, but this is of little importance. Even if no one were to witness such a scene, it should endure in our consciousness. Just knowing that somewhere a mother grizzly is helping her cubs across a wild mountain stream in a primeval wilderness might help us maintain some stability and security, as well as a degree of confidence that we haven't conquered it all—yet.

That was my first one, the first grizzly I had ever seen. I would later see many more grizzlies, a few at close proximity on backcountry trails, but with one exception recounted later in this book, those I met on trails fled like spooked cottontails upon sensing my presence. Before long I caught myself wishing a bear wouldn't immediately run away so I could get a better look. My inherent fear changed to awe and admiration. For me, the grizzly puts the wild in wilderness.

That day on that mountain stream, I learned the grizzly symbolizes an endangered heritage that the nation can ill afford to sacrifice for a higher "standard of living." We must somehow preserve the harmony I experienced along Starvation Creek.

2

The Ninemile Grizzly

Every year I have a bear like the Ninemile Grizzly.
— Kevin Frey, Montana Department
of Fish, Wildlife & Parks

We've all heard about those teenage boys who tend to go a little wild. They're fearless and pumped up with hormones; they believe they're invulnerable and are often struck with an incurable wanderlust. They don't listen to their mother, or anybody else, and they often disrespect authority. They are, of course, wise beyond their years, in their opinion only, as they strike out looking for their place in society nowhere near mother's prying eyes.

Teenage boys can be like that—and male teenage bears, too.

Such is the fascinating story of the Ninemile Grizzly. The travels and exploits of this single boy bear tell the story of the grizzly species in modern America—and, perhaps, foretell its future. The following story is mostly documented and factual, but bear biologists have filled in a few gaps with educated speculation.

It all started in 1995 or 1996 when a female bear decided to leave the Mission Mountains in Montana. Why she did it, who knows?, but she abandoned the security of her wilderness home and somehow made it over to the relative safety of Valley Creek and the lush slopes of Sleeping Woman Mountain in the Jocko Mountains.

The future of the grizzly bear is, in part, dependent on geography, and the Ninemile Grizzly keenly illustrates this significance. Any route from the Mission Mountains to the Jocko Mountains and the Reservation Divide area in the headwaters of the Ninemile Valley is a bear minefield. Several bears have been killed trying to cross U.S. Highway 93, a two-lane but heavily traveled roadway. Others have died in conflicts with local residents. This is, however, also a vital linkage corridor for naturally repopulating the Bitterroot Ecosystem, fifteen million acres of prime, but probably unoccupied, grizzly habitat.

Check a map and you can see two possible routes from the Bob Marshall Complex to Ninemile Creek. The first, and probably the route taken by this female griz, goes down the west slopes of the Mission Mountains; across a 15-mile stretch of flat, agricultural, heavily developed country, probably following Post or Camas Creeks, to the National Bison Range; across the range and U.S. 93; then on to the Flathead Indian Reservation and the Jocko Mountains.

Grizzlies can also go south from the Missions into the Rattlesnake National Recreation Area (where they have been frequently sighted) or west over to the little-known Pitsel Range, across U.S. 93, and into the Jockos. In either case, once on the Reservation Divide, it's a straight shot down the Ninemile to the Bitterroots, with one colossal barrier, I–90.

Valley Creek was hardly as secure as the home the female griz left in the Missions, but, nonetheless, she found a few more of her kind, at least one a male bear, obviously, because she had two cubs in 1998, which were observed several times by wildlife officials from the Flathead Reservation. Most likely, it was one of these cubs that was destined for stardom as the Ninemile Grizzly.

The saga of the Ninemile Grizzly officially began in early May 2001, when a bear came down from the Reservation Divide and found garbage strewn all around upper Ninemile Creek. Up to that point this male bear probably had been hanging out with his mother, eating natural foods and behaving like a model adolescent. Then the three-year-old grizzly got booted out of his mother's world, so he struck out on his own.

Like far-too-many teenagers, he immediately found trouble. He got hooked on bear drugs, an uncontrolled substance otherwise known as garbage. Once addicted, it seems, there's no going back. There's no bear detox facilities. Hence the oft-used adage, "A fed bear is a dead bear."

It all started in the mushroom camps, which could be likened to a seedy section of a big city. That's where teenagers might go to try drugs for the first time.

In 2000 a forest fire scorched the slopes of Squaw Peak (recently renamed Sleeping Woman Mountain). A forest fire launches a surge of fire-following vegetation, including the much-prized morel mushroom.

In 2001 environmental conditions were ideal for a bumper crop of morel mushrooms. This is a big deal most people don't know about. There's a great commercial market for morels, and hundreds of mushroom pickers, mostly migrant workers, flocked to the slopes of Sleeping Woman Mountain. They set up makeshift camps, living in vans and tents, with no toilets or garbage disposal facilities. Before long the bears came in, lured by the smell of food and garbage, and not only black bears as in years past, but also a 375-pound subadult grizzly bear soon to be known as the Ninemile Grizzly.

The USDA Forest Service (FS) manages most of the burned-forest-land-turned-mushroom field, and rangers at the Ninemile Ranger Station knew the mushroom pickers were coming. But the morel crop was better than expected, according to Stacie DeWolf, who handles permits for such commercial activities.

Normally the type of situation the FS carefully controls, the mushroom camps (eight camps with twenty to thirty people per camp) became a horrid mess. To pick morels, the FS requires both a commercial use mushroom permit and a camping permit, both of which were acquired by the mushroom pickers. Both permits contain requirements for garbage and food handling, but these provisions weren't followed, nor did rangers from the nearby Ninemile Ranger Station initially enforce them.

DeWolf went to the mushroom camps to talk to the pickers about handling garbage and food. "They'd bought all their meat for the following week, and then they put it in a cooler and left it out at night. The bears got it, and after that they came back every night."

By the time rangers started managing the situation, it was too late. The mushrooms had been either picked or spoiled, and the migrant workers had started moving on.

"I guess we were caught a little off guard because this hadn't been a problem before," concedes Ken Britton, a ranger at Ninemile at the time. "We didn't know what to expect. We didn't know how many mushroom pickers were coming, and we got a lot more than anticipated."

"Initially they (the mushroom pickers) didn't store their food or handle garbage well. After the first week or ten days, we started picking up the trash daily, and we put a toilet at each camp. We got them to store food in their cars. After that it wasn't a problem."

But it was a problem for the Ninemile Grizzly. The teenage bear was already hooked, or in biologist-speak, habituated to human food rewards.

On June 1, 2001, Jamie Jonkel, a bear biologist for the Montana Department of Fish, Wildlife & Parks (MDFWP), got the call. A few days earlier, May 29, Dave Murray and his wife, who live near the confluence of Ninemile, McCormick, and Fire Creeks, were at home when a bear tripped their motion detector.

"We see bears all the time, but this one was a grizzly," Dave told the *Missoulian*. "It was looking in our son's window." Murray yelled at the overly bold bear, and it took off. But the bear came back the next morning. Murray had just loaded garbage into the back of his pickup truck, and the grizzly jumped in the truck bed, grabbed a pork chop bone, and ran away.

That's when Murray called Jonkel, who sent out game wardens to set a culvert trap. The grizzly visited several of Murray's neighbors in the following days, getting food and garbage at most of them. Five days after its first visit the bear came back to Murray's place, headed right for the baited trap, and got caught.

MDFWP wardens, working with Chris Servheen of the Interagency Grizzly Bear Committee (IGBC), fitted the bear with a radio collar and released him on the Reservation Divide in the headwaters of Ninemile Creek, not far from the Murrays' place. The act of trapping and transplanting creates quite a negative stimulus for a bear, and to add to it, wardens shot cracker shells at the bear when he was released to further send the message—stay wild or die. A few days later an IGBC pilot recorded the grizzly's signal along the divide, indicating that he may have reformed and gone back to natural food.

Sadly, that didn't last long. On June 10 the bear traveled east over the Reservation Divide, down near the little town of Ravalli on U.S. 93. Here the bear went amuck, killing thirty chickens, three ducks, a goose, and a peacock at the home of Shawn Andros.

When Andros came home that night, he saw the chicken coop door ajar and several dead chickens. At first he thought his kids might have forgotten to close the coop and his dog had killed the chickens. Then a bear stood up in the brush. Andros yelled at it, but it wouldn't go away. Then, finally, after more yelling it walked off.

Andros reported the incident to tribal wardens, but he thought it was a black bear so nobody made the connection to the Murray incident. Tribal wardens gave Andros some rubber bullets and told him to use them on the bear if it returned.

It did the next evening. Andros shot at the bear several times and took a video, which Servheen and Jonkel used to identify their collared grizzly. Now they knew they had a problem bear.

From here life got exciting for the residents of the Ninemile Valley, which used to be home to a few sprawling ranches but is now crowded with double-wides, survivalists' cabins, and retirement dream homes, many built on twenty-acre "ranches." This remote, beautiful valley, with a sparkling mountain stream and a horizon serrated with mountain peaks, is now part of the so-called urban interface.

On June 17 the Ninemile Grizzly moved west away from Ravalli, over the Reservation Divide, and back into the Ninemile Valley. Here he went on a rampage, almost daily getting into some sort of trouble—raiding bird feeders, feasting in open garbage dumps, stealing dog or horse feed off porches, killing chickens, feeding on abandoned cattle carcasses, digging up compost piles, and in general doing an excellent impersonation of a bear "habituated to human food rewards."

For two weeks MDFWP wardens, biologists, and volunteers virtually, in their words, "lived with this bear." This was no small task, as the bear kept moving erratically, almost as if he were in some sort of panic to find food. They tried to trap him again, but by the time the culvert trap was moved in and baited, the bear was long gone. They shot cracker shells at him twice, but aversive conditioning wasn't working. The stimulus of getting food rewards from humans far outweighed the negative stimulus he'd gotten from rubber bullets, cracker shells, and culvert traps.

During this two-week period, MDFWP was "shocked" at what they found. "Once we started following the bear around in earnest, we found some horrendous examples of human-related food rewards," claims Bill Thomas, MDFWP information officer. "There were truckloads of kitchen garbage at residences."

MDFWP moved as fast and forcefully as possible. They held two community meetings about removing food attractants like bird feeders, compost heaps, pet food, and open garbage dumps, and they went door-to-door to talk to valley residents. "We'd wake up folks in the middle of the night and ask if we could move their garbage inside," Thomas recalls. "We tried everything, but the bear just seemed to find every attraction available."

Thomas says many people were receptive to changing the way they did things and cleaned up garbage, but others wouldn't change until the bear was already on their land, getting more food rewards, which was too late to have any impact on reversing the downward spiral.

Heather Marstall of the Wind River Bear Institute was in the Missoula area when the Ninemile Grizzly started hitting the headlines, and she volunteered to help out for a few days. She followed the bear around, trying to keep him out of trouble, and talked to landowners about cleaning up food attractants.

"I'd see him along the road and pull up in my truck and yell at him, but he wouldn't even move," she explained. "I shot cracker shells at him, and he'd run off, but not like you'd expect a bear to do. He traveled day and night."

Then on June 30 the Ninemile Grizzly stepped over the IGBC's final line in the sand. The bear walked right into an enclosed porch looking for pet food, which he had done before, but this time the porch was occupied by a woman watching TV. Obviously this scared the stuffing out of her, as it did the bear managers. Even though the bear didn't act aggressively toward the woman, the IGBC threw in the towel on the Ninemile Grizzly. Servheen decided this rebellious teenager would never see adulthood.

By now the Ninemile Grizzly had become so savvy that killing him wasn't that easy. The grizzly was wise beyond his years, not only at getting garbage and other human food, but at staying out of traps and away from people with guns. Wardens radio-tracked the bear twice down to I–90 before he went back north into the Ninemile Valley. Then on July 1 the Ninemile Grizzly did something no other bear has been documented as doing. This bear swam across the lower Clark Fork, Montana's largest river, and crossed I–90.

This was the first real-life example of the dream scenario of environmentalists and biologists who want to repopulate the Bitterroot Mountains with grizzly bears. Having a self-sustaining grizzly population in the Bitterroots would mean, to most, that the grizzly had recovered from the brink of extinction. (See Strange Bedfellows.)

So did our wandering boy bear keep going south, up into the Bitterroots, and help form the foundation for a new population of grizzlies? Hardly. Instead he went to the nearest chicken coop and killed more chickens, then headed back north across the river and freeway, but not back to the Ninemile Valley. Instead he skirted the freeway and traveled northwest toward Superior, 30 miles from where Ninemile Creek flows into the Clark Fork. Here wardens finally caught up with him, and several rifle shots sadly ended the saga of the Ninemile Grizzly.

The moral of the story is: Get ready for more Ninemile Grizzlies—and in more places than the Ninemile Valley.

"Every year I have a bear like the Ninemile Grizzly," reports Kevin Frey, Jamie Jonkel's counterpart in Bozeman. In fact, Frey recently had a similar bear, without a name, that he trapped and released, but it kept getting in trouble. The trap-wise bear was involved in fifty-five incidents before Frey finally caught it again and had to destroy it.

"The Ninemile Valley still isn't close to being bear-proof," Marstall says. "I recommended to the MDFWP that they spend time getting it cleaned up before a female and cubs came through, but they don't really have the manpower to do it."

Jonkel couldn't agree more. To make up for the manpower short-age, he's working closely with landowners to form a neighborhood watch type of program wherein landowners are educated in bear awareness and living with wildlife and work out the problems them-selves, using peer pressure to get the job done instead of having a gov-ernment agency force them into it. He gives out tons of information on removing food attractants, as well as cracker shells and rubber bullets so the landowners can aversively condition bears. And he frequently (and probably gingerly) points out that there's a state law prohibiting people from leaving out food and other items that may attract bears.

This strategy seems to be working, but slowly, in the Ninemile, and Jonkel is doing the same thing in many other areas. There are dozens of situations like the Ninemile Valley's throughout the north-ern Rockies, and these volunteer landowner groups might allow Jonkel to have the impact of a dozen bear biologists.

Black bears have been a problem in the Ninemile for many years, but nobody really cared. That changed dramatically when the Nine-mile Grizzly went on his rampage, but the valley should have been bear-proofed long before a grizzly came calling. If it had, perhaps this wayward teenage bear would be maturing up in the Bitterroot Moun-tains, looking for a mate.

Living with Bears

To reduce the risk of bear problems on or near your property, follow these simple guidelines. It's in everybody's best interest to avoid attracting bears.

Garbage. Store garbage in bear-proof containers or inside a building. Haul garbage to an approved disposal site as often as possible, but at least once a week to avoid a buildup of odors. Bears that become habituated to garbage often have to be killed.

Fruits and vegetables. Fruit trees and vegetable gardens attract bears. Use electric fences to keep bears out of orchards and gardens. Pick all ripe fruit from trees and off the ground as soon as possible. Do not leave fruit on trees through the fall.

Compost. Composting reduces the amount of waste in landfills, but the odor emitted by compost piles attracts bears. Don't put meat, grease, or bones in a compost pile. Put an electric fence around the compost pile, or consider an enclosed composter.

Livestock and pet food. Store livestock and pet food inside a building or in bear-proof containers. Reduce spillage of livestock feed like oats or pellets by feeding from buckets or other containers.

Sheep and pigs. Both sheep and pigs make easy prey for bears. Closely herd sheep. Put electric fences around pigpens. Or better yet, don't keep sheep or pigs in bear country. Bears that learn to kill livestock are usually, in turn, killed.

Livestock carcasses. Don't bury dead livestock. Haul carcasses to a rendering plant or approved disposal site.

Bees. Bears seek out the larvae found in beehives. Put electric fences around beehives, or elevate them on platforms supported by metal poles that bears can't climb.

Bird feeders. Suet and other bird feed, as well as hummingbird feeders, can attract bears. Feed suet only during the winter. Hang hummingbird feeders out of the reach of bears. Take platform bird feeders inside at night.

Children. Closely control children playing outdoors. Keep children indoors at night. Talk to your children about what to do if they encounter a bear.

Once is not enough. If bears get into garbage, pet or livestock feed, orchards, or other attractants, remove the attractants immediately. Bears will move on if they return and can't find food. Repeated use of a site is much harder to stop than a single instance and can teach bears to associate food with humans. These bears can become dangerous and usually have to be killed.

3

Strange Bedfellows

Grizzly bears are dangerous, and people should not be forced to take that risk. Death and injury under any circumstance are unacceptable where they are avoidable. The statistics are meaningless to the person who is killed or hurt.

—Dirk Kempthorne, governor of Idaho

I met Hank Fischer when he was in college in the mid-1970s, earning a master's degree in environmental science from the University of Montana and working for me for a few months as an intern at *Montana Outdoors* magazine. After college he started working as the Northern Rockies representative for Defenders of Wildlife and stayed with it for twenty-five years. He left Defenders in January 2002 and started a small company that offers wildlife-watching tours, specializing in viewing grizzly bears and wolves in Yellowstone and Glacier National Parks. He also spends some of his time trying to raise money to retire grazing allotments in grizzly habitat around Yellowstone.

He has always operated out of his Missoula home office, about a block from the University of Montana, with a view of Mount Sentinel. His rig, an old gray Land Cruiser, sits out front, never seeing the inside of a garage. Here Fischer works hard to cover tuition for two sons, one of them following his tracks toward a master's in environmental science.

In the beginning of his career as a professional environmentalist, Fischer had a tough time because his employer's name implied he worked for one of those evil eastern antihunting groups despised by many westerners. In truth, Defenders of Wildlife didn't oppose hunting, and Fischer loved to hunt. I've been elk and duck hunting with him myself a few times.

It took Fischer a few years to fight through that stigma, but he did. Before long he became a much respected and successful conservationist, with the mental stamina and toughness it takes to stay with such a high-stress job for twenty-five years. His crowning achievement was his pivotal role in reintroducing wolves to Yellowstone Park and central Idaho. I lost a bet with him on that deal. I certainly wanted the wolf back, but I was convinced the political obstacles were too great. That's one bet I loved paying off.

Wolf reintroduction was an incredible environmental and social victory. Many people helped in this effort, but without Fischer's leadership and organizational skills, it most likely wouldn't have happened. While I was still working as the publisher of Falcon Publishing, I asked him to write a book on how it happened, and *Wolf Wars* became an enduring chronicle of one of the most successful environmental campaigns ever, a real inside story of eco-politics at its extreme.

So if Fischer could do it with wolves, could he do it with bears? He obviously thought so, and in the mid-1990s, while the wolves were doing better than expected in Yellowstone, he launched a campaign to reintroduce the grizzly bear into the Selway-Bitterroot Wilderness straddling the Idaho-Montana border.

You've probably heard the old cliché about lightning never striking twice in the same spot. Well, it might be true.

What made Hank Fischer a successful conservationist was his consensus-building philosophy. Unlike many environmentalists, he believed natural resource controversies should be resolved with win-win deals, like business deals normally are—or at least good business deals. As most businesspeople learn, only mutually beneficial agreements result in good, long-term relationships.

In the late 1980s, for example, before the Yellowstone reintroduction, ranchers in northern Montana complained about wolf predation. Most environmentalists had a simple response for the ranchers, something like "tough cookies, the wolves were there first." But that's not how Fischer thinks. His response was a special compensation fund to reimburse ranchers for their losses. He officially launched this fund in 1992, although the first compensation payment dated back to 1987. Since then more than a half million dollars has been raised for the fund, and by 2002 about a third of that had already been paid to ranchers to compensate for wolf predation.

Fischer tried the collaborative approach with the Yellowstone wolf reintroduction, but the consensus broke down and polarization prevailed. When the smoke cleared, many stakeholders felt that the wolf reintroduction had been rammed down their throats. Or as Fischer diplomatically describes it, "There was lots of frustration with how it was done, how much it cost, and how long it took, so could we do it better?"

Fischer, along with Tom France, an attorney working for the National Wildlife Federation, also in Missoula, thought so. For the Bitterroot bear reintroduction, they developed an innovative plan wherein the first step was finding, in Fischer's words, "the most likely detractors."

After ferreting out stakeholders most likely to oppose reintroducing grizzlies into the Bitterroots, Fischer organized a unique group of environmentalists and industry and labor union leaders. He considered the timber industry the main detractor because the grizzly bear and the Endangered Species Act (ESA) sometimes result in the denial or downsizing of timber sales.

Before agencies or enviros did anything to officially promote the Bitterroot reintroduction, this twelve-member group (mostly timber industry and labor leaders and only two environmentalists, Fischer and France) started meeting regularly. Some observers may have considered the group stacked to the right, but those people didn't know Hank Fischer and Tom France. They weren't outgunned.

"It certainly wasn't a love fest at first," Fischer recalls. "The initial meetings were somewhat tense, and both sides occasionally needed to vent their displeasure with each other, but we were surprised to discover that these people who made their living on the land did not object to restoring grizzlies into the Bitterroots.

"We also learned that nearly all of our so-called opponents shared our passion for the outdoors and enjoyed hiking, fishing, camping, and horseback riding. They, too, chose to live in Montana and Idaho because they appreciated the quality of our environment. In short, we had more in common than we ever realized."

After a few short sparring sessions, the group settled into its work with mostly "happy talk," as Fischer puts it.

The first order of business was explaining to the group why reintroducing the grizzly to the Selway-Bitterroot Wilderness was important.

The Bitterroot Ecosystem is twice the size of the Greater Yellowstone Ecosystem (GYE) and also the Northern Continental Divide Ecosystem (NCDE), the two other major recovery areas designated in the recovery plan. Many environmentalists believe recovery can't be achieved without restoring a self-sustaining grizzly population in the Bitterroot Ecosystem. "You can't really have recovery without bears in the Bitterroots," claims Louisa Willcox, former coordinator of the Sierra Club Grizzly Bear Ecosystems Project.

"Our goal is to have populations in all areas in our recovery zone (all areas south of Canada) where grizzlies have traditionally occurred," explains Chris Servheen, coordinator of the Interagency Grizzly Bear Committee (IGBC). "Obviously having bears in the Bitterroot Ecosystem increases the probability of recovery, but it would be technically possible without having bears there."

Similar to the reintroduction of wolves to Yellowstone, the bears would be reintroduced only to the 1.4 million-acre Selway-Bitterroot Wilderness, but everybody expects the grizzly to expand into the rest of the ecosystem. Wolves were only reintroduced to Yellowstone Park and likewise were expected to expand into the rest of the GYE, which is precisely what happened.

Also like the wolves in Yellowstone, the bears in the Bitterroots didn't survive the onslaught of the early 1900s, when we exterminated both the wolf and the grizzly from 98 percent of their original range. It seems rather strange that the big bear persevered in smaller areas like the Cabinet and Mission Mountains but not in the much more expansive Selway-Bitterroot Wilderness, but Fischer attributes this to the area's salmon streams and gentle landscape desirable for grazing cattle and sheep. In the mid-1900s, in fact, sheep and cattle grazing allotments covered all land later included in the Selway-Bitterroot Wilderness. The USDA Forest Service (FS) eventually retired these allotments, but not before stockmen helped eliminate the grizzly from the Bitterroots.

Prior to the building of huge dams on the Columbia River system, large numbers of salmon migrated into the area up the Salmon, Clearwater, Selway, and other rivers. Grizzlies concentrated along these streams to feed on fat-rich salmon, just as they still do in Alaska. "This made them very vulnerable," according to Fischer.

In his classic 1909 book, *The Grizzly Bear: The Narrative of a Hunter-Naturalist,* William Henry Wright wrote eloquently about watching grizzlies feed on salmon in the Clearwater River, describing in detail the bear's fishing techniques. "Once I saw five old grizzlies fishing from one log jam," he wrote. "Indeed, I have watched for hours along the streams, and some of the pleasantest moments of my hunting trips have been so spent; but while I could have killed many a bear in this way, I have never killed but three."

In any major conservation effort, the critical first phase is the development of a Draft Environmental Impact Statement (EIS). "Starting an EIS is probably the single most critical step in any species reintroduction," Fischer explains. "It's the time when opponents typically step forward and make themselves heard. It's the point where politics frequently overrides biology."

Fischer's consensus group, working closely with the Interagency Grizzly Bear Study Team and state and federal agencies, helped to release the Draft EIS faster and less expensively than anybody expected. In the Yellowstone wolf reintroduction, opponents blocked funding of the Draft EIS for nearly eight years, but in this case the so-called opponents signed a letter requesting funds. Remarkably the Republican-controlled Congress approved funding in 1995 in the midst of a hostile political atmosphere caused by the ultracontroversial wolf reintroduction and a court ruling on Pacific salmon recovery that shut down some timber harvesting in Idaho.

"Under any other scenario, the funding certainly would have been denied," Fischer speculates. "Without this collaborative approach, the Bitterroot grizzly reintroduction proposal would not have even been on the table."

The Yellowstone wolf reintroduction Draft EIS cost $6 million and took eight years to complete. In comparison, the Bitterroot grizzly reintroduction Draft EIS cost $500,000 and took less than three years—and you could argue that this project was more ambitious and complex than the wolf reintroduction.

Not only was the grizzly Draft EIS faster and cheaper, it contained some unique features. The consensus group wrote up a plan that addressed their common interests and submitted it to the U.S. Fish and Wildlife Service (FWS), and the agency used it as the preferred alternative in the Draft EIS. It contained three unusual—and controversial—sections.

The first, and perhaps most innovative, section of the Draft EIS recommended a joint management effort between federal and state agencies and local citizens and officially created a Citizen Management Committee (CMC). This idea addressed the core of this controversy, if not the core of all western environmental issues, where locals fear the federal government more than grizzly bears. For the reintroduction to have even the remotest chance of success, in Fischer's opinion, the Draft EIS had to provide for more involvement by local citizens, an idea he had already employed to get to this point in the process.

In the West, eastern environmentalists and "the feds" get verbally shredded every morning in coffee shops and every evening in saloons. Regardless of sincere efforts by scientists, federal agencies, and conservationists, this Big Brother phobia has prevented many needed implementations of the ESA. It's hard to talk to people about biodiversity when they're watching out the window for black helicopters.

The proposal for a fifteen-member CMC specifically addressed this phobia. The consensus group suggested the CMC consist of seven Idaho citizens, including a representative of the Idaho Department of Fish and Game; five Montana citizens, including a representative of the Montana Department of Fish, Wildlife & Parks; and one representative each from the Nez Perce tribe, FS, and FWS. The FWS agreed and in the Draft EIS recommended the exact same composition for the citizens committee.

As stated in the Draft EIS, "The Citizen Management Committee shall consist of a cross-section of interests reflecting a balance of viewpoints, and shall be selected for their diversity of knowledge and experience in natural resource issues, and for their commitment to collaborative decision-making." The secretaries of the interior and agriculture, in league with the governors of Idaho and Montana, would name the committee.

The CMC wasn't another government do-nothing figurehead board. Although the FWS would still be in charge, as required by the ESA, the CMC would have substantial authority to set policy and oversee most aspects of the reintroduction and ongoing management. As long as the actions of the CMC led to recovery and used the best available science to make decisions, it would keep its power. If not, the FWS would take control. This provided a powerful incentive for CMC members to make the entire process work, because they knew environmentalists would be watching carefully and probably could force the FWS to retake control if they believed the CMC's decisions weren't leading to recovery.

The second unusual—and nearly as controversial—section of the preferred alternative in the Draft EIS was designating Bitterroot grizzlies as an "experimental population." The ESA contains this provision to specifically facilitate the reintroduction of a controversial species. The experimental population status permits agencies to allow some animals to be killed as long as the relaxed policy leads to the continued recovery of the species. This controversial section of the ESA was used not only for the Yellowstone wolf reintroduction, but also to reintroduce the red wolf in North Carolina and the black-footed ferret in several states. The provision can be applied only to reintroductions and only in the historic range of the species where the animal no longer exists and has little chance of natural repopulation from other occupied habitat.

Those restrictions fit the Selway-Bitterroot plan, at least according to Fischer. There had not been a viable population of grizzly bears there since the 1930s, and the closest population in the Cabinets was struggling to hang on to viability and most likely couldn't give up enough bears to repopulate the Bitterroots, not to mention negotiate about 100 miles of manmade barriers to grizzly travel, including an interstate highway.

Part of the plan for managing an experimental population was a zero-tolerance policy for any grizzly coming into the private land in the rapidly growing Bitterroot Valley south of Missoula. Wildlife agencies would immediately kill or remove any trespassing grizzlies seen in the valley.

The third special section, which wasn't as controversial as the first two, restricted the reintroduction to the 1.4 million-acre Selway-Bitterroot Wilderness instead of trying to import bears into the entire 15 million-acre Bitterroot Ecosystem. This closely resembled the experimental population application in the Yellowstone wolf reintroduction EIS.

After the Draft EIS came out, a multiyear process began to take public comments. Hearings were held. Some people ranted and raved, but in the end the vast majority of public comments supported the preferred alternative.

When the FWS agreed to use the consensus group's plan as the preferred alternative, the process took a bizarre turn. You don't see it very often, but in this case environmentalists broke ranks, and many enviros publicly criticized the reintroduction plan. No environmental group opposed the basic idea of repopulating the Bitterroots with grizzly bears, but several groups disliked the preferred alternative. The main rub was the amount of power given to the CMC, but making the Bitterroot grizzlies an experimental population also raised some green hackles.

"It's way too full of loopholes," warned Brian Peck of the Sierra Club Grizzly Bear Ecosystems Project. "The Citizen Management Committee had too much power, and it was loaded with industry people. These people are making all the decisions. That's the reason why the grizzly bear is in so much trouble—and they wouldn't do anything different after the reintroduction. Besides that, Martz and Kempthorne would appoint the committee, so you can imagine what kind of people we'd have."

Peck was referring to Montana Governor Judy Martz and Idaho Governor Dirk Kempthorne, both Republican and both living nightmares for environmentalists, or as Peck called them, "obstructionists."

"Don't forget that the grizzly is a nationally imperiled species," Peck wrote in one of his many articles on the subject, "and that the reintroduction will take place almost entirely on public land belonging to all Americans, and that neither the state's governors nor local people are entitled to veto the national will."

Peck didn't buy Fischer's claim that the consensus approach was the only way the reintroduction could ever happen. "Everybody agrees that having a stable grizzly population in the Bitterroots is essential to have a recovery. Since so many people, even people from resource industries, want recovery and the bear delisted (removed from the protection of the ESA), they'll find a better way to do it."

Louisa Willcox also disliked the reintroduction as planned but admitted, "We had decided to hold our nose and let it go ahead, but why shouldn't we try to raise the bar and make it better?"

The Great Bear Foundation joined the fray and became one of Fischer's detractors, even though the organization's president, Chuck Jonkel, and Fischer were good friends and had worked closely together for years on many projects, including the Bear Compensation Fund. This fund, similar to Fischer's wolf fund, was created by the Great Bear Foundation to compensate stockgrowers for losses experienced from bear predation. Fischer helped to transfer ongoing management of the fund to Defenders of Wildlife at the request of the IGBC because the foundation, a much smaller organization than Defenders, lacked the financial resources to make timely compensation payments.

"We strongly prefer augmentation over reintroduction," Jonkel explained. "We support the biodiversity approach. And we don't think the citizens committee is a good idea. There'd be too much political influence. This takes us back to the 1930s. The professionals in the agencies should make the decisions."

"Augmentation" means, in essence, beefing up an existing bear population, obviously making the assumption that the Bitterroot Ecosystem still has resident grizzlies, perhaps enough to constitute a population. To prove this, the Great Bear Foundation launched "The Great Grizzly Search," which dispatched a legion of volunteers into the remotest corners of the ecosystem to look for signs of the great bear. None of their 2001 and 2002 samples of hair and scat turned out to be from grizzly bears.

"We think there are still some bears in there," Jonkel predicted. "This is a huge area, and the agencies have only searched for grizzlies in a small part of it."

Even if Jonkel's army found proof of the grizzly bear, it probably wouldn't result in a major setback for Fischer, who wouldn't discount the possibility that there might be a few grizzlies in the area, but definitely not enough to constitute a viable population.

The absence of a viable population of grizzly bears and any evidence of recent reproduction allowed the inclusion of the ESA's experimental population clause in the preferred alternative in the Draft EIS. If this assumption proved incorrect and the area did have a viable population, it would invalidate the EIS and set the entire effort back years. "But it's inconceivable that there's still a viable population in there," Fischer claimed. "They've been hunting elk and black bear in there for decades, all over the area, and there would have been some evidence. A black bear hunter would have killed one by mistake, or a grizzly would have been in a hunting camp."

In September 2002 a subadult grizzly showed up at upper Rock Creek in the Sapphire Mountains, south of the big bear barrier, I-90. From Rock Creek, the bear moved about 15 miles west and got into garbage around the Burnt Fork area near Stevensville—only a few miles from the Selway-Bitterroot Wilderness. Bear managers decided to trap the bear and move it back into the NCDE, but before they could get the traps set, the bear disappeared. Biologists and environmentalists want to believe that the wandering grizzly went up into the wilderness and made a home for itself, but nobody knows this for sure.

This bear—along with the Ninemile Grizzly and a few more wanderlust bruins—does, however, add strength to the arguments of those who think the grizzly can naturally repopulate the Bitterroots. The bear probably came out of the Bob Marshall Complex and crossed the Garnet Range south of Ovando before dashing over the freeway. It definitely proves grizzlies can travel far and wide and could make it into the Bitterroots.

The movement of these bears across I-90 is quite significant because Fischer and other proponents of reintroduction believe the freeway creates a major barrier that prevents the grizzly from repopulating the Bitterroots naturally. "It's not so much about individual bears being there (in the Bitterroots)," Fischer explained. "It's more about a population being there. There has to be evidence of reproduction to constitute a population."

"The grizzly population is expanding," he admitted. "But look at how long it takes bears to expand into a new area. The dispersers tend to be young males who are kicked out of the core area and wander around a bit."

All of this is déjà vu for Fischer because he has faced off with the Sierra Club and other enviros before on the same issue. When the FWS, with Fischer's support, used the same experimental population clause for the Yellowstone wolf reintroduction, the Sierra Club opposed it and claimed there were still wolves roaming the park. That issue went to court, and even though the plaintiffs had documentation of wolf DNA in the park, the court nonetheless allowed the use of the experimental population clause, mainly because there wasn't a viable wolf population nor was there much chance of one in the future.

Fischer won that fight, but will he win this one?

Probably, but Fischer faces a much bigger opponent than the Sierra Club in winning approval for the Bitterroot bear reintroduction. When he lined up his most likely detractors, he may have missed the biggest detractor of all, John Q. Public, who has an ingrained primordial fear of the grizzly bear. Concern for human safety, or "irrational fear," as Fischer describes it, definitely percolated up to the highest political levels and caused core opposition to reintroducing grizzly bears into any area where they didn't already exist. Upon reflecting on the overall process, Chris Servheen agrees. "Public safety turned out to be the number one concern."

The local John Q., perhaps the proverbial silent majority in places like Stanley, Idaho, or Hamilton, Montana, probably doesn't care much about things like experimental populations or citizens management committees or whether augmentation is better than reintroduction. Some people just don't want grizzly bears, period, primarily because of concern for public safety. In Stanley, in fact, the local sheriff told reintroduction proponents that he couldn't protect them if they went ahead with a public meeting on the subject.

This issue came up in Yellowstone, too, and Fischer had to overcome what he called the "Little Red Riding Hood Syndrome." But in the Bitterroot reintroduction, he had a much different animal, a critter that did indeed kill and eat people, and Fischer may have underestimated his real opponent.

With a huge body of research on his side, Fischer could successfully claim that a nonrabid wolf had never attacked anybody anywhere in North America. People accepted the facts, and the issue of public safety never became a major obstacle in the Yellowstone wolf reintroduction.

Not so with the grizzly bear. Fischer had plenty of statistics on bear-human encounters—about mosquitoes and milk cows and vending machines killing more people than bears—but those numbers fell on deaf ears. Statistically grizzly bears kill an average of less than one person per year. Apparently, though, one is too many for some people.

Fischer also compared the Selway-Bitterroot to the Bob Marshall Wilderness, the latter approximately the same size but with a healthy population of grizzly bears. In the Bob Marshall a wounded grizzly killed a hunter in 1939, but that had been the only documented fatality since records were kept until the 2001 incident on the Blackfoot-Clearwater Game Range. He additionally brought in outside experts and took them on tour to talk to people, but nothing worked.

Officially public comments didn't reflect an irrational fear of bears. Only 12.5 percent of the people who sent in public comments cited safety as a major concern, but unofficially many did fret about it—and obviously a few people in high places did, and they apparently ruled the day.

At this point the roof started to cave in. "Basically what happened was the politicians told us to get together with industry and work something out that we could all agree on and then bring it to them and they'd support it," recalls Fischer. "Well, we did that, but when we brought it to them, they wouldn't support it."

Some did, including then Montana Governor Marc Racicot, who called the consensus group's proposal "superb" and went on to insist that "without the detailed and intensive involvement of Idaho and Montana citizens, the chances for success of the reintroduction would be greatly diminished."

The media liked it, too. Most local newspapers editorialized in favor of the citizen management approach, and the national media also joined in. *ABC Nightly News* did a special Earth Day segment on the proposal, and several national newspapers such as the *Washington Post* ran features or editorials supporting this nontraditional approach.

U.S. Senator Michael Crapo of Idaho, a conservative Republican, saw the editorial in the *Washington Post* and was so impressed with the idea that he sent the editorial to the members of the Republican

Task Force on the Environment, a group that decides Republican positions on major environmental issues. One of the group's goals was to counter the growing perception that Republicans were, in general, antienvironmental.

"One of the key challenges we face as Republicans is to develop a proper framework within which we can address environmental issues," Crapo wrote in a cover letter sent with the editorial. "We are forced to make a decision between people and animals or between jobs and animals. There is no middle ground because the debate is too polarized, the regulations too restrictive to allow for anything other than a win/lose scenario. There must be better options. It takes creativity, consensus-building, and a willingness to work together."

But the politicians who really mattered couldn't stomach the idea, regardless of how collaborative and reasonable it seemed to be. They just couldn't bring themselves to support such a thoroughly green idea. So they reneged on their deal, not only pulling support for the consensus plan, but also working underground to torpedo it. Fischer doesn't like to name names, because he hopes for future support from some of these politicians, but admits, "It wasn't that hard to figure out who was on board and who wasn't, but in the end, Kempthorne was the one who really stopped us."

Governor Kempthorne, along with retired U.S. Representative from Idaho, Helen Chenoweth, were certainly among the most vocal opponents of the plan. Chenoweth likened it to "introducing sharks at the beach," and, likewise, Kempthorne didn't mince words. In his 2001 State of the State Address he asked, "Can you believe the Clinton administration's proposal to reintroduce the flesh-eating grizzly into the Selway-Bitterroot Wilderness? Folks, this could be the first land management action in history to result in the sure death and injury of citizens."

Fischer heard this loud and clear: "The reintroduction probably won't happen as long as Kempthorne is in office." On November 5, 2002, Idahoans elected him to another four-year term as governor.

Brian Peck is more pointed in his criticism: "This is a political payback by the right wing, pure and simple."

Chris Servheen doesn't go that far but says, "This whole ordeal wasn't even about grizzly bears. It was about state versus federal control, about a struggle to keep the states in control. Somehow they thought we (the feds) were taking control, and the politicians played the fear factor expertly to this end."

Louisa Willcox thinks the proponents were partly at fault and shouldn't have proceeded without a better foundation of support from local communities, especially in Idaho. "This worked beautifully with Yellowstone wolves, but we didn't do it with this plan," she notes, "and that's why it went sour. You can't have a project based in Missoula when most of the affected area is in Idaho. We just didn't have a base of support in Idaho."

Ironically, according to Willcox, the rapid pace of the proposal might have helped defeat it. "In the wolf reintroduction we did seven years of groundwork while waiting for the funding."

When Marc Racicot moved on after two terms as governor of Montana to chairman of the National Republican Party, former Lieutenant Governor Judy Martz replaced him and quickly joined Kempthorne in opposing the grizzly reintroduction. This left Fischer with few friends in high political places. Most politicians wouldn't even discuss how it might be done—they simply didn't want it done, period, end of discussion. So what to do?

Keep pushing. The next step was the Final EIS, which the FWS prepared, again using the consensus group's plan as the preferred alternative. This was followed by what's called a Record of Decision, the final official bureaucratic document signed by the FWS after receiving approval from the secretary of the interior, if not the president himself, who at that time was Bill Clinton. In other words, it was essentially the end of the game, a done deal. The reintroduction was scheduled to start in the summer of 2002.

Lightning did hit the same guy twice. Fischer had won again—or at least he thought he did, but we can never forget about the political world we live in.

If you're a politician, you can make up your own rules instead of following legal mandates such as those cast down in the ESA. If politicians disagree with something, it really doesn't matter what the law of the land might be.

The Record of Decision was signed in November 2000, in the last days of the Clinton administration and in the midst of the bitter battle between George W. Bush and Al Gore over who won the election. Bush won, but Hank Fischer—and the grizzly bear—lost.

"That's what really went wrong," Willcox reminisces. "Gore lost the election."

Shortly after Bush was elected, he named Gale Norton as secretary of the interior, and, in short order, in June 2001 she decided to reevaluate the Record of Decision, an unprecedented turn of events. Nonetheless, Norton officially asked for reevaluation, and yet another public comment period took place. Once again the pro-bear public— about 97 percent of comments, in fact—strongly supported the reintroduction.

Anti-bear forces pointed out that most of the comments came from outside the affected area, but legally that probably didn't matter. It sure did politically, though, and it put Norton in a bind.

Technically, and perhaps legally, she couldn't overturn the Record of Decision. There was no scientific basis for overturning it, as required by the ESA, and the public strongly supported reintroduction. Several prominent Republicans did not support it, however, so what's a defiant secretary of the interior to do after painting herself into a corner?

Nothing.

And a brilliant strategy it was.

Norton made no official ruling on the reevaluation. She probably couldn't legally overturn the Record of Decision, but politics dictated she do so. By not ruling one way or the other, she accomplished her goal. She stopped the reintroduction, and she quashed plans for a lawsuit to force the process forward.

"Technically the Record of Decision wasn't changed, so we couldn't litigate it," Fischer explains. "It was good strategy on her part. There was some general language in the ESA about moving forward as rapidly as possible, but no real time limit, so nobody knows what an unreasonable amount of time is. We might have to wait until the current administration gets ready to leave office."

"There's no law that says the government can't change its mind," agrees Tom France. "It's certainly awkward for them to walk away from all this public comment and the best science available, but it's hard for us to find a rationale for litigation."

Strange bedfellows. That's one way you could describe the Bitterroot bear reintroduction. Think about it: The primary environmentalists pushing the project, Hank Fischer and Tom France, developed strong alliances with the leaders of the timber industry and with federal and state agencies, normally their opponents in an environmental debate. And conservative politicians who normally side with industry leaders on environmental issues more or less allied with the Sierra Club and other liberal environmental groups in opposing the reintroduction.

Strange bedfellows can bond together into a cohesive force, as witnessed by one remarkable turn of events in 1994. Fischer recalls a memorable meeting the day after election day, when both the House and Senate went Republican and the outlook for environmental protection looked bleak. He went to that meeting of his consensus group, expecting the industry partners to reconsider their involvement, because it was obvious that they now had the political horses to prevent any reintroduction for the foreseeable future.

To Fischer's surprise, the election only reaffirmed the timber industry's commitment to the collaborative process. "We're sticking with this process because it's the right thing to do," said Bill Mulligan, who represented the Resource Organization on Timber Supply. "Yes, we could block grizzly restoration now, but at some point in the future, the pendulum would swing the other way. If we can find a solution today that meets the needs of local people and the bear, we're all better off. This approach takes the politics and the polarization out of the issue."

Mulligan's comments generally reflected the opinions of the consensus group, and they kept working.

Strange bedfellows can come together when everybody has the same goal, which is actually the case with most efforts to preserve endangered species. Nobody wants species listed under the ESA. Everybody wants them delisted. Environmentalists want to believe they saved a species. Industry detractors might personally like to believe this, too, but they also want the species recovered so they don't have to deal with restrictions on resource development and worry about the feds looking over their shoulders.

So maybe it wasn't strange bedfellows after all.

Fischer's major opponent wasn't the timber industry. Instead his major challenge was overcoming an "irrational fear" of bears so strong that it withstood the best efforts of a truly effective environmentalist. "It sure shows you how the extremes of an issue can control it," Fischer reminisces, "and that it's easier to stop something than to make something happen."

Was overconfidence a problem? Probably not. Fischer attributes the current setback to plain old bad luck. "With the wolf reintroduction, we simply had the right people in the right places in government to get the job done, but with the Bitterroot bears, we just didn't have those people with the ability to carry the ball into the end zone."

Fischer and his consensus group made a big investment in this deal, and they won't walk away from it. But they might be forced to file a lawsuit to get the plan off the shelf. This, of course, follows the path of polarization, precisely what the group wanted to avoid.

In any case, this study of eco-political intrigue will continue to play out over the next few years, possibly for decades. And eventually, someday, somehow, the grizzly bear may reestablish residence in the Bitterroots.

The Governor and the Grizzly

Idaho governor Dirk Kempthorne played a pivotal role in defeating the Bitterroot grizzly reintroduction, and based on his answers to my questions, he isn't likely to lessen his resolve to prevent it in the future.

"Reintroducing grizzly bears into Idaho is unnecessary, unsafe, and undesirable," the governor insists. "Grizzly bears are dangerous, and people should not be forced to take that risk. Right now the Selway-Bitterroot Wilderness is one of the largest wilderness areas where people from all over the world can hunt, hike, ride, and camp without fear of grizzly bears. Death and injury under any circumstance are unacceptable where they are avoidable. The statistics are meaningless to the person who is killed or hurt.

"People should have a choice, and our choice is 'no.' The people of Idaho have overwhelmingly opposed reintroduction; our legislature, in a bipartisan vote, opposed it; and our congressional delegation has also voiced its objection to this grizzly bear plan. This experimental program would violate state sovereignty and, as we alleged in our lawsuit, the Tenth Amendment to the U.S. Constitution because it infringes on Idaho's ability to manage its own wildlife."

Governor Kempthorne and other Idaho politicians obviously opposed the reintroduction, but they don't necessarily want credit for the defeat of the proposal. Instead they, like many others, blame it on the federal government.

"The reason this project never got off the ground is that not even the U.S. Fish and Wildlife Service was wholly committed to it, and the Idaho Department of Fish and Game opposed it," Kempthorne insists. "They (the FWS) delayed the paperwork and had no plans to fund the project."

Idaho already has grizzly bears, of course. The Yellowstone population is expanding deeper and deeper into the Targhee National Forest and the Centennial Mountains east of the park, and the Selkirk Mountains of northern Idaho also support a few grizzlies. But, Kempthorne notes, "More bears mean more expense, more danger, and more opportunity for frivolous lawsuits. Where the bears go, an expensive program is sure to follow. And bears—like spotted owls and bull trout—are routinely used by special interests as the basis for lawsuits that delay, derail, and disrupt land management."

One part of the Bitterroot proposal the governor seems to like is the citizen management approach, but not enough to support the plan. In fact, he considers local control essential.

"The Endangered Species Act cannot work unless local, state, and federal governments agree to work together on a cooperative program," according to Kempthorne. "By sharing responsibility for species conservation, we are more likely to make durable decisions and provide sustainable staffing and funds to reach the goals. As for bears that show up in the Selway-Bitterroot, we can consider citizen management for them if and when that happens. Reintroduction of bears should not be the price of citizen management."

Idaho and its governor support delisting, and environmentalists have argued that the state should support the reintroduction to expedite recovery and then delisting, but Kempthorne doesn't see it that way. He says delisting would be more likely if Canada's grizzlies were included in population estimates, which is something neither the FWS nor environmentalists do, even though they all know bears freely move back and forth over the border.

"It is important to note that the reintroduction proposal would have moved bears out of populations that are healthy and poised for delisting on their own," Kempthorne explains. "Keep in mind that listing and delisting are bureaucratic decisions reflecting our country's confidence in the future of a species. Current plans are to delist grizzly bears by ecosystem; for example, the Yellowstone population will be delisted independently of other areas, and these existing bear populations must be kept intact."

At the end of the day, however, environmentalists and Governor Kempthorne agree on one point. The Bitterroot reintroduction isn't going to happen unless the governor changes his mind, and it wouldn't be wise to hold your breath until this happens.

Is One Too Many?

For as long as records have been kept, grizzly bears have killed an average of less than one person per year in North America. Clearly we take much greater risks doing just about everything we do, even staying home, than we do by going into grizzly country. Yet some people still harbor an irrational fear of bears and believe even one is too many, especially when they can avoid any risk by refusing to allow the grizzly to expand its range into their backyards. When asked why we should take the risk of a bear attack when, to the inquisitor, even one is too many, here's what the experts have to say:

"This is the flip side of people criticizing enviros for saying that one tree getting cut down is too many or any amount of pollution or pesticides is too much. There's risk in anything you do in the outdoors. The risk the grizzly bear poses is very, very low."
— HANK FISCHER, former Northern Rockies
representative for Defenders of Wildlife

"If I get asked that question, I say you can make a choice. Most of the world doesn't have grizzly bears, so you can go there. So why not give the rest of us the choice of going where there are grizzly bears?"
— KATE KENDALL, project leader, Northern
Continental Divide DNA Monitoring Project

"For some, that's too much, but for other people, it's not too much. To make it totally safe, we'd have to pasteurize the wilderness so a tree can't fall on you or you can't fall off a rock, and it would take trillions of dollars. We can't even make homes safe. How could we make the wilderness safe? And the bigger question is, do we want to?"
— BRIAN PECK, consultant, Sierra Club Grizzly
Bear Ecosystems Project

"If I get asked that question, it's a tough one for me, and I might not have a good enough answer to change that person's opinion. Anything we do has a cost. All I can do is do everything I can to make sure nobody gets hurt by a bear."
— GARY MOSES, chair, Wildlife Management
Committee, Glacier National Park

"When I'm asked this question, I try to overwhelm them with statistics on how people die. Tobacco kills 700,000 people annually, 60,000 die in auto accidents, and 4,000 guys get killed by their wives every year. Bees, wasps, and hornets kill about 400 people every year, but do you ever see a sign at a trailhead that says "Trail Closed Because of Yellowjackets"?
—CHUCK JONKEL, bear specialist and president
of the Great Bear Foundation

"Some people can't manage fear, so perhaps hiking in grizzly country is not their cup of tea. We live in a culture where we're afraid of everything. Fear is a personal thing. You can't tell people where to put it."
—LOUISA WILLCOX, former project coordinator,
Sierra Club Grizzly Bear Ecosystems Project

"What I like to tell people is that more people have committed suicide in Yellowstone than have been killed by bears, so you're more likely to kill yourself than be killed by a bear."
—KERRY GUNTHER, bear management specialist,
Yellowstone National Park

"These are people who live next to Rottweilers, and Rottweilers kill 260 people every year. Everybody has a threshold, and grizzly bears could easily be somebody's threshold. I think what people are really scared of is the wilderness. They're afraid of the unknown."
—JOHN VARLEY, director, Yellowstone Center
for Resources

"Grizzly bears do kill people, and I agree any death caused by a grizzly is regrettable. If the risk were great, it would be unacceptable, but the risk is so low that it's acceptable. If people are unwilling to take any risk, then grizzly bears are unacceptable."
—CHRIS SERVHEEN, coordinator, Interagency
Grizzly Bear Committee

"There are people deathly afraid of airplanes or heights, too. I just assume that there will be some people who are so afraid of grizzly bears that they will never want to recreate in grizzly country, just like people who never get on airplanes."

—DAN CARNEY, director of wildlife research, Blackfeet Reservation

"There's no real counter to that. The risk is minimal and acceptable, but if that's too much risk, well, there's nothing you can do about it."

—STEVE HERRERO, professor emeritus of environmental science at the University of Calgary and leader of the Eastern Slopes Grizzly Bear Project

"I try to avoid these conversations, but what I tell people is that we have proven without a shadow of the doubt that we can share the landscape with grizzly bears. All we have to do is want to do it."

—BOB SANDFORD, coordinator, Heritage Tourism Strategy

4

The Great Grizzly Gamble

Why would we consider delisting the grizzly bear in the Yellowstone ecosystem, even if it could be unequivocally demonstrated that the population has recovered? Recovery of a single population unit such as the Yellowstone population would be only the first step in a multistep recovery program for long-term persistence in the contiguous forty-eight states. With such long-term consequences, we don't have the option to delist.

Delisting, if it occurs at all, must await population recovery throughout the Northern Rockies. Current delisting efforts may serve bureaucratic and political agendas, but a rational biological agenda should require no deadlines, no near-term declaration of accomplishment, and no change in protective status.

—John Craighead, Wildlife-Wildlands Institute

I had read about her, and I had seen her quoted in the papers many times, but all I could think of when I finally had a chance to meet her was that here's somebody you definitely want on your side. If you owned a mining company and wanted a government permit, you'd want her to get it for you. If you were the director of a federal agency battling state agencies or enviros, you'd want her representing you—assuming you wanted to get something done, that is. If you were the Sierra Club, you'd want her in charge of your efforts to save the grizzly bear, which is exactly what Louisa Willcox has done for two decades. There's no chance of her giving up anytime soon, but she concedes, "It's a hard business to be in."

I guess she's a master of the understatement, too.

I recently spent a few hours with her in her office in the stately Emerson Cultural Center, in downtown Bozeman, Montana. Here—from a covey of offices cluttered with maps, stacks of scientific research reports, and "Guard the Grizzly" posters—as leader of the Sierra Club Grizzly Bear Ecosystems Project, she coordinates the grand environmental battle plan to make sure the grizzly bear has a future. She manages a staff of eight—make that nine if you count her not-so-little office dog named Little Guy, obviously named as a puppy without thinking much about the potential for future growth. If a poll were taken, Louisa Willcox would most likely be voted the most influential environmentalist in the endless campaign to save the grizzly bear. A few months after I talked to her, she switched ships over to the National Resources Defense Council but continues to do the same work.

When you listen to Willcox talk, you get the feeling you're hearing the unabridged history of the grizzly in fast-forward. And that's what you do when you're with her, you listen, because it's hard to get a word in when she's juiced up and rolling on about what society needs to do to preserve her favorite animal. Or at least her favorite wild animal.

"The grizzly bear is a living symbol of the American West," she has written, "a wilderness icon, and the essence of what makes Yellowstone Yellowstone, an ecological canary in the coal mine, whose well-being indicates health for many other wildlife species, as well as human communities which rely upon the land."

She compares the grizzly to an inner-city youth, born into the world with many strikes against it—low reproductive rate, small litter size, long rearing period, the need for a large home range, an undeserved reputation as a man-eating beast, a voracious appetite in a food-short habitat, enemies who would shoot it for its claws or gall bladder, and the need for remoteness in a world rapidly becoming less remote. Perhaps worst of all, it's an animal with no friends in high political places.

You get the picture? The grizzly isn't the silver-spoon child in the animal kingdom. Because of the multiple strikes against it, according to Willcox, "grizzlies tend to die young and not of natural causes."

Before going to the Sierra Club, she worked for the Greater Yellowstone Coalition, but she left in 1995 to start a small environmental group called Wild Forever, which later morphed into the Grizzly Bear Ecosystems Project.

Her thoughts on the future of the grizzly bear? "In the short-term, we could definitely lose the grizzly in the Cabinet-Yaak and Selkirk Ecosystems. The agencies may have already written off these populations. We're probably not going to lose the bear in the other ecosystems in the short-term, but we're setting the table for the future."

Willcox and her coworkers have been involved in virtually every facet of preserving the grizzly bear, but the delisting debate has soaked up most of their time, energy, and money of late. The Interagency Grizzly Bear Committee (IGBC) has set the goal of delisting the grizzly in the Greater Yellowstone Ecosystem by 2005.

This means government wildlife managers think the Yellowstone grizzly is well on its way to recovery and by 2005 will no longer be threatened with extinction. Delisting would remove the bear from the protective umbrella provided by the Endangered Species Act (ESA) and transfer responsibility for grizzly management from the U.S. Fish and Wildlife Service (FWS) to the state wildlife agencies in Idaho, Montana, and Wyoming.

The IGBC believes the Yellowstone grizzly population has recovered from its downward spiral of the early 1970s, after the National Park Service (NPS) abruptly closed garbage dumps in Yellowstone National Park, much to the chagrin of renowned bear scientists Frank and John Craighead. The dump closures instantly eliminated a huge percentage of the Yellowstone grizzly's diet, and the number of encounters skyrocketed as bears scrambled to find alternative food sources. Many of these encounters ended in dead bears. The Craigheads believed at least half of the grizzly population died in the killing fields of the 1970s and subsequently predicted extinction for the Yellowstone grizzly by 1981.

Fortunately that prediction proved to be overly pessimistic. Instead, after hitting its low point around 1981, the Yellowstone grizzly population started crawling back to the level estimated by the Craigheads in the 1960s, around 400 to 600 bears. At the same time, grizzlies began pioneering new habitat farther and farther from the park. "We now have bears occupying habitat where they haven't been for a hundred years," notes Chuck Schwartz, leader of the Interagency Grizzly Bear Study Team (IGBST). "We may be at our zenith for the grizzly bear in the Yellowstone Ecosystem. This is an island, and once it's occupied, we can't have more bears."

The Sierra Club and all of the other major environmental groups strongly disagree with the timing of delisting. So far, enviros have successfully fought efforts to remove the protections afforded by the ESA. In 2002 it looked like this battle was still in the fourth inning with a score something like Sierra Club 7, IGBC 2, with Willcox calling the delisting process "a five-ring circus."

Ironically, everybody wants the grizzly delisted, even Louisa Willcox. Delisting is everybody's victory. Enviros want delisting because it represents a tremendous success story. Industry wants delisting because it removes a major obstacle to development and prevents enviros from playing the bear card to trump energy and mining development and timber sales. Federal agencies want delisting so they can devote money and staff to other priorities and wouldn't have bear-crazy ecofreaks pounding on them every day. State agencies want delisting because it means they won the war with the feds and earned back the state's right to manage wildlife. Even politicians want delisting so people will stop calling them about it.

But there's no such agreement on when or how to do it. "Delisting is ultimately all about politics, not science," Willcox believes. "How can they (government agencies) even say with a straight face that they can delist the grizzly now in the Yellowstone Ecosystem when all the science says the opposite?"

She also likes to point out that the public (about 95 percent of recorded comments, in fact) overwhelmingly opposes premature delisting. The FWS has, according to Willcox, ignored public opinion in its headlong dive for delisting.

"The park itself is no longer the problem," she explains. "The problem is outside the park."

Willcox refers to what she sees as unbridled development of areas surrounding the park, on both private and public land. She's particularly concerned about the absence of any recommendations for meaningful regulation of this development in delisting discussions, even though, again, roughly 95 percent of public comments supported increased protection of grizzly habitat. Instead, and incorrectly in her opinion, the major push for delisting is based on population estimates. All, or almost all, funding has gone to counting bears, not to regulating development nor to improving or acquiring key habitat.

The recovery plan sets fairly easy-to-reach goals for removing the bear from the threatened species list, according to Willcox, but does nothing to limit the activities that made the grizzly extinct in most of its original range in the first place, such as logging roads and energy development. The recovery plan and delisting process turn over responsibility for habitat protection to the USDA Forest Service (FS) and state and local agencies, yielding to the incredibly intense political push for "local control." But, Willcox notes, the performance of forest supervisors is, in part, rated on their ability to cut as many trees as possible. They aren't rated on their ability to protect wildlands, close roads, hold back oil and gas drilling, reduce off-road vehicle use, or, in general, limit resource activities that in the past led to the near-demise of the grizzly bear.

"The best way to ensure that grizzlies will survive into the future is to restore them to a bigger landscape," Willcox says. "Fortunately the Yellowstone region is blessed with good habitat for bears to move into, including habitat that connects Yellowstone to other grizzly ecosystems, which would increase overall numbers and the long-term health of the population."

What she's referring to is another political hot potato, the size of the recovery zone. She thinks the Greater Yellowstone Ecosystem is much too small to ensure the future of the grizzly and points out that the IGBC's own radio telemetry studies show regular use by grizzly bears in 4.5 million acres outside the current recovery zone. "Unfortunately the recovery line does not include areas bears currently use or will need if displaced from other habitat by development or declines in key food sources."

Chris Servheen of the IGBC disagrees with the idea of increasing the size of the recovery zone and points out that this was never part of the deal. "We never said habitat outside the recovery zone would be protected," he claims. "Certainly it isn't protected now, but maybe it will be in the future. I think the Forest Service will make some management changes outside the zone."

Actually, when you talk to Willcox and Servheen on separate occasions, you have to wonder if they're on the same planet, politically speaking. Willcox has no doubt that politics carries the day and that politicians are forcing the FWS to prematurely delist the grizzly. "A decision has been made, basically, to delist the bear," she claims. "We expect a delisting proposal by the end of the year (2003)."

Servheen says what politics, what decision, what proposal, and what is she talking about?

"As usual," he lashes back, "Louisa Willcox is making stuff up. There's been no decision to even propose delisting, and I cannot see that happening by the end of this year. I am the grizzly bear coordinator and have been so for twenty-two years. Nobody has given me any political pressure to do anything about delisting. That's not even on the table right now."

Servheen also pooh-poohs the Sierra Club's concern over disappearing habitat. "Logging is a minimal problem. The Shoshone, Gallatin, and Bridger-Teton (national forests) are hardly cutting any trees, and the Targhee has pretty much cut them all already. And are we really going to see full-field development of oil and gas near Yellowstone National Park? I doubt it. Basically I don't see development of public land as that big of a deal."

Private land is a problem for the grizzly bear, he agrees, even though it amounts to a small percentage of the recovery zone, but he points out that the ESA never had any impact on private land development, so delisting won't change that fact.

So there you go. That should clarify the political situation. I guess you could say there isn't much common ground, and I'll go out on a limb and bet that Willcox and Servheen don't get together on Friday nights for a few brewskis.

Servheen's confidence notwithstanding, after talking to Willcox and reading the stack of documents I carried out of her office, the argument against premature delisting looks powerful.

First and perhaps foremost, delisting proposals contain no assurance that habitat destruction won't continue unabated. "This proves the FWS is determined to remove ESA protections for the Yellowstone grizzly bear under any circumstances," Willcox insists. "They set the bar for habitat protection so low it doesn't even protect bears where they live today, much less consider future threats to the forests and mountains where they range."

Researchers have proven that Yellowstone grizzlies range freely in and out of the park. The same research tells us the grizzly depends heavily on the public and private lands surrounding the park. Bear experts like Kerry Gunther, who supervises the park's bear management efforts, readily agrees with this. "The park is not enough," he says without reservation.

On January 5, 2001, during the infamous last days of the Clinton administration and after 600 public hearings over three years and 1.6 million public comments, the FS adopted a rule banning new road building on 58.5 million acres of national forest land, including 4.2 million acres in the Greater Yellowstone Ecosystem. This sounds like a lot, but, in reality, it's less than 2 percent of the U.S. land base.

Environmentalists, including Willcox, were elated and believed this rule could make a difference for the grizzly, but their revelry was short-lived. A mere two months later, the incoming Bush administration suspended it—illegally suspended it, according to the Sierra Club.

Nobody really disputes the need to protect roadless lands to help the grizzly. "For grizzlies to survive into the future," notes Servheen, "as much roadless land as possible must be protected." Scientists back this up with several studies that prove roads fragment habitat, cause grizzlies to underutilize key food sources, and increase bear mortality.

Even if reimplemented, however, the roadless rule still wouldn't apply to private land in the GYE, which is about 11 percent of the land considered part of the ecosystem. Although minor in percentage, private land is major in importance because it includes low-elevation valleys and riparian areas, often among the highest-quality habitat for both *Ursus arctos horribilis* and *Homo sapiens*.

John Varley, director of the Yellowstone Center for Resources and in charge of all research activities in the park, doesn't completely share the IGBC's optimism for the future of the grizzly.

"I'm concerned about the long-term future of the grizzly bear," Varley says. "The long-term is definitely not as bright as the short-term."

Varley knows the private land around the park is vital to the future of the grizzly. He also knows the park isn't, for the most part, prime habitat, so bears must go outside the park, especially to expand their range, something that needs to happen to meet IGBC recovery goals.

"What do you do with all those people with their little homesteads?" Varley asks. "The one thing we can't do is camp out on private property and talk to everybody about horse food and apple orchards and bird feeders. We have no control over what happens on private land, and this results in too much human-caused mortality."

Varley volunteers the obvious. His view is counter to that of the NPS, his employer. "To be honest, I don't personally believe we'll see delisting of the grizzly bear in my lifetime."

Gunther, who works for Varley, agrees there's a problem outside the park. "We've cleaned up the park, but outside the park we need to keep working on public education on living with bears. I'm worried that state and local agencies are giving up too early on trying to clean up private lands."

A major focus of the Sierra Club's criticism of the delisting proposal, in addition to the small size of the recovery zone, is the avoidance of any meaningful discussion on the isolation, or "islandizing," of the Yellowstone grizzly population. Scientists believe the GYE must be genetically and geographically linked to other grizzly populations. To achieve this, key linkage zones must be protected. This would prevent a possible problem with genetic inbreeding and provide avenues for the Yellowstone population to be augmented by other grizzly populations, and vice versa.

"The Yellowstone Ecosystem is not enough," Willcox warns. "We really need to connect it with other populations."

And it will be a challenge. The most logical link is along the Montana-Idaho border through the Centennials, across I–15, along the Italian Peaks, through the West Big Hole area, and into the Bitterroots, assuming, of course, the grizzly is able to reestablish a population there (see Strange Bedfellows).

The other potential route goes from the Gravellies to the Tobacco Roots and through the mountains west of Helena to the Continental Divide and into the Northern Continental Divide Ecosystem. On a map this linkage zone looks shorter, but it may present an even bigger challenge for the grizzly because much of it is private land.

On the issue of linkage, there's some agreement. "Developing these linkage zones isn't essential for recovery," Serveheen contends, "but it certainly would enhance the probability of recovery."

Where the grizzly walks, controversy follows. And any effort to provide linkage corridors, where the grizzly could walk from ecosystem to ecosystem, could be very controversial.

Another powerful argument against premature delisting is the tenuous status of major grizzly food sources. Yellowstone Park is not high-quality habitat because the fairly dry, high-elevation park doesn't support an abundance of succulent vegetation and berries, which bears depend on in other areas such as some national forests surrounding Yellowstone and in Glacier National Park. Because of this, the GYE may never support the density of bears found in Glacier.

One key vegetative food source Yellowstone does have in relative abundance, however, is whitebark pine seeds. The seeds are full of vegetable fat and much-needed calories and are ready to eat in October, when grizzlies really need high-quality food.

Grizzly bears usually stay in their winter dens for five or six months, which means they have to live on food they consume during the other half of the year, with part of May and June commonly taken up with mating activities. So grizzlies need to consume a year's worth of food in about four or five months. In August grizzlies enter a physiological condition called hyperphagia, which lasts until they go to their dens in November or early December. During hyperphagia the search for food becomes an all-out panic. The constantly famished bears must pack in 20,000 calories or more per day to put on enough fat to survive the winter sleep, when they don't eat or drink.

It's apropos that the grizzly would depend on the whitebark pine, a wilderness species in its own right. The stately whitebark pine, like the grizzly, is considered a "keystone species" because of its ecological significance. It grows on windswept, high-elevation ridges and plateaus, and is fancied by some as a weather-beaten Old Man of the Mountains. In fact, the whitebark pine's ability to prosper in colder, drier, windier sites than other trees allows it to dominate around timberline.

In high-altitude whitebark pine stands, the grizzly has an ally in its pursuit of fatness, the red squirrel. The squirrel collects vast quantities of whitebark pine seeds and stores them in underground middens. Grizzlies find these middens and devour the squirrels' winter caches. Not only do these squirrel middens provide prehibernation meals, but grizzlies can also find them under snow before or after denning when other foods are scarce.

It's difficult to overestimate the importance of the fat-rich pine seeds. Biologists estimate that the grizzlies in Yellowstone get 23 percent of their yearly intake of energy from them, only second in importance to red meat from elk, bison, and other ungulates. Female grizzlies in Yellowstone that consume high quantities of pine seeds have higher reproductive rates. When Yellowstone has a bad crop of pine seeds, grizzlies look elsewhere for food, often moving them into low-elevation areas and closer to logging roads, which increases mortality. Roughly twice as many females and three times as many subadult males die from bear-human conflicts in years with poor pine seed crops.

Also like the grizzly, the whitebark pine is vulnerable—and threatened. This time, though, we aren't the killer, at least not directly. In the same way as the chestnut blight and Dutch elm disease decimated those species, a seemingly unstoppable disease, white pine blister rust, threatens to wipe out a large majority of these trees. Blister rust has already purged most whitebark pines from Glacier National Park, the Bob Marshall Wilderness, and the Selway-Bitterroot Wilderness, and now it's killing them in Yellowstone. By 2001 Grand Teton National Park had lost 44 percent of its whitebark pines to the disease, but to date blister rust has claimed only 7 percent of Yellowstone's population, mainly because the park's drier climate impedes the spread of the disease. However, bear biologists consider it a matter of *when*, not *if*, the disease will destroy most of the whitebark pines in the GYE. As if that weren't enough, the dramatic 1988 forest fires that swept through Yellowstone claimed 28 percent of the park's whitebark pines.

The FS is trying to find a blister rust-resistant strain of whitebark pine. If successful, the agency will plant them to replace infected trees.

Unfortunately, again like the grizzly, the whitebark pine is a slow-maturing species, and doesn't produce sizeable crops of seeds until at least fifty years old.

Does the FWS worry about this? Not really. "The whitebark pine has been wiped out in Glacier Park and the Bob Marshall, and we still have bears everywhere," Servheen points out. He does, however, consider blister rust "the biggest habitat problem in Yellowstone."

"When the whitebark pine goes away, the carrying capacity will go down," notes Chuck Schwartz (IGBST), who isn't as pessimistic as some. He reminds us that blister rust has been in Yellowstone since the 1930s and hasn't significantly reduced the whitebark pine yet. Perhaps, he theorizes, there's something about the climate in Yellowstone that will prevent a 90 percent die-off like Glacier had.

The shortage of quality vegetative bear food, such as whitebark pine seeds, increases the significance of protein in the Yellowstone grizzly's diet. Researchers have already documented a higher percentage of protein in the grizzly's diet in Yellowstone compared to Glacier, and with the potential devastation of the whitebark pine, the Yellowstone bears may become even more meat dependent. Regrettably all three major sources of that extra protein have uncertain futures.

Besides digging up marmots and ground squirrels and licking up a few ants or grubs here and there, the Yellowstone grizzly gets its protein from three main sources—cutthroat trout, army cutworm moths, and ungulates (mainly elk and bison)—all three threatened food sources.

Park biologists estimate that perhaps half of the grizzly's calories comes from ungulates. With the return of the wolf to Yellowstone, there have been fewer winter-killed elk and bison to feed grizzlies in the spring. However, the amount of red meat available to bears may have actually increased on a year-round basis because grizzlies often chase wolves off kills and claim the carcasses. Biologists still haven't determined the impact of the wolves on the ungulate populations, but reduced populations of elk, bison, and other large ungulates would definitely have a negative impact on the park's grizzly population.

Bison management is a white-hot debate all by itself, notwith-standing any impact on the grizzly bear. Montana stockgrowers don't want bison leaving the park and possibly infecting cattle herds with brucellosis, a feared disease that causes abortions in domestic bovines and is commonly carried by Yellowstone bison. Consequently current management calls for hazing the bison back into the park or shooting them if they cross the park boundary. The Montana legislature has also decided to open a bison hunting season north of Yellowstone Park.

"Pound for pound, bison are much more important to the grizzly bear than elk," Willcox points out. "Our current bison control pro-gram, killing them at the park boundary, makes another important food source unavailable to the grizzly."

Another valuable food source is the countless thousands of cut-throat trout that move out of Yellowstone Lake into small streams to spawn. Yellowstone grizzlies fish for cutthroats like Alaskan brown bears fish for salmon, and Kerry Gunther suspects as many as 30 to 40 percent of the grizzlies in the park feed on cutthroats. However, another fish, the lake trout, illegally introduced to Yellowstone Lake, threatens this vital food source (see Killing Trout to Save Bears).

And the moths? These wayward insects provide the fattest feast of all for grizzlies. Army cutworm moths are by far the most concen-trated source of energy for Yellowstone grizzlies, and the bears feed heavily on the fat-rich insects that gather in the talus slopes in and around the park, with most of the good feeding sites in the Shoshone National Forest on the eastern flanks of the park. Grizzlies have been documented as eating as many as 40,000 moths per day—equal to 20,000 calories, or 70 candy bars.

The moths are, however, a fickle food source. The number of moths on the talus slopes fluctuates widely from year to year, mainly because of natural conditions.

But this vital food source also has an unnatural problem. The moths migrate to the Yellowstone high country from grainfields around the park, but farmers consider army cutworms an agricultural pest. Consequently they're doing everything possible to eradicate them. So far the resilient insect has survived all efforts to wipe it off the face of the earth. If the farmers find the silver bullet for army cutworms, concern that the moths provide supplemental protein and fat for the Yellowstone grizzly isn't likely to deter them from killing every single one.

The Sierra Club could go to the Farm Bureau and request the preservation of cutworms to help the grizzly bears, but I doubt the idea would be well received. And in the end Yellowstone grizzlies will have to find food elsewhere.

The grizzly is amazingly adaptable and has often been able to find new food sources, but when will the pantry be bare? What quality food source will the bear turn to if the wolf reduces elk populations, if bison management diminishes bison numbers, if blister rust kills most whitebark pines, if the lake trout conquers the cutthroat trout, and if agriculturalists win their war with the army cutworm? Where will the grizzly go for its next meal?

No bear scientist knows the answer to this question. And the likely decline of major food sources has not, apparently, ruled out delisting of the Yellowstone grizzly. "Those food sources are erratic anyway," says Chris Servheen. "I suppose this (loss of food sources) could cause some adjustment in the population, but will it lead to extinction? No way!"

Steve Stringham, a bear scientist and director of the nonprofit organization called the Bear Communication and Coexistence Research Program, wrote a technical article in *Wild Earth Magazine* (Fall 2002) condemning the delisting proposal. The report, "Smokey and Mirrors: The War Between Science and Pseudoscience in Conserving the Grizzly Bear," basically said methodologies currently in use would lead to the extinction rather than the recovery of the grizzly bear, which he calls the "flagship of the conservation movement."

Stringham said that if we had used the same type of research we are now using to delist the Yellowstone grizzly on remnant populations back in the 1800s, it would indicate that "nearly all those populations would still be flourishing. In fact, they have nearly all disappeared."

"It's only smoke and mirrors to claim that long-term risks can be kept in check," he wrote. "It would be highly irresponsible to remove the grizzly's ESA protections without compelling evidence of true recovery, much less when the weight of evidence suggests that long-term risks are increasing."

Proponents of delisting point out that the ESA now has little or nothing to do with stabilizing ungulate herds, saving the cutthroat, stopping blister rust, or keeping farmers from killing cutworms. That's true, of course, but opponents voice this counterargument: If the drastically reduced food sources cause a severe decline in the grizzly population, the ESA could make the difference between survival and extinction.

Dramatically reduced food sources could cause large numbers of bears to come into conflict with various types of human development, much the way bears did when they were forced to find new food sources when the NPS closed the park's garbage dumps between 1969 and 1973. In the four or five years following the dump closures, at least 130 grizzly bears died due to various types of conflicts, and some people, including Frank and John Craighead, believe that number was much higher. This increased human-caused mortality brought the Yellowstone grizzly to death's door, perhaps only a few dead females away from an irreversible slide to extinction.

The FWS listed the grizzly under the newly passed ESA in 1975, when the bear most needed protection. Environmentalists, along with some bear scientists like Kate Kendall in Glacier, believe that the ESA saved the grizzly from extinction. If a scenario similar to the dump closures is played out again and grizzlies rapidly needed new food sources, with hundreds of hungry bears being killed for various reasons and the population plummeting, could we stop the downward spiral again? Could we do it without the ESA? Is this a gamble we want to take?

Last but hardly least on Louisa Willcox's list of concerns is the huge increase in grizzly mortality. In 2000 alone the human-caused mortality in the GYE reached thirty-three, the highest level since 1972, during the dump closures. Hunters killed sixteen, or 53 percent, of these grizzlies.

"While hunting accounts for over half of known bear deaths, poaching exacerbates the problem," according to the Sierra Club. "It has been estimated that for every known dead bear, there is one additional bear poached."

Actually this might be a conservative view, because in certain parts of the world, they haven't heard about Preparation H. There's still an active black-market trade for grizzly parts, especially gall bladders, which in Asia are considered a potent cure for many aliments, including hemorrhoids. Because of this invisible drain on the grizzly population, some estimates of illegal mortality go as high as three unrecorded deaths for every one recorded.

Again, Servheen disagrees. "In the short-term, the Yellowstone-area bears are doing well and increasing the population 3 or 4 percent per year . . . and we are not exceeding our mortality limits for either females or the population as a whole."

But is this just an exercise in the obvious? Apparently so, according to Servheen. "The reason we're seeing more mortality is because there are more bears. We expect more mortality."

In supporting the park's stand on delisting, Kerry Gunther concurs. "I think the bears in Yellowstone are doing fine right now. It amazes me how easy it is now to see a grizzly bear. I've been here since 1983, and I've never seen so many bears."

After hearing this you could assume the obvious: We're seeing more grizzly bears because there are more grizzly bears. But even this is arguable, as is, it seems, just about every statement with the word "grizzly" in it. Enviros wonder if the increased number of sightings could be the sign of a desperate grizzly population traveling far and wide to find food, both inside and outside the park. Some bear researchers also consider this a good possibility. Far-ranging bears would be more likely to come closer to developed lowlands and near roads, where they're more likely to be counted—and more vulnerable to poaching or anger over federal regulation. And there's ample opportunity to see grizzlies from roads because there are so many roads. Prior to 1990 the GYE had around 10,000 miles of logging roads, and the FS added almost 1,000 miles in the 1990s.

Could it be an optical illusion? The numbers indicate a growing population, but could increased human use and number of roads create the image of an expanding bear population because there are more opportunities to see bears?

"One problem that will come back to haunt the FWS is its continued adherence to the 'females with cubs' surrogate measure for counting bears," Willcox warns. "As long as the FWS relies on this measure and current methodologies, they cannot reliably count bears or assess population trends."

Before this delisting discussion goes any further, perhaps we should check the scorecard. Threatened food sources, escalating human-caused mortality, geographic and genetic isolation because of no links with other grizzly populations, and the eventuality of greatly increased development around the park, particularly on private land. This looks like 4–0 against delisting—or perhaps 4–1, if you buy population trend figures based on increased sightings of females with cubs. You'd think this combination of factors would create a powerful case for retaining the protection provided by the ESA until we can clearly see the future. But state wildlife agencies believe delisting is in the best interest of the grizzly bear, and Chris Smith is always anxious to explain why.

Smith, chief of staff of the Montana Department of Fish, Wildlife & Parks (MDFWP), spearheads the agency's efforts to achieve recovery and delisting of the grizzly. He disagrees with the theory that everybody wants delisting because "some people (translate: the Sierra Club) wouldn't have the grizzly as a poster child for fund-raising."

Actually, Smith agrees with John Varley and also doubts he'll see delisting in his lifetime. Good news for enviros: He's much younger than Varley.

Smith has a fresh take on why delisting will benefit the grizzly. You could call it the state perspective.

Not only is delisting "the right thing biologically" in Yellowstone, he explains, but eliminating the "Big Brother problem" will make working out conflicts much easier because local people prefer to deal with state bear managers rather than the feds. "We're better off without the baggage of the ESA. It creates a tremendous schism."

"Look at the mountain lion," he proudly points out. "We have mountain lions everywhere, and it has never been listed. There isn't the perception that the federal government is forcing people to live with mountain lions. They don't feel the heavy hand of the federal government."

True enough. Mountain lion numbers have greatly increased since the 1960s. Today the big cats venture into most Montana cities at night, stalking urban deer and causing dogs and cats to disappear. At the same time the mountain lion was prospering under state management, with no oversight by the feds, listed species such as the wolf and the grizzly bear struggled to survive.

"We need to demonstrate that an ESA listing is not a one-way trip," Smith claims. "We need a few examples of success." Nobody would argue with him on this point. In recent history, graduating to extinction is about the only way an animal or plant gets off the endangered species list.

Smith believes many people don't understand the current management situation. "Right now we (MDFWP) have a significant amount of the responsibility and very little of the authority."

The FWS is officially in charge, but because of budget shortfalls and lack of personnel at the federal level, the burden of day-by-day management activities often defaults to the state wildlife agencies. "We have four full-time biologists in grizzly bear management and a $250,000 annual budget," Smith boasts (see The B Team).

Another part of this that most people don't understand (or believe?), according to Smith, is the MDFWP's plan to expand the amount of habitat available to the grizzly far beyond the current recovery zone and into any area that's "biologically suitable and socially acceptable." Wyoming proposed this in its management plan, too, and used the same language. However, defining one of these two terms might be a bit tricky for the state bear managers.

The bear itself will decide what's "biologically suitable," so that's easy, but figuring out what's "socially acceptable" might be dicey. Basically it's where local folks will accept grizzlies, and it won't have anything to do with what the Sierra Club considers socially acceptable. Smith doesn't know how to define this term, "but obviously having grizzlies in downtown Bozeman is not socially acceptable."

The Montana grizzly management plan, again like Wyoming's, stresses education, but will the state succeed in convincing people they should live with grizzlies and make the big bear "socially acceptable"?

Education is one part of the plan that has everybody's approval. "The education portion is extraordinary," Willcox noted after reviewing the Wyoming plan. "It's the key to survival in these sprawling times."

Smith thinks the Big Sky area northwest of Yellowstone Park might be the test case for social acceptance. The ski resort and exploding residential development surrounding it sit right smack in the middle of prime grizzly habitat, squeezed between the two sections of the Lee Metcalf Wilderness, the Spanish Peaks and the Taylor-Hilgard.

Right now this high-rent community could be described as one of the proverbial "bear black holes" where grizzlies go but do not return. However, as the Yellowstone grizzly population expands into new habitat, which is necessary to achieve recovery goals and delisting, will the residents of Big Sky accept grizzlies walking through the golf course? Many houses here are pricey trophy homes, commonly not the owner's primary residences. Perhaps this makes it difficult to reach the owners with educational messages. Perhaps these homeowners haven't grown up in Montana with grizzly bears. Perhaps they'll never have an "educated attitude," as Chuck Jonkel, president of the Great Bear Foundation, puts it.

"Making the grizzly socially acceptable is mainly people management," Smith says. And he insists Montana plans to make a big effort to increase tolerance for the beleaguered bear.

Smith explains that under state management and within the official recovery zone, which would not be expanded, grizzlies will "get
the benefit of the doubt" in any resource developments. "Outside the
zone we're going to accommodate the bear as much as possible, but
we'll balance the needs of bears with the needs of people. In some
cases the decision will be based on economic opportunities."

That type of bureaucratic talk scares the pants off ardent environmentalists. They interpret it as a license to approve any development by saying it has minimal impact on grizzlies. But Smith strongly
disagrees with this pessimistic view. "We're looking at the entire
ecosystem, whatever that is, as habitat for grizzly bears, not just the
recovery zone."

The Montana plan also includes a section on linking the Yellowstone grizzly with other populations, but Smith is as realistic as any
environmentalist as to the difficulty of this task. "It may be impossible to link the Yellowstone grizzly with other populations," he admits.

After talking with Chris Smith, you find it hard to believe that
powerful western senators call him up every day to see if he's gotten
the grizzly delisted yet so they can rid themselves of this bothersome
bear and build more roads or drill more oil wells. Instead you get the
feeling Smith truly believes the state can do a much better job of managing grizzlies than the federal government. But will he ever get a
chance to prove it?

And what if he's wrong? What if local economics dictate every
resource decision; food sources disappear, sending the hungry bears
into developed "black holes"; and bear mortality skyrockets? What
then?

If this happens, and he won't rule out the possibility, Smith says
the bear can simply be relisted. Legally this could be done in fifteen
days, but politically it would hardly be so simple. Political pressure in
opposition to relisting would be intense. Even though Smith admits
politicians would be driven "mainly by commodity interests," he
points out that relisting is not a political matter—"it's a judicial
issue." This means if the grizzly bear were indeed threatened with

extinction, the ESA would require relisting. Hopefully Smith is politically correct, not politically naive.

So where is the delisting debate going? Here, finally, we have something on which everybody agrees. It's going to the courthouse. "I'm sure that sometime in the future," Smith predicts, "we'll be at one side of the courtroom, and the Sierra Club will be on the other side."

State agencies, perhaps prodded on by powerful politicians, will continue to push for delisting. They might get it through the bear bureaucracy, but that won't be the end zone. Environmental groups will definitely drag it into court, where they have a good track record.

Like many debates heading for court, there could be an out-of-court settlement. Perhaps there should be because the stakes are so high. The enviros could lose in court, and the agencies could be incorrectly interpreting the numbers. If the grizzly population took a sudden dive toward extinction, politicians probably would block relisting.

Delisting has the potential of becoming a tragic irony in the history of the environmental movement. It's the high wire act in Louisa Willcox's five-ring circus, obviously not meant for the risk-adverse among us. We think the grizzly is doing great because we're seeing more bears. We're filled with confidence that delisting will allow us to improve management of the great bear. So we give up the safety net provided by the ESA. But then, what happens when we fall?

An Unacceptable Species

Not everybody wants more grizzly bears, as witnessed by the following resolution unanimously passed by the Fremont (Wyoming) County Commission on March 12, 2002. Fremont County includes the southern Wind River Mountains, an area sure to be recolonized by the expanding grizzly population in the Greater Yellowstone Ecosystem. The resolution has no force of law, but apparently the Fremont County Commissioners wanted to make a statement.

I say "apparently" because I tried a half-dozen times to get the chairman or vice-chairman to discuss it, but they wouldn't do it, except for one proclamation by Chairman Scott Luther: "There's a place for grizzly bears, but not in Fremont County." The resolution may have turned out to be somewhat of an embarrassment for Fremont County. It was intended to win support for keeping the big bear out of the county.

RESOLUTION 2002–04
"GRIZZLY BEARS DEEMED UNACCEPTABLE SPECIES"

WHEREAS, the health, safety, and livelihood of the citizens of Fremont County is the responsibility of the Fremont County Commissioners who are duly elected by the citizens of Fremont County, State of Wyoming; and

WHEREAS, the five elected County Commissioners of Fremont County do hereby condemn any effort, under the Endangered Species Act (ESA) or otherwise, which allows for the presence, introduction, or reintroduction of any animals within the boundaries of Fremont County, which are deemed by the Fremont County Commissioners to be a threat to public health, safety, and livelihood; and

WHEREAS, the following duly elected officials of Fremont County openly oppose the introduction or reintroduction of grizzly bears: County Assessor, County Attorney, County Clerk, Clerk of District Court, County Coroner, County Sheriff, County Treasurer; and

WHEREAS, the Board of Fremont County Commissioners hereby deem grizzly bears, *Ursus arctos horribilis,* to be a threat to public health, safety, and livelihood;

NOW, THEREFORE, BE IT RESOLVED that the Board of County Commissioners, Fremont County, State of Wyoming, by the authority vested in us, do hereby prohibit the presence, introduction, or reintroduction of grizzly bears within the boundaries of Fremont County.

DATED this 12th day of March, 2002.

BOARD OF FREMONT COUNTY COMMISSIONERS

Signed by Scott Luther (Chairman), Lanny Applegate (Vice-Chairman), Thomas R. Satterfield, T. Crosby Allen II, and Douglas L. Thompson

5
A Most Delicate Balance

Early writers and orators took the Lewis and Clark Journals and repeated, magnified, and glamorized the bear's bad reputation until it became so ingrained in American tradition that today it's nearly impossible to introduce the real grizzly to a preconditioned public.

—from *Where the Grizzly Walks* (1977)

Can you say "dee-vo-shun"? If you can, you already know a lot about Chuck Jonkel.

Jonkel isn't the type of guy who hides his feelings. Unlike many bear experts who work for agencies and environmental groups, he doesn't hold anything back. He has studied bears—all kinds of bears, not just grizzly bears—and for all of his adult life, he has lived and breathed bears. To this day, since he started working on bears in the late 1950s, he puts everything he has—every word, every breath, every step, into saving bears.

Wildlife scientists have theorized that biologists tend to take on some of the physical characteristics and behavioral traits of the animals they study, and some people might think Chuck Jonkel looks and acts like a bear. He does sort of resemble a bear—a majestic old silvertip, living in harmony with his environment and with little concern about what the other animals think about him.

And his office, well, if grizzlies could read, it's probably what a bear's den would look like, full of pillars of research papers, government reports, and news clippings climbing towards the ceiling, leaving just enough room for one old bear to get comfortable. But not enough room for a pesky writer, too, at least not until I moved several piles of documents and squeezed into a dusty chair that hadn't seen a backside for months. Jonkel has retained at least one of his academic traits from his years as a professor at the University of Montana—never saying no to anybody and then being too busy to get things done on time. Fortunately he remains open, friendly, and big-hearted enough to let everything else wait another hour or two to make time for me. He had helped me research the first edition of this book twenty-five years earlier, and I was anxious to get his perspective on how the grizzly had weathered those years.

Plaques, awards, casts of grizzly tracks, cartoons, clippings, posters, letters, and every other conceivable form of bear stuff cover every square inch of every wall of his office—and have seeped out of his office and spread throughout the rest of the building, like a vine gradually covering a building leaf by leaf. You'd now have a hard time finding a spot big enough to tack a business card on the wall anywhere in the offices in the entire building.

"I put everything up on the wall because if I file it I'll never find it again," Jonkel explains. Ironically this proved to be true. He wanted to give me a copy of a letter to the editor he had recently written, but he couldn't find it because, of course, his "wall files" were full. If you really want to know a lot about bears, spend a few days reading the walls at the Great Bear Foundation.

I've known Chuck Jonkel for a long time. I met him back in the early 1970s when I was first writing about bears. At that time he headed the Border Grizzly Project, a massive multiagency effort created to research grizzlies in northwestern Montana and southern Alberta and British Columbia. After a few years it became clear that he wasn't cut out to be a "bearacrat," and amid ongoing disagreements over agency policies, which helped to earn him the handle "Dr. Doom," the project slowly imploded.

But that didn't change Chuck Jonkel. He kept on living and breathing bears, and in 1994 he became president of the Great Bear Foundation, a nonprofit organization located in an old house on the edge of the university campus in Missoula, Montana. That's where I found him, and clearly he hadn't really changed much. He was still old and wise and gray and knew everything there was to know about bears.

Instead of fighting agencies over obscure government rules and regulations and ingrained attitudes about which agency should be in control, Jonkel now emphasizes education. That's also the main goal of the Great Bear Foundation, which has done a terrific job of it, but regrettably only around Missoula.

Like many of the dedicated bear people featured in this book, Jonkel believes the existence of the grizzly bear depends on a delicate balance of social acceptance. It hasn't always been like this, but in the first years of the twenty-first century, most people tend to accept the status quo regarding the grizzly. They accept the current level of danger and the disruptions to outdoor recreational activities and resource development, but they might not accept more. They accept the grizzly the way it is, where it is. They accept it in the remaining 2 percent of the bear's original range, but might not accept it in much more of the 98 percent where the grizzly no longer walks.

You could say Missoula is located in both areas. It's on the edge of occupied grizzly habitat, with verified sightings in the Rattlesnake National Wilderness, which abuts the city limits. But it's also on the edge of the Bitterroot Valley, a flash point in efforts to reintroduce the grizzly into the Selway-Bitterroot Wilderness. Many people here haven't accepted the idea of having grizzly bears in their backyards, the traditional NIMBY problem, i.e., grizzly bears are okay, but Not-In-My-Back-Yard.

"In distant areas like California, people are too frightened, too unsure, to ever accept grizzly bears back into their areas. People in Montana are not concerned about having a few more," Jonkel says optimistically.

In the near future we'll find out if he's right. The grizzly is obviously expanding its range in all directions, so people in Montana will soon get their chance to accept "a few more."

He admits fear and misunderstanding still dominate attitudes towards grizzlies, but he predicts that patience and a diligent educational effort will lead to acceptance, just like it has in the flatlands east of the Rocky Mountain Front west of Great Falls, Montana, where grizzly bears now venture out among the wheat fields and cattle pastures. People previously opposed to allowing grizzlies to roam the prairie, among agricultural communities, now live peacefully with the bears, 40 miles from the nearest mountain. Some people are even quite proud of it.

When asked about the concept of social acceptance, Jonkel gets excited. "This is so crucial," he explains. "I call it perception. If people get educated about grizzly bears, then they have an educated attitude about grizzly bears."

As a good example of this, Jonkel recalls a situation that occurred in the 1980s when researchers found a few bears in the North Cascades near Seattle. This was, at best, an extremely endangered remnant population. Many people wouldn't even include the North Cascades as part of the last 2 percent.

"We went looking for allies for these bears in Seattle, but we really couldn't find much support," he recalls. "It was hard to find the right people to talk to in such a large urban area."

This situation is hardly among Jonkel's fondest memories. While trying to find support for the grizzlies, he went to The Mountaineers, a large group of outdoor enthusiasts based in Seattle, and asked them to support efforts to stabilize and expand this remnant grizzly population in the club's favorite playground, the North Cascades. You'd think the demographics were perfect, mostly upper-income, well-educated folks who would rather stay in a four-pound backpacking tent than at the Hilton. But would The Mountaineers step forward to support the grizzly? No. Instead, according to Jonkel, they opposed the idea of restoring this population of grizzly bears in the North Cascades, mainly because of concern for public safety.

"If you can't get these types of people to support you," Jonkel points out the obvious, "we're going to have a hard time saving the grizzly. It goes to show you that there's little tolerance for the bear in places where there aren't established populations. I guess this also shows us that we really need to educate people that they can live with the grizzly bear and that the bear might even add a little thrill to it."

A more current version of this same debate flared up in 2003. British Columbia wildlife officials proposed augmenting the seriously threatened grizzly population in the North Cascades area north of the border as part of the province's recovery efforts. Washington state senators were afraid that the Canadian bears wouldn't stay in Canada and instead cross the border ("without going through customs") to attack farmers and hikers and cause the USDA Forest Service (FS) to close roads. To make their point, they were able to convince the Washington legislature to pass a resolution urging British Columbia to stop trying to recover bears next to the border.

So how do you create "an educated attitude"?

"You get to the kids," is Jonkel's answer. The Great Bear Foundation has an active program that sends people into elementary schools, with props like bearskins, skulls, and imprints of tracks, to talk to kids about living with bears. "Unfortunately," he notes, "we only reach out about 100 miles around Missoula, but we're applying for grants to expand this program."

Jonkel's experience with the North Cascades grizzlies convinced him that educational efforts should target urban areas, but he clearly shows some frustration with the smallness of his educational effort. "Our kids in Montana grow up with bears, and they understand how to live with bears, but in big cities kids learn about how to catch a bus and who has switchblades."

Talking with Chuck Jonkel about the delicate balance of social acceptance gets interesting in a hurry. Along with many others who understand this precarious situation, he frets about it. Most bear experts have concerns about the long-term future of the grizzly bear, primarily because of incremental habitat degradation. However, most of them also believe the short-term future seems fairly secure—unless, of course, something upsets the delicate balance of social acceptance. Jonkel and I spent most of our time discussing potential events that could result in a dramatic change in the public's perception of grizzly bears and possibly jeopardize the bear's short-term future.

One of his concerns is the possibility of more deadly encounters. "The number of maulings is definitely going to increase," he predicts. His reasoning is threefold.

First, he believes the amount of human use in the national parks will steadily increase, and, second, the grizzlies in the parks aren't getting enough aversive conditioning to keep them wild and scared of animals wearing shoes.

Third, the grizzly is expanding its range into new areas such as the Blackfoot Valley northeast of Missoula, the Gravelly Range northwest of Yellowstone Park, and the Wind River Range south of Jackson, Wyoming. Unlike folks hiking the trails of Yellowstone or Glacier, people using these new habitats might not expect to encounter a grizzly and may not take the recommended precautions. If the number of maulings escalates and gets dramatized by the media, Jonkel thinks it could cause a downturn in the public's ability to tolerate grizzly bears. People just aren't realistic about the threat posed by bears, he claims. "Tobacco kills 700,000 people annually, 60,000 die in auto accidents ... and bees, wasps, and hornets kill about 400 people every year, but do you ever see a sign at a trailhead that says "Trail Closed Because of Yellowjackets"?

Jonkel gets lots of support for his concern about how the media covers bears, but some supporters aren't as diplomatic, for example, Chuck Schwartz, leader of the Interagency Grizzly Bear Study Team, who says, "The media is responsible for our fear of bears."

Because of this unrealistic public perception and how the media covers it, Jonkel worries about what would happen if the number of people killed or injured by grizzly bears suddenly increased. Perhaps everybody who believes the grizzly is safe for the short-term should worry about this.

"The park service needs to do more aversive conditioning in the parks," he claims. "All the rangers should have thumper guns and shoot any bear they see that's aware of people around but doesn't get out of there fast."

Thumper guns are modified shotguns that shoot a capsule of liquid plastic that hits the bear over a six-inch area. It hurts the bear enough, hopefully, to get the message across but doesn't injure the bear as much as shooting it with a rubber bullet.

In the beginning, of course, before Europeans invaded what is now the United States, the only thing a grizzly bear had to fear was a larger grizzly bear. Guns changed that.

"If a bear sees you in the backcountry and doesn't hightail it out of there," Jonkel points out, "that bear is challenging you bear to bear. You need to show it you're the bigger bear. A man with a gun is a bigger bear."

He theorizes that if enough grizzlies get this negative stimulus, they will consider all humans as bigger bears, even if they don't have shotguns slung over their shoulders, and will more diligently avoid encounters. Fewer encounters would prevent human injury, reduce the number of dead bears, and avoid circumstances where unfounded fear might cause society to reject the grizzly—even in the national parks, which Jonkel is quick to say "could happen."

"All it would take is one train wreck to change social values," Schwartz predicts. "If a grizzly bear killed a little girl at Big Sky Resort, the media would go crazy. It would only take one."

"Obviously you have more anti-bear sentiment in years when people get killed," Steve Herrero of the Eastern Slopes Grizzly Bear Project adds. And bear mortality, too: "People just grab their guns and start shooting."

Jonkel concedes that the current track record really doesn't support this theory. In the 1990s there wasn't a dramatic increase in human use, at least backcountry use, in the parks, nor has there been an increase in the number of bear-caused injuries. In fact, the statistics show a downtrend in the number of injuries caused by bears.

Then again, Jonkel and all of the other bear experts know the grizzly bear has an amazing ability to disprove just about any theory.

Through the years there have been documented incidents of predatory bears killing or injuring hikers and campers, but nowhere in the history of the grizzly bear has there been a clear case of what Jonkel calls "repeat predation." This would be a grizzly killing somebody and then developing what biologists call a "predator-prey relationship," doing it again and again. That would certainly change the public's attitude toward grizzly bears, now wouldn't it?

There have been bears that have injured more than one person, such as the infamous Whiskey Creek grizzly in Banff National Park that mauled three people in separate incidents before it was killed, as detailed in *Bear Attacks: Their Causes and Avoidance* by Steve Herrero. Likewise, in *Alaska Bear Tales* Larry Kaniut profiles five Alaskan bears that have injured more than one person. But the ominous predator-prey relationship Jonkel mentions has never really developed. No grizzly has ever tasted human flesh and then consciously gone back for more by stalking and preying on humans.

Why hasn't this happened? One reason might be the common policy of immediately killing any bear that displays predatory behavior, or "unnatural aggression," as it's technically called. Regardless of this policy, there have been a few cases where authorities weren't able to get the killer bear, but the bear didn't become a repeat offender. A good example is the 1984 White Lake incident in Yellowstone National Park, where a grizzly came into Brigetta Fredenhagen's camp and tore down and consumed her food cache, which was properly stored 12 feet off the ground between two trees 90 feet from camp. But the bear didn't stop there. It ripped into her tent, killed her, and dragged her body about 250 feet from camp and devoured it.

Fredenhagen had increased her risk by hiking and camping alone in prime grizzly country, but otherwise she had carefully followed bear awareness rules, setting up her camp correctly and properly handling food and garbage. Nonetheless, she may have been stalked and killed by a predatory bear. Despite major efforts by the National Park Service to find and kill the predacious grizzly, the bear was never found. More significant, however, is the fact that the bear didn't become a repeat predator.

Even after studying incidents like this and Banff's Whiskey Creek grizzly, Herrero still considers repeat predation a "nonissue." But will it ever happen? "No," he quickly answers. "We're too good at finding and killing predatory bears." Strongly agreeing, Schwartz calls it "science fiction." Another reason it probably won't happen is, according to Jonkel, that "we're just another bear, and bears don't develop predator-prey relationships with other bears."

In talking to all of the experts about the issue of repeat predation, it's clear most believe there's only the slimmest chance of it happening. In fact, they don't like to talk about it (or have people write about it) because they worry that the very thought of it will further deepen an already too-deep fear of bears.

Jonkel and I discussed one more event that could cause a sharp downturn in social acceptance—the threat the grizzly poses to the sport of hunting. Consider this: In Montana, Idaho, and Wyoming, last home of the grizzly bear, big-game hunting is extremely popular, and hunters as a group are extremely powerful politically. Ditto for Alberta and British Columbia. Like most people, hunters tend to accept the grizzly where it is, how it is. But in recent years a storm cloud has appeared on the horizon. In areas with large big-game populations, grizzly bears may have started to equate a rifle shot with a dinner bell. Grizzlies are learning that a rifle shot might reveal the location of 60 pounds of high-quality food in the form of a gut pile from a field-dressed elk or, in some cases, 500 pounds of quality food in the form of a hunter-killed elk. Nowadays, for this reason, some grizzlies may run towards rifle shots instead of away from them.

Chris Servheen of the Interagency Grizzly Bear Committee estimated that each year big-game hunters leave 350,000 pounds of gut piles strewn over the landscape. Until recently nobody really thought much about this. That's the way it's always been. Hunter kills elk, guts it, skins it, quarters it, drags it to his rig, hangs it in his garage, cuts it up, freezes it, eats it, end of story.

Now, enter the grizzly bear.

Scavengers like ravens and coyotes have long sought out gut piles as a highly nutritious supplement to their diets. But now there's a new scavenger in town, probably smarter than the others, and definitely bigger and meaner. In fact, this silver-tipped scavenger might even be audacious enough to consider a downed elk its property, not that of the successful hunter. Now, there's a conflict!

There have been documented cases of grizzly bears being attracted to rifle shots because that's part of "grizzly bear learning" as Jonkel puts it, which is all related to finding food. If you can teach a rat in a maze to find food in a few minutes, how hard would it be for a grizzly bear to learn that a rifle shot signals the start of a feast? That's an easy question for Chuck Jonkel. "Obviously grizzly bears are going to gunshots."

A grizzly rushing to the sound of a hunter's rifle certainly creates a hazardous situation, but, unlike most hikers, hunters have guns and know how to use them. The result? Well, no big surprise here. These conflicts frequently end with a dead bear—but can also result in a dead hunter.

"Right now not too many people are thinking about grizzlies keying in on gunshots, but five years from now, this will be a big issue," Jonkel predicts. (See Running the Trapline.)

In a population of any animal struggling to survive, especially an animal with the slowest reproductive rate of any North American mammal (with the possible exception of the musk oxen), increased mortality obviously reduces the chances of recovery. Conflicts between big-game hunters and grizzlies have definitely increased mortality, but there could be a worse impact on the grizzly bear. Much worse.

Let us not forget that the grizzly bear has been officially protected as a threatened species under the Endangered Species Act (ESA). The ESA prohibits the killing of listed species. Any circumstances commonly leading to the killing of a threatened species, officially called "illegal taking," need to change. In other words, if hunters are killing grizzly bears when there's no open season on the big bruin, something needs to change.

Politically and realistically, though, it's unlikely anything will change. No politician in a stronghold of the National Rifle Association, like the northern Rockies, would consider siding with bears over hunters. That would be a recipe for instant political suicide, akin to supporting gun confiscation. So, assuming hunters accepted the extra risk of attracting a grizzly and assuming recovery efforts could sustain hunter-caused bear mortality, would anything have to change?

Possibly not, unless something forced a change. Consider this: Any environmental group familiar with the ins and outs of the ESA could claim big-game hunting causes illegal taking and diminishes the grizzly bear's chances of recovery. Environmental groups are also familiar with the ins and outs of our legal system, so one could file a lawsuit to restrict or stop big-game hunting in certain hunting areas or at certain times of the year.

Politically this would resemble the eruption of Mount St. Helens. Or more appropriately, compare this to the magma only one kilometer below the surface in Yellowstone Park. If that ultrahot rock ever broke through the surface, it would cause an indescribably huge eruption, like the one that created the Yellowstone Caldera. The possible magnitude of the "political eruption" is a concern of EarthJustice, the feared "law firm for the environment." EarthJustice spends most of its time and money suing agencies to protect endangered species and environmental quality.

When I talked to them in March 2002, EarthJustice had no plans to go to court to stop or restrict hunting in grizzly habitat, but when asked about the killing of grizzly bears by elk hunters and hunting guides, Douglas Honnold, managing attorney for EarthJustice, didn't pull any punches. "It's prohibited under the Endangered Species Act, but there are mechanisms to allow the taking of certain species under some conditions." However, according to Honnold, those mechanisms haven't been employed to allow the killing of grizzly bears by hunters.

"The agencies are breaking the law," Honnold confidently stated. "What they're doing is illegal, and it's resulting in dead grizzly bears."

If this issue reaches the courts, what would happen to the delicate balance of social acceptance, primarily but not completely among hunters, people who normally would support having a viable population of grizzly bears in the northern Rockies? Hopefully nobody will ever have to answer that question.

You'd expect environmental groups to be concerned about this, and they are—but not in a way you'd expect. Enviros definitely worry about any additional human-caused bear mortality, but they worry even more about eco-politics. Subsequently hunters have a best friend they don't know about, the Sierra Club.

Large environmental groups like the Sierra Club understand the political backlash such litigation could create, so they aren't considering going to court over any hunting issue. However, they fret about some fringe group going ahead with a lawsuit to limit or stop hunting.

"We'd be on the phone to them immediately," predicts Brian Peck of the Sierra Club. "And they'd be getting lots of other calls from environmental groups, too."

Actually, unknown to all but a few enviro insiders like Louisa Willcox, former coordinator of the Sierra Club's Grizzly Bear Ecosystems Project, an eco-political disaster has already been averted. In 2001 a small group decided to "go after the hunting season," according to Willcox. "We called them and told them they would have no support from other environmentalists. We told them they'd be on their own, and we'd say bad things about them in the press. We told them we'd disown them."

Willcox won't name the group, but, significantly, she and other environmental leaders kept this issue out of the courts—and out of the newspapers. However, this near miss should rattle the nerves of lots of people concerned about the future of the grizzly bear. "We try to control the agenda, and our friends," Willcox warns. "But as we all know, you can't control your friends."

What is it about the grizzly bear that makes us work together in ways we've never tried before? Who knows? But it's definitely a measure of the power the species has over us.

The moral of this story is one of caution—spiced, perhaps, with a bit of overconfidence. A battalion of bear people who have dedicated their lives to preserving the grizzly universally express concern for the long-term welfare of the great bear, but few express any major concern for the short-term future of this majestic mammal.

Yet they all agree that the grizzly depends on a tenuous level of social acceptance. It's likely this level can be kept within an acceptable range, mainly because many keen-minded people are working diligently on issues that could upset this delicate balance.

Park managers understand the need for aggressive people management and aversive conditioning of bears to limit the number of maulings and maintain the current excellent track record. Some people believe the parks should do more, and they probably will do more in the future.

Wildlife agencies, hunting organizations, and large environmental groups understand the political explosiveness of any litigation to restrict hunting. Instead of going to court, they have decided to work together to reduce the number of bears killed by hunters and the number of hunters killed by bears. And, of course, to avoid the need for litigation.

It's amazing what you can do when you work together instead of against each other. As Chuck Jonkel reminds us, "Grizzly bears are still here because of us."

A Few Bears I've Met
and What I Learned from Them

Date: July 14, 1986
Place: Camas Lake, Glacier National Park
Lesson: If you don't have dreams, they can't come true.

This really happened.

When I had finally finished writing *Where the Grizzly Walks* in 1977, my publisher asked me about the dedication. "You don't have to include one," he said, "but most people usually have one and make it something personal."

So I did. I dedicated the book to my two young sons, only five and two years old at the time, as follows:

> This book is dedicated to Russ and Greg, my two sons.
> May they grow up and see a wild grizzly.

This was sort of a dream I had. It's good to have dreams. If you don't, they can't come true, and this one did in grand style.

Since my experience at Starvation Creek, I had revered the grizzly bear, and, of course, I hoped my children would join me in enjoying wild nature. I only wish my daughter Heidi would have come along earlier so she could have been included in the dedication and old enough to go on this particular hike.

When I planned the trip to Lake Evangeline, I didn't tell Russ and Greg about my ulterior motive. We talked about the beauty of the remote lake with big trout. I didn't tell them that the entire Camas Creek Valley was known for its high grizzly population, and I secretly hoped they'd be able to see one. I didn't tell my wife either, but I suppose I should have, so I guess you could consider this a public confession.

I didn't have much time for hiking in those days, so I tried to pack in as many miles as possible when I had time off. Most people would take two days to cover the 14 miles to Camas Lake, where the trail ends at a designated campsite. Lake Evangeline is 2 more miles up the valley, but it's a tough bushwhack to get there. Since we only had three days, we planned to hike to Camas Lake in one day and camp two nights there, spend the second day at Lake Evangeline, and hike out on the third day.

I also kept to myself the fact that this schedule would put us in the best grizzly habitat, the area above Arrow Lake, late in the first day and early in the third when wildlife, including bears, should be moving around and more visible.

As I write this, it has been seventeen years since that July day, and like most people my age, I tend to forget a few things here and there. In this case, however, I'll always remember that day as if it happened yesterday.

The weather, for instance, was ideal—clear, cool, and no wind. The first 11 miles to the upper end of Arrow Lake went by uneventfully, just another great hike in wild country. After taking a break on a small alluvial beach at the inlet, we started up the steep grade to Camas Lake, another 3 miles away. It was late afternoon, about six o'clock, and it had already been a long day. We had left Helena around five in the morning and didn't hit the trail until about eleven. Russ was thirteen and Greg almost eleven, both good hikers, but, nonetheless, progress slowed as we moved up the big hill with big packs. About a mile from Arrow Lake, the trail goes through some thick brush before opening up into a gorgeous, open valley. In the middle of one of those brush patches, we saw it.

Not a grizzly bear, but where one had just been. Right on the trail was an enormous pile of bear dung, so fresh it was still steaming. This may have been the biggest bear scat I had ever seen, and obviously it had been deposited only minutes before we found it.

I still vividly remember the chill going up my spine. At that exact point in time, with the thick brush limiting visibility, I definitely did not want to see a grizzly. I'm not sure Russ and Greg completely understood that we were in a dangerous situation as I urged them to join me in yelling "Hey bear! Hey bear!" I also took out my coach's whistle and started blasting away every minute or so as we inched up the trail.

Incidentally, I learned some things about noise that day. For example, I learned that whistles might not be a good idea. After blowing on mine for a few minutes, I noticed that marmots were answering. I guess the whistle sounded like a marmot, and grizzly bears do eat marmots, right? I put away the whistle, and we continued shouting. We kept this up for a mile or so until the trail crossed Camas Creek and broke out into the huge alpine meadow about a mile and a half from our destination. We hadn't been covering ground very fast, and it was already about seven-thirty. However, the good visibility calmed our fears of surprising a grizzly, so we hiked on quietly.

About a half mile into the meadow on a bench above a sharp V-shaped ravine that Camas Creek had gouged out of the rock, I stopped to glass the slopes, hoping to see a bear. To the east, along the lower slopes of Heavens Peak, looked promising, but no bear. Then I looked west, across the deep ravine, at a small swale above the stream. I remember saying to myself that this would be a great spot to safely see a bear.

As I glassed around the edge of the opening, the bear walked into the field of my binoculars. It was the biggest grizzly I had ever seen. This had to be the same bear that left us shivering with fear with its scat. And here it was, right on cue.

You didn't need binoculars to see the bear as it walked across the swale, but the boys fought for turns with them to fully appreciate the massiveness of this grizzly, a true king of the mountain. I remember Russ comparing him to the size of a Volkswagen Beetle. We watched the bear for two or three minutes before it disappeared into the forest on the other side of the opening.

It was just as I had dreamed. I wanted the boys to see a grizzly in a truly wild environment, not in a zoo or along a highway. There we were, 13 miles from the nearest road but still in a safe viewing situation. And this was not just any bear. It was a monster of a bear, dark brown with beautiful silver-tipped guard hairs shining in the last sunlight, probably an old male and the dominant bear in this drainage, the proverbial top of the food chain around here. It was the best thing my sons could see. It was perfect, truly a defining moment.

It was also getting late, probably after eight by now, so I encouraged Russ and Greg to move faster so we could get camp set up before nightfall claimed the Camas Creek Valley. Russ, the eldest, always wanted to go first, of course, so I took up the rear. I didn't say anything, but I worried about the path of the big bear. If it stayed on its current course, it would probably come close to the foot of Camas Lake—and our campsite.

I also remember thinking that this bear had obviously not been very far from the trail, probably within earshot. Either it had not been able to hear our shouting or had heard it and ignored it. I couldn't decide which was worse, but, in any case, that was the day I lost confidence in the value of human voices as a deterrent. Either natural conditions muffled them so much they couldn't be heard, or some bears weren't scared by them.

I kept all this to myself, hoping Russ and Greg were thinking about supper and fly-fishing. We had hiked about another half mile to a small knoll above the lake when Russ saw them.

"Bear," he said loudly. "Two of them."

Sure enough, about 300 yards ahead and only about 20 feet below the trail were two more grizzlies, neither of them the bear we had just seen, but two different bears. Through the binoculars I could see the average-sized grizzlies were occupied with digging up camas roots. These were probably two subadults still traveling together after being cast out of the nest by their mother to make way for her new cubs.

Now, what to do? The bears didn't give any sign that they noticed our presence. They kept digging while I tried to decide our next move. We couldn't go up the trail with the bears so close to it, but we had more than 13 miles under our belts and needed to camp. We also only had about an hour of daylight left.

I decided to try scaring the bears away. I didn't want to reveal our location, although I'm not sure that was a good decision. I theorized a loud noise might scare them off, and we could safely continue to our campsite. Having learned that my whistle sounded like a marmot, I decided not to use it. Instead I dug into my emergency pack and pulled out a mini air horn I had carried hundreds of miles but never used. As we fixated on the bears, I gave the air horn an extended blast. I'll never forget what happened next.

The bears went crazy. They started running around wildly. One of them uprooted a log, and it went flying. Rocks loosened by the bears tumbled into the creek. It was a scary moment. After a few seconds of wildly running around, one of the bears disappeared into the brush along the stream, heading generally in our direction. If it stayed along the brushy stream bottom, it would pass less than 100 feet from us.

At that point I made a bad mistake and have since learned to be careful about what you say about bears when you're around young minds. I said something like "We better get out of here." I had decided it was too dangerous to continue—we had to abandon our campsite and go back to Arrow Lake for the night. I don't remember using an alarmist tone, but I must have, because by the time I put the air horn in the pocket on top of my pack and turned around, Greg was already 200 yards down the trail and going as fast as his little legs would take him, obviously scared to death.

Russ and I had to almost run to catch up to Greg. After we did, finally, I tried to assure him we weren't in danger, even though I did not completely believe it myself. Even with supper long overdue, there was no whining from the boys about having to tack another 3 miles onto our day, making it a total of 16 miles with overnight packs, and it sure was a noisy trip. I'd be surprised if three people could make any more noise than we did on the way back to Arrow Lake.

One problem we all knew about was the absence of a designated campsite at the upper end of the lake. This meant we'd have to camp illegally, not the kind of lesson you want to teach your children, but we had no choice under the circumstances. We couldn't camp at Camas Lake, and it was already dark when we reached Arrow Lake. The boys, especially Greg, were exhausted. Not a great situation. I had no choice but to set up an illegal camp.

In later years I had several conversations with the National Park Service while researching my book *Bear Aware* and conducting bear awareness seminars. I learned that most rangers would agree with the decision and not cite me for illegal camping. Safety prevails over policy. Most regulations have safety as the prime consideration, but no set of regulations can cover all situations.

That night, for the record, I was meticulous in my efforts to set up a zero-impact camp. I doubt any ranger could have found any sign of our camp a week after we left.

If we had not been so exhausted, I'm sure it would have been a sleepless night. Every night sound would have been a monster bear approaching our tent. Fortunately, I suppose, we were so tired, we had a good sleep.

In the morning the fear of the previous evening gradually turned to exuberance. Over instant oatmeal and hot chocolate, we relived every second of the incidents several times, an exceptionally joyous experience for me.

Undeterred by bears, we hiked back up to Camas Lake that morning and camped there that night before heading out the next day. We didn't make it to Lake Evangeline that year, but we came back two years later, caught some nice Yellowstone cutthroats, and saw a female grizzly and two cubs on our way out, at a safe distance, on the slopes of Heavens Peak.

To this day I'm sure Russ and Greg remember the foregoing as clearly as I do. Sometimes we joke about how Greg got interested in cross-country running, but mostly we just relish the experience. It was perfect, and it really happened. A dream that came true.

6

The B Team

What would we do without the Kevin Freys of the world?
These guys provide the essential link between landowners and
agencies. That's where the rubber hits the road.
— Chuck Schwartz, leader,
Interagency Grizzly Bear Study Team

How things change! When I worked for the Montana Department of Fish, Wildlife & Parks (MDFWP) throughout the 1970s when it was still the Department of Fish and Game, insiders correctly called it a "deer and elk agency." About 99 percent of the department's resources and money went into programs benefiting major game species. Now that's changed, not completely but at least in one area—dealing with high-profile, charismatic megafauna such as wolves and grizzly bears.

In the 1970s MDFWP higher-ups probably wouldn't have even discussed the idea of devoting significant resources to a nongame species. Now, however, they've created what I'll call the "B (for bear) Team," a dynamic group of four bear management specialists who spend most of their time managing people. These four guys—Kevin Frey of Bozeman, Jamie Jonkel of Missoula, Mike Madel of Choteau, and Tim Manley of Kalispell—form the proverbial front line in the battle to save the grizzly. They certainly don't do it all. They get invaluable help from colleagues in their own agency, other agencies, reservations, and nonprofit organizations. Without them, though, the grizzly landscape in Montana, the major remaining stronghold of the great bear, certainly wouldn't have the budding aura of peaceful coexistence that it has today. They're only four hard-working guys, but almost everybody I interviewed while researching this book said the B Team made the difference.

All this became quite clear to me the day I went for a little drive through the Blackfoot Valley with Jamie Jonkel, who is, incidentally, the son of Chuck Jonkel, president of the Great Bear Foundation. When we drove by the Blackfoot-Clearwater Game Range, the younger Jonkel pointed out the exact location, only about a mile from a major highway, where a grizzly killed a hunter as he field-dressed his elk. (See Running the Trapline.)

The game range is on the western edge of the valley, a large, open stretch of productive agricultural land with the famous Blackfoot River and U.S. Highway 200 running through it. It's on the southern edge of the Northern Continental Divide Ecosystem (NCDE), but is not officially listed as occupied grizzly habitat.

But Jonkel, who has been studying bears and managing people in bear country for more than twenty years, knows differently. "Some folks are in denial about this place because the bears are here, on both sides of the highway. They ask me why the bears are here, and I say look around. This is another Hayden Valley," referring to the famous Serengeti-like basin in Yellowstone Park that provides fertile habitat for a large number of grizzlies. "With these drought conditions, more bears are moving out of the Bob Marshall Wilderness and into these valleys looking for better habitat."

Some wildlife managers consider U.S. 200 the southernmost boundary of the grizzly's range in Montana, excluding the Greater Yellowstone Ecosystem (GYE). But Jonkel has found many grizzlies south of highway throughout the Garnet Range and even over into the Clark Fork Valley near I–15. Like the grizzlies living on the prairie's edge along the Rocky Mountain Front west of Great Falls, these bears have been here a long time, but now, according to Jonkel, the grizzly population is increasing.

Also increasing is the chance of more conflict between ranchers and grizzlies, because the Blackfoot Valley is great cattle country. Many people, especially Jonkel, worry about this growing conflict.

That's what we discussed as we drove up U.S. 200 and turned south toward the tiny, isolated burg of Ovando—but not isolated enough to escape the "Espresso Age." "When Ovando has an espresso shop, you know they're everywhere," Jonkel joked as he filled up his pickup truck there instead of Missoula to help out the small-town economy.

We were on our way to check a culvert trap Jonkel had left at a rancher's boneyard, a pit where dead animals are dumped. "I'm trying to get them to stop using these boneyards," he explains. "If the ranchers don't want grizzlies around, then they should stop leaving carcasses lying around."

Decomposing livestock carcasses put out a ferocious smell that can attract grizzly bears. A grizzly had been visiting this boneyard, which was dangerously close to the rancher's home on his large spread south of Ovando—and a long way south of U.S. 200. The bear had been coming in at night and feeding on a dead horse.

On the way Jonkel chewed on Twizzlers and mumbled something about never having time for breakfast or lunch. That's because he puts in long hours working with ranchers and other government agencies to keep things cool in the Blackfoot Valley. He does, however, take every Monday off to spend some quality time with his daughter. During the rest of the week, he starts early, works late, and has a hard time getting to his mundane office work, such as filling out his time sheet so he can get paid. But he always has time to talk hour after hour with ranchers about bears, or fishing, or what's happening in the Middle East and to help them haul away carcasses so they won't become food rewards for grizzlies and teach the bears the taste of beef.

I can't imagine that hauling away bloated cattle carcasses in his government rig is in Jonkel's job description, but it certainly helps accomplish his goal of developing a good relationship with ranchers, the same people who'll have to allow the grizzly bear to live in the Blackfoot Valley. Or not allow it.

Once off the pavement and on a gravel road heading south from Ovando, Jonkel points out several places where he's spotted grizzlies. This would surprise most people, as it did me, because we weren't driving through forested high country. Instead, we were driving though mostly open rangeland, hardly matching common perceptions of grizzly habitat.

When we arrived at the ranch, Jonkel drove in and waited in the front yard a respectable distance from the house, a rural protocol, giving the rancher a chance to come out at his convenience to talk to us. After about fifteen minutes he decided nobody was home, so we drove around back to check the trap, which was unsprung but smelling really bad from the rotting cow placenta Jonkel had used for bait.

Since Jonkel had to leave for a meeting in northern Montana the following day, he decided to close and lock the trap. He didn't want to catch a bear when he couldn't get there instantly to take it off the rancher's hands.

On the way out we met the rancher driving his ATV. Jonkel chatted with him for a half hour about what the bear might be up to, another grizzly the rancher had recently seen on a spring snowmobiling outing, canoeing the river, bow hunting, a little politics, and lots of other stuff Jonkel didn't need to discuss. The rancher seemed genuinely interested in bears and bear behavior, not adverse to their presence, and anxious to help Jonkel with his work. He volunteered to burn the horse carcass, but Jonkel said bears liked them cooked, too. "It would have to be a very intense fire to do any good," he said, so they decided to haul it away instead.

Just another day at the office for Jamie Jonkel, not unlike those of his three comrades on the B Team.

Mike Madel, like Jonkel, spends the bulk of his time working with ranchers. Unlike his three fellow B Team members who work out of regional headquarters in Bozeman, Kalispell, and Missoula, he works in a satellite office in Choteau, a small agricultural community in north-central Montana.

Madel has been dealing with an amazing sequence of events. When Lewis and Clark came through Montana back in 1804–05, they "discovered" the grizzly bear and tested their muzzle-loaders on quite a few of them. They observed the "great white bear" along the Missouri River, a long way from the mountains of the Bob Marshall Complex but not too far from Choteau. For many years bear scientists believed this prairie population had long ago disappeared. Then in the 1980s it was "re-discovered," sort of. The ranchers knew the bears were there, and that they'd always been there, but most biologists wouldn't believe them. Much to the surprise of many bear experts, grizzlies had been coming out of the mountains and onto the prairies, and even living there all year long. This had been going on for many years, maybe even since the days of Lewis and Clark.

In recent years, as the grizzly population increased, more and more bears have ventured onto the cattle pastures and grainfields, creating a fascinating wildlife phenomenon. Madel has found three different groups of bears. He has "lowland grizzlies" that stay on the prairie all year and a population of "mountain grizzlies" that stays in the mountains all year. He also has "immigrant grizzlies," bears that spend part of the year on the plains and the rest in the mountains. In fact, 70 percent of the mountain bears spend part of the year on the mostly privately owned flatlands, particularly in the spring, a critical time when food is scarce and needed badly by all grizzlies.

Like his teammates and most other dedicated bear people, Madel has been working with grizzlies most of his life. He started in 1978 working for Chuck Jonkel's Border Grizzly Project and spent a few years studying grizzlies in the Mission Mountains with Dan Carney, now in charge of wildlife management on the Blackfeet Reservation adjoining Madel's region on the north. He then did a stint studying bears in the Kootenai National Forest before moving to the Rocky Mountain Front in 1983 to study its unique prairie bear population. Three years later the MDFWP made him the agency's first regional bear management specialist, making him the senior B Team member. The other three positions were more or less patterned after his.

"Our major problem is on private land," Madel reports. "We really don't assess the changes going on there." Because of this, he spends most of his time working with about 150 large-scale ranchers. "We have the greatest ranchers around here. They're very easy to work with."

The fruits of his labor are clearly noticeable. Even with grizzlies roaming virtually everywhere in this agricultural community, the locals have started accepting the grizzly as part of the neighorhood. This certainly wasn't always the case. When he started this job, people were scared and intolerant. He recalls a parade that year where several floats bore signs saying "Save Our Kids. The Bears are Here!"

"Social acceptance has improved," he says. "In 1985 people wouldn't allow grizzly bears around their homes. Now they do."

Why, you might ask, are grizzlies out on the prairie where they're less secure, when they could stay up in the more secure mountain valleys? The answer is simple: The prairie provides a much more productive habitat for them. "We have bigger bears here because of better and more reliable food sources."

Madel has trapped yearling males weighing 290 pounds and mature males over 750 pounds. He also trapped a 465-pound female, the largest ever caught in Montana. Then in May 2003, he hit the jackpot.

While trying to capture a female grizzly to change her radio collar, Madel snared "the most magnificent bear I've ever seen." He and his coworkers had to estimate the big male's weight at 830 pounds because their scale only went to 800 pounds. Since this bear had recently left his den after a long winter sleep where he lost several hundred pounds, Madel estimated he would weigh well over 1,000 pounds in the fall. And at only eleven years old, the bear had not stopped growing. Adult males continue to grow throughout their lives.

"All of our bears eat cattle carcasses," he explains. "And they eat oats, barley, and wheat, but they like oats the best. I once saw a bear lying on top of a pile of oats, just shoveling them in as fast as he could."

Ranchers in this area normally experience the loss of about 200 head of cattle each spring, mostly stillborn calves or other casualties of calving. "Bears eat these carcasses, but it doesn't translate into killing live cattle," Madel says like a coach proud of his players. "There are only two or three cows killed each year. That's amazing because there are cattle throughout the forests of the Rocky Mountain Front."

But he doesn't know why.

He'd like to think the bears are smart enough to know that killing cattle seals their fates. It also could be that the bears simply haven't learned how to effectively kill cattle—yet. Instead, however, Madel speculates that grizzlies don't kill cattle because they face a lot of risk in doing it, even in killing calves. Cows are big and can be mean, and he's even observed them chasing grizzlies away from their calves. So the bears eat oats instead because it's readily available and doesn't defend itself.

Whatever the reason, this good behavior has helped change attitudes towards grizzlies. Amazingly, to Madel at least, most ranchers and farmers seem okay with bears in their backyard. Most, but not all. Some complain about a particular bear, but in most cases Madel doesn't capture and move the bear. Instead he tells the ranchers about the grizzly working the area and encourages them to live with it. Most of the time they do, "and they appreciate being told about it." He captures and moves the bear if it gets in trouble, but most don't.

He also helps ranchers put up, and shares the cost of, electric fences around bee hives, residential areas, and other sensitive places. Like Jonkel, he sometimes hauls away livestock carcasses and works closely with the ranchers on ways to live peacefully with bears.

The fertile habitat around Choteau has also increased the reproductive rate of the local bears. Females have cubs every two years instead of three, usually with two or three cubs per litter.

And these bears are adapting to their new environs. "It's all about learned behavior," Madel notes. "These bears are learning to live here on the lowlands. Grizzlies walk right through Choteau at night."

He is, however, realistic about how far this can go. In his mind, two factors limit the grizzly's expansion, "a social line and a biological line," which he believes overlap each other near the north-south line following U.S. Highways 287 and 89. Nonetheless, he's found bears 40 miles east of that line.

"There's no doubt in my mind that the grizzly bear could reestablish a population in the Charles M. Russell Wildlife Refuge (CMR) and the Missouri Breaks," he says confidently, a thought that might give the ranchers out there a heart attack. To get to the CMR, though, bears would have to make it through about 100 miles of pure farmland, not the mostly ranching country found west of the highways. "I don't know if they could ever establish a population in this farmland," Madel says.

But wouldn't it be something if we let them do it?

I was just getting ready to leave to meet Tim Manley, Jonkel's and Madel's counterpart based in Kalispell, when he called to cancel. He had just gotten a call from somebody who found two small grizzly cubs, one dead and one alive, on the outskirts of Whitefish, and he needed to deal with it. Later, when I finally caught up with him, I asked him what happened.

It turned out that a female grizzly had been living on the edge of Whitefish for several years. She had been repeatedly sighted and trapped, but started getting into more and more trouble, including coming right into the town of about 10,000 people at night. Then she disappeared—most likely dead, probably shot or hit by a car, because mother grizzlies rarely abandon their cubs.

A sad story, to be sure, but to Manley, not uncommon or surprising.

Manley has been working for the MDFWP since 1984, and during that time he's seen "a positive change" in the agency. "The department now sees the value of working with landowners." And it's a good thing, the veteran wildlife biologist notes, "because 80 to 90 percent of my work is people management."

Manley has a camper on his pickup truck so he can better cover his territory. If he gets caught out late in a remote area, he can stay on the scene and be ready to start again at first light—indicative of the collective work ethic of the B Team. Government employees often get criticized for not putting in their time, but nobody ever accused the B Team of clock-watching.

Like his teammates, Manley has made bear management his life. After starting in 1984 studying grizzly bears in the Cabinet-Yaak Ecosystem, he moved to his current job in Kalispell, with responsibility for the Flathead Valley and northwestern Montana, another area experiencing runaway development in rural areas. Here he spends his time talking to landowners and dealing with problem bears. Through the years, though, he has changed his philosophy on dealing with bear problems.

Since 1993 he's trapped sixty-seven grizzly bears. All of these bears were in some sort of trouble. Only thirty-one of them survived.

Until recently the policy was to move the problem bears as far away from the site of capture (i.e., where they got in trouble) as possible and hope they didn't come back. Regrettably they frequently did and got into more trouble either when they got back or while traveling through strange country on their way home, and so were eventually removed from the population.

Manley theorizes that part of the problem is the "somewhere else" solution. Moving the grizzlies somewhere else, usually a remote area with a bear population already at or near carrying capacity, causes more stress for the bear than on-site releases. So now he releases bears in familiar country near where he caught them and uses aversive conditioning to put the fear of man in them. He chases them with Karelian bear dogs, shoots them with rubber bullets, and bangs them with cracker shells.

In addition, the actual trapping and release process sends a seriously negative message to the bear about being around humankind.

It's hard for a bear to have a good time crammed into a culvert, starved, deprived of water, and jabbed with a needle loaded with sickening chemicals causing headaches, dizziness, and other side effects. It's hard to imagine an intelligent animal like the grizzly going back for more.

"I give grizzly bears a lot of credit," Manley says. "I think bears have personalities. Some are cranky, but most are not golden retriever bears (i.e., they keep coming back to you). Most bears have good personalities. Most are nonaggressive bears."

It's too early to tell, but it looks like this new policy might greatly improve the survival rate among bears in trouble. Soon after the on-site release, Manley works with the landowners to make sure they understand the bear is still there and encourages them not to tempt the bear with food attractants, which is like leaving a lit cigarette in front of somebody trying to quit.

Preventing bear trouble is still the ultimate goal, Manley emphasizes, but his new on-site release policy might reduce human-caused mortality, which is already exceeding limits in northwestern Montana. "The responsibility is still on the landowner. The bear can't just go somewhere else." Because, of course, there really isn't a "somewhere else."

But, Manley concedes, "We're not even close to solving this problem." Like Jonkel, Manley is trying to educate landowners with welcome wagon-like groups: established neighbors talking to new neighbors about lots of things, including not letting bears get food rewards.

Gradually this should work, because the landowners should start to realize that they won't always have the option of calling up somebody like Tim Manley to take away their problems. There simply won't be enough Tim Manleys to go around as the grizzly population expands. They've chosen to move into bear country and live with bears, not displace them, so now they have to learn how to do it.

"We're making some headway," Manley believes. "Tolerance is improving, but people need to be more tolerant."

So what happened to that forlorn cub Tim Manley picked up on the day he had planned to spend with me? His teammate Kevin Frey took care of it for him.

Frey grew up on a Montana ranch, and in 1973 he started working on grizzly bears for the MDFWP, then spent a few years with the Interagency Grizzly Bear Study Team (IGBST) in Yellowstone Park. He took his current job in 1993 and now spends about 90 percent of his time working on grizzly bear problems in south-central Montana around the park.

The main problem is, of course, the expanding populations, both people and bears. Hundreds of new homes go up every summer, and grizzly bears are showing up everywhere. "We used to go a long time to find a grizzly bear," Frey notes. "Now it's not hard to find them. I have grizzly bears within sight of Livingston and Bozeman."

Through the years Frey has had a lot of orphaned bear cubs, usually resulting from the untimely death of the mother, but also a few every year that are brought in by unthinking people who find them and assume they're orphans when, in fact, mother bear is healthy and nearby, watching them drive away with her cub, dooming it to death or worse.

What do you do with an orphaned grizzly cub? Officially biologists consider it "removed from the population," and it goes into the human-caused mortality stats for that year. There are only three options: try to return it to the wild, place it in a zoo, or execute it.

The third option might be the most humane and least costly, but killing cute little bear cubs doesn't pass the test for political acceptability. Returning a cub to the wild dooms it to a slow, agonizing death. Without the knowledge and protection of the mother grizzly, the cub has no chance of survival.

That leaves zoos, but even this is a problem because they're already full and sometimes won't take more grizzly bears. Frey has, however, spent many hours trying to place cubs in zoos and has developed enough contacts to usually allow him to find a spot for an orphaned grizzly. This means, of course, committing a majestic creature to prison with a sentence of life without parole. Instead of living the good life in a lonely mountain cirque, eating glacier lily corns and digging up marmots, the cub now gets hordes of schoolchildren gawking through fences and a diet rich in horse pellets.

"I hate to place them in zoos," Frey agrees. "Grizzlies live so long, and it's not a noble ending for a grizzly bear."

We talked nervously about just killing them instead, but bear managers like Frey know the consequences of seeing this in the newspaper, so they can't do it. Instead they do as much as they can to prevent the situation by trying to educate people to never take home supposedly orphaned wildlife and by preventing the conditions that cause cubs to become motherless.

Or, in a word, garbage.

"Garbage is still the number one killer of grizzly bears," Frey confidently says. And you wouldn't want to argue with him on this point because he faces this frustration every day. Rural development in south-central Montana is booming, to say the least. Hundreds of new homesteads go up every year, often built by well-meaning people who don't know that garbage kills bears. For the most part, these new residents like wildlife, including bears. That's one reason they invested in their dream home or wilderness cabin. But they present an almost overwhelming challenge for people like Kevin Frey. Just reaching all of them can be mind-boggling.

Frey considers the wealthy out-of-state homeowners the most difficult to reach. Sometimes they only spend a few weeks in Montana—perhaps not imagining that one food reward can kill a mother bear and orphan two cute, cuddly cubs. "These folks still think grizzly bears only live in Yellowstone Park, but bears can't see those boundary lines."

In Frey's extensive experience, here's how it goes. At first the new residents see a bear eating garbage or pet food or apples, and it's a novelty. It seems fairly innocent to put food out or leave it out. Then the novelty wears off, and it's a problem bear. "That's when I get the call," Frey says.

You can see that Frey would like to tell the concerned rural home-owner on the other end of the line, "Nice going. You just killed another bear, and maybe one of your neighbors, too." But, of course, he's much too professional and diplomatic to say that. Instead he goes out and traps the bear, which he knows is probably doomed. "You can't leave a chronic problem bear out there very long," he insists. "It ends up killing several other bears through a negative backlash."

"Sometimes you feel pretty defeated when you see all this devel-opment," Frey admits. "I don't know if we can win. I want to believe we can win, but I'm not 100 percent convinced we can."

What really frustrates Frey, along with his teammates, is the sim-plicity of the garbage problem. Few people disagree with the goal, and the solution is obvious and simple.

"We know how to fix this," Frey points out, raising his voice a bit from its normally calm, controlled level. "We need to secure the garbage any way we can, but will we do it? That's the question."

"There's no way to fix the backcountry encounter problem com-pletely. A certain level of risk has to be acceptable to people. We can't eliminate every encounter in the backcountry. But the goal of fixing the garbage problem in developed areas is achievable."

Most people would let the voice mail take over or grab a handful of hair, pull it out, and yell "Take that damn thing off the hook!," but not Jamie Jonkel.

A few weeks after our little drive up to the Blackfoot Valley bone-yard, I was back in his office, pawing through a thick file on the Nine-mile Grizzly situation. While I was there (about an hour), the phone kept ringing. As soon as he finished a conversation and hung it up, it rang again. This made it impossible to get my questions answered, but it was enlightening to eavesdrop on the phone conversations.

Every call came from a rural resident who had a bear problem—bears eating chickens, bears knocking over garbage cans, bears dig-ging up the compost pile, neighbors complaining about neighbors who fed bears and made it scary for their kids, bears in the backyard apple tree, all kinds of bear problems. And Jonkel took the time to help them all. He repeatedly and politely explained to people that they were killing bears by letting them get garbage and other food rewards. He told one person to come in to the office to get some rubber bullets to use on the bear the next time it came back. He promised to bring out a culvert trap and remove one bear. And on and on and on. It sure made me think Jamie Jonkel and his three teammates would be good choices for cloning, because Montana, Idaho, and Wyoming—and the mountains north of the border—need a lot more than four of them. All four told me they'll soon be overwhelmed with bear problems— and you could effectively argue they already are.

"I'm trying to get these local communities to self-police them- selves," Jonkel explained during a brief moment between calls. "All that garbage is still out there like a time bomb."

Obviously he doesn't have enough time to deal with all the bear problems, sort of like city police not having the chance to prevent all crime, so he's taking a cue from them and setting up the rural version of neighborhood watch groups made up of volunteers who look out for trouble and deal directly with minor problems instead of calling for the cavalry.

Peer pressure can be powerful. Don't mow your lawn or spray your weeds or shovel your sidewalk, and you'll feel it from your neighbors. Can the same subtle pressure within communities help solve the rural garbage problem? Jonkel thinks so. Let's hope he's right, because it might be the only answer.

Raising Grizzly Bears

Dusty Crary has been ranching on the Rocky Mountain Front his entire life. He, along with his wife and two children, live on a picturesque cattle ranch west of Choteau, Montana, along the Teton River.

And he has bears.

For twenty-five years, he has been raising grizzly bears. "I'm very pro-wildlife," Crary assures. "I spend lots of time in the outdoors. Wildlife is a big part of my life, and I very much appreciate grizzly bears and the role they play in the ecosystem. I'm proud to live on a place that's good habitat for grizzly bears."

Not all ranchers agree with him, he admits, but he thinks most on the Rocky Mountain Front do. He also believes the future of the grizzly bear on the Front hinges on private land, an opinion shared by most bear managers and environmentalists.

"This is a public species for the benefit of all the people in the United States," he explains, "but only a few people are responsible for saving the habitat. I don't know if that message gets out there. Only a few people are making it happen. Someday I'd like to have somebody from Ohio call me up and thank me for supporting grizzly bears instead of being mad at me for being a rancher."

Crary's coexistence with grizzly bears hasn't gone on for decades without problems. He had to move his calving area out of the river bottom (used heavily by grizzlies) and near his home to avoid conflicts with bears. At his expense, of course. "Some ranchers say this is my land and I shouldn't have to do this. That's a viable argument that'll probably never be settled."

He's lost a few cows to grizzlies, but not many, and he's never even kept track of it or considered it a serious problem, nor has he ever sought compensation for his losses. Instead he just considers it part of the deal, just part of the ranching biz. "You'd almost have to witness it to know for sure if a grizzly killed the cow or if it just died and was fed on by a bear.

"We like living here. We don't do it for the bucks. Most of us (ranchers) are positive about having grizzly bears around here, as long as there's some management if there's a problem. I don't live in fear, but the fact that you have grizzlies on your property changes your life. It's very important that people understand that we're altering our lives and our business for the benefit of a public wildlife species."

For example, when he was a little buckaroo, he used to go fishing in the river by himself, but now he won't let his kids do it. The reason is the big bear. "My kids can't enjoy the same freedoms I did. It's hard to put a dollar figure on some of the concessions we make."

Like most westerners, Crary has strong feelings about government intervention. "I have a good relationship with Mike Madel of Fish, Wildlife & Parks (MDFWP). He has done a good job up here. But I'm very critical of the U.S. Fish and Wildlife Service (FWS) on how they've handled this. They mandate how the species will be managed, and then they let the state (MDFWP) do the dirty work. I really don't have much use for the FWS. I've never even been contacted by anybody from the FWS. The MDFWP does the best they can, but their hands are tied by the FWS. Ultimately it's Chris Servheen's call."

So would he support delisting to get the FWS out of the picture? Perhaps.

"That's a bureaucrat's deal," he says. "The Endangered Species Act employs lots of people. There's lots of resistance to delisting because it could cost some people their careers."

In summary, Crary says, "I don't have many complaints. The bear causes me very little economic hardship. Bears and humans have coexisted on the Rocky Mountain Front for a long time, and we're coexisting very nicely. There isn't much trouble. People are tolerant, and the grizzly bears are doing well."

May it always be so, Dusty Crary, and not only on the Rocky Mountain Front.

7

The Hair of the Bear

Wilderness is temporary. Development is forever. It's easier for bears and bear managers if it's wilderness.
— Chuck Schwartz, leader,
Interagency Grizzly Bear Study Team

After spending years carefully following the debate over the future of the grizzly bear, one thing has become abundantly clear. There's no shortage of emotion in what people say about the grizzly bear—or how they say it. The grizzly bear does that to you. It makes you emotional. Look at some of the disputes—preserving more wilderness, open-pit mining in roadless areas, reopening grizzly hunting seasons, stock-killing habits of a few grizzlies, reintroducing "man-eating beasts" into formerly safe backyards, removing Endangered Species Act protections, safety of hiking trails in our national parks, and on and on. There rarely seems to be much middle ground.

Nor facts.

Emotion often rules over facts. And the facts we do have often get cooked and recooked to support a certain point of view until you cringe every time somebody uses statistics. A mining company might say, for example, that the proposed mine would only displace five grizzlies in the Cabinet-Yaak Ecosystem, a small price to pay for the creation of hundreds of high-paying jobs. But an environmental group might use the same stats to say the mine would displace at least a third of the Cabinet-Yaak grizzlies, ensure extinction for that population, and make recovery nearly impossible. Or a park ranger might say grizzlies kill only one person per year, but a fearful park visitor might say grizzlies kill somebody every year and "I don't want it to be me; in fact, I'm sure it will be."

They say facts are stranger than fiction, and in the grizzly debate they're scarcer, too.

The problem, of course, is that *Ursus arctos horribilis* is horribly hard to study. Grizzly bears live a long time (up to thirty-five years) and reproduce slowly (one to three cubs every two to three years after age six). And the grizzly is hard to observe in the field and hard to capture, too, all of which makes it difficult to estimate population size or trends. Add the wildly variable behavior common among grizzlies and the obvious fact that studying this animal can be dangerous, and before long even the unscientific mind starts to get a feel for the challenge.

But all those obstacles certainly haven't kept us from trying. The grizzly is, in fact, one of the most studied animals on Earth. Yet, ironically, we really don't know much about this amazing animal. For example, why do some bears become bold and aggressive and others remain secretive? And wouldn't we like to know how a bear lives six months without eating or drinking? That could help us travel through space or eliminate obesity. Or how a bear can eat a high-fat diet yet have no cholesterol build-up in its arteries? That might dramatically reduce heart disease. And what would we give to understand the miracle of delayed implantation? That would allow us to have children on our schedule, not Nature's.

Today, as you read this book, all this might be pipe dreaming. Right now we'd be satisfied just knowing the answer to this question: How many grizzly bears do we have?

That's the question Kate Kendall plans to answer.

Kendall officially works for the Biological Resources Division of the U.S Geological Survey (USGS), but she has an office in the science center at the National Park Service (NPS) headquarters in Glacier National Park. For all practical purposes, she works for the NPS. Explaining why she (and many other national park researchers) gets her paycheck from the USGS, the federal mapping agency, would be a pointless exercise in bureaucracy, nor does it matter.

What does matter, however, is what the current dean of bear scientists does. She spends her non-field days writing up her research and talking on the phone in a tiny, dimly lit office—the shelves filled with books and reports and the walls covered with awards for her scientific achievements. She's been studying grizzly bears since 1977, and, like most scientists, her mind-set demands making order out of chaos (otherwise, her office would likely be so packed with paper, she couldn't open the door). Unlike many scientists, though, she's always willing to answer questions from the media or talk at the local outdoor club or school, even when she doesn't have time for it.

"The Endangered Species Act turned the tide," she believes. "Before the bear was listed, the population was not stable or increasing like it is now. Looking out ten years or more, I'm pretty optimistic about the future. Grizzly bears are so flexible and adaptable. They'll do fine if we give them enough space."

But will we?

As to the answer, she's not so sure. She worries about the trend of only allowing grizzlies in high, mountainous wilderness with minimal resource uses. "We want grizzlies there, but not on private land. This relegates the grizzly to its present range. The parks are not enough, and the isolation of habitat is getting worse and worse."

Kendall strongly believes, for example, that we need a stable population of grizzly bears in the Selway-Bitterroot Wilderness. And we must protect travel corridors between occupied grizzly habitats. This fragmentation of habitat is, in her opinion, the greatest threat to the grizzly bear.

"The more opportunity we have for an intact ecosystem, the better," she says. "We're starting to see how species depend on each other. An ecosystem operates differently when it's missing the big predators."

Kendall sees the big picture, but on a daily basis her life is all about a much smaller universe, hair follicles and DNA genotypes. What she does in the field is much more interesting than what she does in her dimly lit office. Instead of bear scientist, you could call her "bear hair scientist," and she's using this hair to more or less revolutionize bear research.

For forty years grizzly bear research has depended on radio telemetry. This involves capturing a bear and then tracking its movements with frequent flights in a small plane or helicopter to record current positions.

This traditional research method is fraught with problems. It involves capturing, drugging, collaring, tagging, and frequent flying. "Not only do these techniques disturb bears," Kendall notes, "but they are expensive to conduct and involve long-term commitments."

But that's not the end of it. Frequent overflights in wilderness areas and national parks infringe on visitor solitude and happiness, which means the following Monday mornings, agency heads get the calls they don't want to get. And when a wilderness traveler sees a wild grizzly, perhaps a first, he or she doesn't want it to look like somebody's science project—with orange radio collar, ear tags and tattoos, and missing teeth.

And who would believe the bear likes all this? There have been, in fact, claims that the drugs used during the capture-and-release process might make a bear more dangerous. One compound, an anesthetic called phencyclidine, or PCP, which was previously used to sedate grizzlies, is also sold illegally on the street as "angel dust." This hallucinogenic, addictive drug causes agitated, delusional, and irrational behavior in humans, not to mention a seriously bad temper. Did it do the same for bears, which are physiologically similar to humans?

There's no evidence that this ever happened (nor have biologists used PCP for several years), but plenty of scientists believe this traditional research process is tough on the bears. Kendall calls her new methods "an innovative process, friendlier to bears and the scientists studying them," mainly because it doesn't involve handling bears. It's now all about what she calls "the hair of the bear."

In 1998 Kendall launched a study of the northern one-third of the Northern Continental Divide Ecosystem (NCDE), including the "keystone" of the ecosystem, Glacier National Park. She divided the study area into 126 "cells," each 64-kilometer square, and put at least one scent trap in each. She also set up established routes where rangers and volunteers collect bear scats from along the trail and hair from "rub trees," usually trees already used by bears to scratch their backs with the addition of barbed wire to catch more hair.

Grizzly bears heavily depend on their sense of smell, and this new methodology plays to that strength. But in order to do this, Kendall and her coworkers must have highly tolerant olfactory lobes.

In West Glacier, Montana, you'll find a small shed enclosed with electric fencing. The shed is about the size of a four-hole outhouse (rumored to be called, among other things, "the Brew House"), but inside, you'll find three fifty-gallon drums, one filled with cattle blood donated by local slaughterhouses and two filled with rotting fish donated by grocers and fisheries biologists.

When Kendall gets the cattle blood from a slaughterhouse, she adds an anticoagulant to prevent clots from forming. She then pours the blood into five-gallon jugs and dumps them into the drum in the shed.

The fish have to be the right kind of fish. Saltwater species like salmon or shellfish put out a stronger smell when fermented than freshwater fish like trout or perch.

Using the decomposing blood and fish as her ingredients, she cooks her stew for about two weeks to maximize the smell. Then she pours it into one-liter Nalgene water bottles, mixes in some glycerin to preserve the smell, packs the bottles in zip-locked bags, and puts them in Pelican camera cases (airtight, waterproof cases used by scuba divers). Researchers then pack the triple-protected containers into the backcountry for use in scent traps.

After picking a good site for a scent trap, the researchers surround it with barbed wire strung 20 inches above the ground so bears can't get over or under it without leaving a present for Kendall. Then they pile up rotten wood in the middle of the barbed wire "corral" and pour the blood-fish concoction on it. They also hang a long-distance lure, or "love scent," about 15 feet above the flavored wood pile. The love scent, contained in a film canister stuffed with wool, is punctured just before leaving the site.

Kendall varies the smell used in the love scent in order to attract more bears, even those that have already visited another trap and did not find a food reward. She tested the effectiveness of various scents on captive bears at the Grizzly Discovery Center in West Yellowstone, Montana, and Northwest Trek in Seattle, Washington, to see what worked best. Anise (black licorice) oil had been highly touted as the world's best bear lure, advertised to "wrinkle a bear's nose with fits of desire," but that didn't prove to be the case in her tests. Instead she found that the bears favored skunk essence, beaver castor, bacon oil, fermented egg essence, and shellfish essence. (You'll just have to imagine what these items smell like.)

Researchers check and move the traps every two weeks and carefully collect all bear hair. These samples, along with hair samples from scats and rub trees, go to a high-tech DNA laboratory at the University of Idaho, and the bear's genetic fingerprint goes into Kendall's database. From this genotype she can identify the bear in the future, as well as determine the species and sex (but not the age) of the bear.

After identifying more than 200 individual bears, she used a capture-recapture computer model based on the frequency rate of bears revisiting traps to come up with a population estimate. And the results are in.

Kendall estimates the grizzly population in the two-million-acre study area at 273 bears, a high-density population. About half of the study area is Glacier National Park, and the other half is mostly Flathead National Forest and Blackfeet Reservation land. Scientifically this number could vary from 234 to 339 animals, but it's more accurate than the previous estimate, dating back to the 1970s, of about 200 bears.

"This population (in and around Glacier) appears fairly healthy, with a high density of bears," Kendall notes, but her findings can't be used to say the population has increased. "Because the 1970s estimate was based on bear sightings only," she explains, "its numbers would not stand up under today's scientific standards for reliability."

Nor can her findings be used to compare or estimate populations in other ecosystems. "We have a richer and wetter habitat with more topographic variation than other recovery areas to the south."

Nonetheless, it's fairly safe to bet that the grizzly population in her study area has increased in recent years, at least in Glacier. But outside the park, who knows?

Nobody right now, but Kendall also wants to solve that problem. Starting in 2004 and backed by a $3 million congressional appropriation, she plans to expand the study to the entire seven-million-acre NCDE in search of a better population estimate for the entire recovery area, with results due in 2006. She'll be the project leader, but the research project will be a huge, multiagency effort.

Don't generalize about grizzly bears unless you want to be proved wrong, they say, but one generalization has never been disproved: Everything about the grizzly is controversial, even Kendall's research.

Paranoid environmentalists worry about the motive. In the aftershock of the stock market downturn and huge government deficits, finding money for any wildlife research can be more challenging than the research itself, but suddenly Congress found $3 million to study bears in the NCDE. Enviros worry this money appeared for only one reason—to justify premature delisting.

"The bad news is that it (the funding) was approved at the request of Montana Senator Conrad Burns and Governor Judy Martz, both long-time champions of industry on public lands and opponents of grizzlies and sound conservation," warns Brian Peck of the Sierra Club. "In all likelihood, they hope to 'spin' numbers to delist NCDE grizzlies and turn loose industrial-scale logging, mining, and oil drilling in grizzly habitat."

Nonetheless, Peck continued, "It is important for the conservation community to be supportive of this landmark research, which will provide us with a key piece of the puzzle in grizzly recovery."

The Great Bear Foundation (GBF), in fact, supports extending the study and repeating it periodically to gather crucial population trend data. However, as an article in the GBF's newsletter, *Bear News,* warned, "At the same time, we must be on guard against those who would attempt to twist good science for narrow political purposes."

To this the always gracious and eloquent Kendall replies, "We need this information to responsibly manage bears. Now we're spending a lot of time and money to manage bears, and we have no way to assess those efforts. We need data, and this project is the best first step toward that goal. My assignment as a scientist is to make a reliable population estimate."

She implies, of course, that the tough decisions such as when to delist the grizzly belong to somebody else. "The goal is to establish optimal density for certain types of habitat and to establish parameters for delisting, but the real question is how many bears are enough? Ultimately this will be a judgment call. On the scale of things, a population of a thousand isn't very many for any animal. And the box keeps getting smaller."

So, now you heard it. "How many bears are enough?" is one question Kate Kendall won't be able to answer.

Another concern is priorities. Is counting bears the best use of this money or other limited bear management budgets?

Bear managers need money for many other priorities besides getting a good estimate of the population size. Bear people aren't prone to criticizing the work of their peers, but there are other priorities like beefing up the B Team, buying bear-proof dumpsters, installing more electric fences, or instituting more educational programs to teach rural residents to live with bears.

"We probably could put some of this money to better use," speculates Dan Carney, director of wildlife research for the Blackfeet Reservation, who regularly helps Kendall with her work. "But if you want to delist the grizzly bear, you need to know how many bears are out there."

The other key point that troubles many bear people is the "snapshot in time" problem. After the research results come in, we'll have the best possible population estimate that money can buy, but what does that tell us? It doesn't tell us whether we have enough bears or a viable population. It doesn't tell us whether the population is healthy or unhealthy, growing or shrinking. It doesn't tell us if we have enough bears to delist. It doesn't tell us how much habitat we must protect to achieve recovery. Or, as bear management specialist Mike Madel asks, "What good is a one-time population estimate?"

Kendall answers this question by agreeing that the research has limited value, but at the same time, insisting that you can't really do much without it. "This study provides one of two things we need to determine if the bear has been recovered. We come up with a baseline for the population. The other component is long-term monitoring. This project is not set up to do that. This research project doesn't tell you whether the population is increasing or decreasing, but you could make some inferences about how the population is doing based on density by comparing densities in the NCDE to other places. For example, if we have a population twice as dense as Yellowstone, you'd feel good about that.

"You need trend monitoring to get the complete picture," she continues. "You can do that two ways. One would be to repeat the hair trapping and compare it to the baseline. The other way would be to get out there and put radio collars on a bunch of bears and look at birth rate, mortality, and other factors to come up with a trend."

A few misgivings aside, most bear experts line up with Kendall. Steve Herrero, leader of the Eastern Slopes Grizzly Bear Project in Alberta, for example, agrees wholeheartedly with her. "We need the baseline for where the population is."

Kendall has an intriguing agenda, but she isn't the only bear scientist in town. Hardly. Many more log the long hours to grind out the facts we need to manage the beleaguered bear. One, for example, is Chuck Schwartz, leader of the Interagency Grizzly Bear Study Team (IGBST), which he calls "the hub of the science."

The IGBST coordinates and supports all scientific work, including Kendall's, relating to grizzly bear recovery. "The role of the study team is long-term research and monitoring of the bear population. We put the science behind the decision-making," explains Schwartz, who reports to Chris Servheen, coordinator of the Interagency Grizzly Bear Committee. Schwartz is based in Bozeman, Montana, and has been studying grizzly bears since 1973, most of it in and around Yellowstone National Park. In 2002 he became team leader of the IGBST.

"The reality is that the grizzly bear is a threatened species," Schwartz answers when asked about criticism over spending too much money to count bears. "The only way the public will be comfortable that the population is healthy is to have good numbers. The only way we can determine the impact of a new development like the increased use of snowmobiles in grizzly habitat is to have research like this."

Schwartz and many of his team members are doing the same thing Kendall is doing, counting grizzly bears, the animal he describes as "the great umbrella," in preparation for eventual delisting. However, they use a completely different method—counting females with cubs and comparing observations year to year and the continuance of radio telemetry studies that have been going on for decades, combining this data to calculate population trends.

Herrero uses the same methods, particularly females-with-cubs observations. "It's one of the better nonobtrusive methods we have for following population trends," he notes.

Some environmentalists believe politics, not science, dictates management decisions such as delisting, but Schwartz disagrees. "I've never had a call from a politician."

At the same time he acknowledges that the current controversy has a political undercurrent, but points out that bear scientists actually have a reason to resist political pressure to delist the grizzly. "I compete with the rest of the world for money and delisting might mean less research money."

If Schwartz is right, there might be less money for future research—but not less need. "I don't see our role going away. Instead I see it getting more important."

Not many people would argue with him on that point, and in the end it's quite likely that Kendall, Herrero, Schwartz, and the other scientists will, ever-so-gradually and unemotionally, save the day.

Why Do We Need Grizzly Bears?

One question comes up over and over when talking to people about grizzly bears, especially people not familiar with them or those who have never seen a wild grizzly. These people commonly and legitimately want to know why we need grizzly bears. During the course of writing this book, I asked bear experts this difficult question, and here are their answers:

"I should refuse to answer that question. The grizzly bear is a native species. It was here before we were. It's the bear's world, too. One of our responsibilities as stewards of the land is to provide a place for the grizzly bear."

—CHRIS SERVHEEN, coordinator, Interagency
Grizzly Bear Committee

"Basically it's a moral issue, wanting to maintain all parts of our environment, and grizzly bears are a significant part of our environment. I believe in not only taking care of bears but people, too. We have to make sure our livelihood is not endangered by bears. Some enviros are anti-people, but I'm not like that."

—HANK FISCHER, former Northern Rockies
representative for Defenders of Wildlife

"Whether you love them or hate them, you have to admit this is a magnificent creature. You can't just wipe out two million years of evolution, which is about what it took to create the grizzly bear. Are we ready to kill the last one? I don't think so."

—CHUCK JONKEL, bear scientist and president
of the Great Bear Foundation

"It's the ethical thing to do. It's in the best interests of all human beings. We must preserve biodiversity. We want to save all the parts because you never know when you'll need them. The more opportunity we have to study intact ecosystems, the more we see how species depend on each other. The ecosystem operates differently when you're missing the big predators. Besides, it's the right thing to do. Who are we to say we'll let the grizzly bear go extinct?"

—KATE KENDALL, project leader, Northern
Continental Divide DNA Monitoring Project

"I'm not sure that's the right question because it carries with it the assumption that the only reason we need something is because it's good for human beings. This wonderful area we live in here in northwestern Montana, well, the grizzly bear is an important part of it. And you don't throw away any part just because you don't like it or it's convenient to do so. Aldo Leopold taught us. He told us not to tinker with the parts until we knew why we needed them. We should listen."

—BRIAN PECK, consultant, Sierra Club Grizzly
Bear Ecosystems Project

"For starters I should say that having grizzly bears is part of our mandate here in Glacier. For me it's the essence of our mandate to preserve the park in its natural state. You wouldn't have a sense of wonderment, a sense of the wilderness, without the grizzly bear. Without the grizzly bear it wouldn't be wilderness. Personally I feel more alive when I'm in grizzly country."

—GARY MOSES, chair, Wildlife Management
Committee, Glacier National Park

"Lots of reasons. The grizzly is the heart of the wilderness, an emblem of our frontier past. The grizzly gives us humility. This animal reminds us that we aren't at the top of the food chain. It teaches us about nature. Grizzly bears are great teachers. They remind us of ourselves."

—LOUISA WILLCOX, former project coordinator,
Sierra Club Grizzly Bear Ecosystems Project,
now with National Resources Defense Council

"In Yellowstone Park it's our mandate. We have to preserve grizzly bears. To me the grizzly is a good indicator of the health of our environment. If we degrade the habitat enough to lose the grizzly bear, other species would go, too, and this will affect us."

> —KERRY GUNTHER, bear management specialist,
> Yellowstone National Park

"Let's face it: This is one of the greatest creatures ever placed on the earth. Just look back at the role of bears in our history and mythology. If grizzly bears weren't so significant, we'd have gotten rid of them long ago. I also buy into the ecological argument. We need to keep the ecosystem whole. To me, as a dyed-in-the-wool conservationist, it would be like taking a brand-new Mercedes Benz and pulling out one of the spark plug wires. You obviously wouldn't have a fully functioning vehicle."

> —JOHN VARLEY, director, Yellowstone Center
> for Resources

"I have a short answer for that—why do we need people like that? I've got no patience with that kind of person."

> —ANDY RUSSELL, outdoorsman, author,
> and filmmaker

"Maybe we don't need them, but our chances of surviving as a species are increased by demonstrating that we can live with nature."

> —STEVE HERRERO, professor emeritus of
> environmental science at the University of
> Calgary and chair, Eastern Slopes
> Grizzly Bear Project Steering Committee

"When I look at the whole world, it seems to me that in order to keep it a habitable place for people, we need to keep it a habitable place for wildlife."

—DAN CARNEY, director of wildlife research, Blackfeet Reservation

"I tell them that the grizzly bear is an icon of what it means to live in this place, a symbol of what the West means. If we're able to preserve that symbol, we're not only preserving the ecosystem, but we're also preserving a unique western way of life. The grizzly is a symbol of what's important about how and where we live."

—BOB SANDFORD, coordinator, Heritage Tourism Strategy

8

Minimal and Acceptable

Giving people the impression that no danger exists can be as bad as scaring people with over-dramatized accounts of maulings. If misinformed and unprepared hikers converge on grizzly country, the number of encounters will surely increase. Not only must bears be made aware of people, but also people must be made aware of bears. Otherwise, more frequent encounters will prompt hatred, fear, and intolerance for the grizzly.
— from *Where the Grizzly Walks* (1977)

It doesn't happen that often, but once in a while in any profession, such as the science of understanding the relationship between humans and bears, somebody comes along and—through hard work, dedication, and step-by-step credibility building—emerges as the true leader of the pack. Such is the case with Steve Herrero.

For thirty-five years Herrero has been analyzing this emotional human-bear relationship, recording as much information as possible on encounters and building the best database available on bear attacks. In fact, he considers this database "the only scientific sample" of bear encounters. His analysis of 414 encounters from 1960 to 1980 became the basis of his classic book, *Bear Attacks: Their Causes and Avoidance,* which contains the time-honored principles on what we should do—or not do—in bear country. His research and book have directly or indirectly shaped the way we do things today. Bear managers have used his research in league with their own findings to establish regulations for parks and forests. And as for recreationists, well, every time we're out there hiking, hunting, camping, or mountain biking and being blissfully bear aware, we're following the teachings of Steve Herrero.

Most people don't even know this because his research and recommendations have been recycled and rewritten and regurgitated thousands of times to fit the mold of agency managers and book authors. If you diligently follow the information trail, however, you'll discover it leads to the ultimate source, Steve Herrero.

Soft-spoken Herrero might consider this an exaggeration. And it's certainly true that many other dedicated people have been involved in developing the principles of bear awareness, but many of them worked with Herrero on his research or studied under him at the University of Calgary, where he still enjoys supervising about sixty graduate students. But I doubt many people, perhaps not even Herrero himself, would argue the profound impact he has had on managing—and, in fact, vastly improving—the always controversial and occasionally bloody relationship between bear and man.

So if you read up on bear awareness, follow all the recommendations, and have a safe, enjoyable trip in grizzly country without an encounter, you probably owe him a thank-you note. If you do have an encounter, do all the right things, and escape uninjured, you definitely owe him a thank-you. For all of us who enjoy the wilderness, Herrero has helped reduce the risk of a bear attack to what he calls "minimal and acceptable."

The quality information on bear awareness now available has allowed millions of people to more safely hike, camp, fish, hunt, and otherwise enjoy grizzly country. The resulting terrific track record of steadily declining numbers of injurious encounters has gradually improved the public's ability to accept the grizzly bear as a key element of western ecosystems. It has helped many people to control their primal fear of bears, and it has helped to secure a future for the king of the western wilderness.

Back in 1967 the big story of the year was, of course, the Vietnam War, which was going strong at the same time Herrero earned a doctorate in psychology and animal behavior from the University of California, Berkeley. "When I left Berkeley, I was a disenchanted American," he admits. "I was not happy with the Vietnam War or the country's attitude toward it." But then he switched his focus to another big story that came along in 1967, and he never went away. Grizzly bears killed two young women in Montana's Glacier National Park in separate incidents on the same August night.

After spending many years acquiring an education, Herrero decided to take a breather and travel for a year with his family before entering the workforce. They went to Yosemite, Mount Rainier, Jasper and Banff National Parks. Their next destination was to be Glacier, but after the news of two young women dying a horrible death, the stuff of nightmares, his wife said "no way," so instead they stayed at Banff.

To this day nobody knows for sure the true story behind that fateful August night in Glacier, but one thing definitely happened: That night changed bear management forever. And it left many questions to answer. Why, after fifty-seven years (Congress created the park in 1910) without a bear-related fatality, did two grizzlies in two separate locations in the park suddenly go crazy and kill somebody? Why in the same night? Could these tragedies have been prevented? How? Will there be a sequel?

With his intense interest in both animal and human behavior, Herrero became keen on trying to answer these questions, and one other very big question—are grizzly bears too dangerous? If so, perhaps they should be removed from the national parks. That question came up during the "morning after" discussions following the 1967 Glacier incidents.

Shortly after the fatalities, for example, Gairdner B. Moment from Goucher College, Baltimore, Maryland, suggested in an article in the scientific journal *BioScience* that perhaps Glacier and Yellowstone should be purged of grizzly bears. Moment's ideas stunned bear biologists, who rose to the grizzly's defense. They criticized Moment's stand and emphasized the need to preserve the grizzly as part of natural systems, which is key to having national parks in the first place. Of those defending the grizzly, Herrero was especially ardent. In 1970 he replied to Moment in *BioScience:*

"(Several) outstanding biologists including Charles Darwin have presented the case for preserving maximum diversity in our remaining natural areas. They argue convincingly that one way in which the diversity of people and their behaviors is well served is by offering the widest possible range of experience in nature. There is no doubt that grizzly populations in Glacier and Yellowstone can serve this role.

In deciding the value of the grizzly in these circumstances, we must look beyond the present and into the future. With increasing urbanization and automation, man will become even more removed from nature, and the contrast and stimulation offered by the wilderness experience will be even greater . . . to many people the grizzly symbolizes wilderness, makes it come alive in both our minds and our hearts. If relatively undisturbed museums of natural history cannot exist in National Parks, then where will they survive?"

While visiting Banff and Jasper National Parks in Canada, Herrero fell in love with the area and decided to put down roots there. Only about halfway through his allotted year of travel, he went to the University of Calgary and talked to the head of the biology department, who quickly offered him a post-doctoral fellowship. He accepted and launched his long career in studying bear behavior and encounters.

He immediately wrote a proposal to the Canadian Wildlife Service (CWS) to study grizzly bears in Banff, but because of his lack of experience, the CWS rejected it, so Herrero started out studying black bears in Jasper. Then he turned to researching grizzlies in British Columbia's Glacier National Park before finally getting back to the grizzlies of Banff. He took a few breaks along the way to study brown bears in Italy and reintroduce the endangered swift fox to Alberta, but his heart stayed with the big bears of the northern Rockies.

He worked his way up through the ranks at the university and became head of the biology department, but it didn't take long for him to decide that being in charge fell short of the advance billing. After only two years at the helm, he'd had enough administrative life and returned to teaching, research, and answering those tough bear questions. As he says, "I try to make things cause the rubber to hit the road, not fill file drawers with reports."

Herrero now serves as project leader for the Eastern Slopes Grizzly Bear Project, a massive, eight-year research partnership consisting of tour operators, resource extractive industries, recreational groups, and government agencies. "You can make a lot of progress with the soft sell, and that's one reason this project has been so successful."

He still lives in Calgary, Alberta's largest city, where he graciously invited me into his stately old house to spend a few hours talking about something we had in common, our bear obsessions.

So why did Steve Herrero decide on this career when he could have put his stake down in many other scientific fields? "I felt I could have more influence on our environment by working with grizzly bears. We're all really moralists. We'd like to see the world as we'd like to see it. We can get our message out with the grizzly bear. When we talk about environmental protection, it all keeps coming back to bears. That's what keeps us all going."

Sound familiar?

If it doesn't, it will by the time you finish this book. Herrero embodies the same fierce dedication expressed by most bear managers and scientists. Once they join in the effort to save the grizzly, they can't quit—sort of like a cult, only the mind control is self-imposed.

Perhaps he explains addiction better in his book, *Bear Attacks.* "Few biologists can study bears without seeing in them traits that are distinctly human. Such traits make people feel a strong attachment toward bears."

Which only proves he has also mastered the understatement.

In Herrero's case, he not only dedicated himself to studying bears, but also decided to focus on the all-important issue of how we can peacefully coexist with the grizzly, because if we can't learn to do this, well, there won't be a future for *Ursus arctos horribilis.* "We have clearly demonstrated our ability to eliminate the grizzly. Today, we're faced with a task more difficult: to coexist with it."

Unlike some scientists, Herrero has gotten the message out of academia and into the public consciousness. He not only wrote the book on it, but it's also hard to find a documentary on bears without his face in it or a magazine article that doesn't contain a quote or two from him. He somehow squeezes time out of his schedule to talk to various groups about bears, too.

Herrero has not only changed bear management and regulations, but attitudes, too, even his own. In his book he explained how he worked with bear scientists Frank and John Craighead in the early 1970s on the most famous bears of them all, the garbage dump grizzlies of Yellowstone. "Many Yellowstone grizzlies had lost their natural wariness of people but retained their aggressive nature—a dangerous combination," he wrote in the introduction to his book. "I knew this firsthand because in 1968 and 1970 my family and I camped in Yellowstone. While we were there grizzly bears prowled at night among the tents and trailers, searching for garbage or improperly stored food. If I had known then what I know now, we would have packed and left."

When I read that I recalled a scene when I, as a twelve-year-old, went to Yellowstone on a family vacation in 1958. We saw what seemed like hundreds of roadside bears—two kinds of bears, black ones and brown ones. I didn't even know there were two species, but I do remember peeking out the tent at first light one morning and seeing a really huge brown bear that I now know was a grizzly walking through the campground.

Herrero is so interested in animal and human behavior because he considers avoiding encounters a pivotal issue. Feeling safe in bear country makes people feel comfortable, and if people feel comfortable around bears, they're more likely to let the grizzly have a future.

Getting the masses comfortable with bears is, however, a grizzly-size challenge—and Herrero has a problem. The media has much more influence on the masses than he does and commonly overdramatizes maulings, strengthening the image of the grizzly as a bloodthirsty beast.

"Hollywood has fed us a bum story over and over," he says while attempting to explain why people so irrationally fear bears. "We still see the same images of grizzly bears tearing up people in all the films. I hate to see people's lives crippled by fear based on ignorance."

Herrero refers, in part, to the exploits of Bart the Bear, a 1,500-pound Kodiak brown bear that played about as many key roles as Clint Eastwood has, including *The Bear, Legends of the Fall, The Edge,* and *Clan of the Cave Bear.* Bart's resume lists forty feature films, made-for-TV movies, and documentaries, but doesn't list the hundreds of television ads and still pictures of his canines on dozens of book covers and in countless magazine ads and articles. Nor does it list two blood-and-guts, Grade-D movies, *Grizzly* and *Claws,* made in the 1970s. Good Old Bart wasn't in these gore flicks, but other captive bears were used to give the grizzly the image of a serial killer.

Raised by trainer Doug Seus of Utah from the time he was a cub, Bart passed away in May 2000 at the age of twenty-two. Seus is a well-meaning guy who loves bears. He created a nonprofit organization, Vital Ground, with Bart's earnings to purchase key grizzly habitat faced with destruction. Nonetheless, the roles Bart played helped reinforce the public's primal fear of bears and probably hampered efforts by Herrero and others to allay those fears and build social acceptance for the species.

Herrero has concluded, scientifically, that bear attacks are "rare events," but more than most people, he also knows bears are dangerous. He has had thousands of interactions with bears. "If grizzly bears readily attacked people, there would be far more injuries, and I, for one, would not care to coexist with them. The challenge of continued existence, however, does require that we accept some small chance of injury and even death."

And we're talking veerrryyyy small. Even at the high point, around 1970, it was statistically slim, to say the least. After the dramatic deaths in Glacier, Herrero addressed this issue in a technical article in *Science,* a magazine written by and for scientists. He called

A Few Ways to Die	Deaths per year, 1999
Drownings	1,887
ATV accidents	948
Choking on food	648
Hypothermia	600
Bicycling accidents	510
Falls from ladders	328
Falls from chairs	178
Violent storms	128
Falls from cliffs	83
Bitten or struck by mammals other than dogs	68
Lightning	64
Contact with hot tap water	51
Bitten or crushed by reptiles	45
Avalanches	44
Hornets, wasps, and bees	43
Unspecified forces of nature	39
Bitten or struck by dogs	25
Overexertion	21
Trained Asian elephants	12
Household appliances	11
Nonvenomous insects and arthropods	10
Venomous spiders	6

Source: Centers for Disease Control and Prevention, 1999

the probability of getting mauled by a grizzly "negligible," and calculated it at about .00007 percent.

"During the almost 100-year history of North American national parks that harbor the grizzly, there have been a minimum of 150 million visitors," he wrote. "Only 77 persons have been injured by grizzly bears in 66 separate incidents. This gives an injury rate of about 1 person per 2 million visitors. The death rate is 1 person per 30 million visitors. This may be compared to 1.9 million human beings injured in motor vehicle accidents in the United States during 1967. This was about 1 percent of the total population of the United States, or 1 out of 100 people."

And that was 1970. Since then the number of grizzly-caused injuries has declined.

As Herrero knows, though, to some people statistics simply don't matter. They still can't get over that irrational fear and spend their time in the wilderness wondering when they'll become a statistic.

When I asked him about this, I could tell he had talked about people who won't accept any risk a few too many times. A touch of impatience showed through his polished academic veneer. "The risk is minimal and acceptable. We all accept some element of risk in our daily lives. That risk is not appreciably higher in bear country. If that's too much risk for some people, there's nothing you can do about it."

Through the years, Herrero's advice for avoiding encounters hasn't really changed. He still strongly advocates trying to avoid encounters on the trail by making noise, staying alert, and hiking in a large group, and in camp by carefully selecting and setting up campsites and meticulously handling food and garbage. His standard rules came from both his personal observations of bear and human behavior and his analyses of encounters. He found, for example, that a grizzly had never attacked a party of six or more people.

I see no need to repeat in detail his recommendations for avoiding encounters. That's not the purpose of this book. If you've read Herrero's book, or my slim volume *Bear Aware*, or several other excellent books on the market, or the brochure you received when you went through the park entrance station, or any of the thousands of news-paper or magazine articles on the subject, you've already read his advice. And for the most part, the principles of avoiding encounters hasn't changed since Herrero wrote the book on it back in 1985. (See page 144 for The Bear Essentials of Hiking and Camping in Bear Country.)

Bear Attacks definitely made grizzly country safer for anybody who takes the time to prepare, but it didn't answer all the questions. Perhaps one of his new research projects will.

Herrero and biologist Tom Smith have been involved in a long-term research project in Katmai National Park in Alaska to answer a new question posed by hikers and hunters, as well as bear scientists: What colors, scents, and sounds attract or repel bears?

Basically Smith and Herrero have confirmed what many have sus-pected: Any unusual stimulus in the backcountry can attract the atten-tion of a grizzly bear, always a curious creature. So, in general, it's probably wise not to make loud unusual sounds, carry strong artifi-cial scents, or use bright nonnatural colors.

Building on this basic fact, the researchers are finding some inter-esting new revelations. They found, for example, that grizzlies mostly ignored dull green and other camouflage colors but sometimes reacted to bright colors such as yellow. Some bears would go right up to a brightly colored tent and bite it and roll on it, which is "not what you want a bear to do," Herrero notes, but others would have the oppo-site reaction and run from the tent.

Some of these new findings came about by accident. A few years back, Smith's boss at Katmai decided that the brightly colored tents the park used violated the scenic sanctity of the wilderness and created "visual scars" on the tundra landscape, so he replaced them with cam-ouflage tents. "Immediately bear visitation to our camps decreased markedly," Smith notes. "It didn't take a genius to realize that our bright yellow-and-blue tents had been attracting bears."

Smith now believes camouflage tents are the safest choice, espe-cially when camping in open terrain, where bears can see long dis-tances. He also believes any large unbroken splash of color, even natural colors, might attract a curious bear. In a visually crowded forest, though, the choice of colors wouldn't be as critical.

Today you might have a hard time finding camouflage tents and backpacks in retail stores. However, as this research gets more fine-tuned and distributed, that might change.

While testing scents, the researchers found that some bears would go to the scent and roll in it, but other bears would ignore it or be repelled by it. Specifically, they found that strongly scented, fruity shampoos (peach and strawberry) and citronella, an ingredient of some insect repellents, attracted some but not all bears.

When testing noises, they discovered that bears almost always "noticed" human voices, "but we didn't see bears running off when they heard them," Herrero notes. "They keyed on human voices but didn't really react to them." They also tested bear bells and found that they didn't get a reaction from bears one way or the other. The bears "just ignored them," according to Herrero. He said the best sounds (translate: bears fled when they heard them) the researchers tested were "bear growls" and the sound of breaking sticks.

Smith set up a blind on top of a cliff and lowered a string with a bear bell attached down to some brush near a well-used bear trail. Fifteen grizzlies came by, and he rang the bear bell each time. "Not a single bear investigated the bell or even turned to look at it," he notes. But when he snapped a twig in his hiding place, all the bears became "acutely alert" and either froze in place or ran away. He had the same reaction when he made a loud "huff" sound. In both cases he thinks the grizzlies got worried about another bear (not human beings) in the vicinity. Smith also likes loud clapping, because he thinks it sounds like a twig breaking.

After doing this research, Smith now likes the "blend in" strategy. This means, in general, don't do anything to pique a bear's curiosity. Instead try to be one with nature. Sounds good, right? That's why most people go hiking and camping anyway.

All of these findings are preliminary and haven't been scientifically published yet, but when Smith and Herrero get done, these facts, like those from earlier research, will gradually meld into the way we enjoy the wilderness. In the meantime recreationists should still be quite safe by using the wisdom gathered to date.

Herrero's main advice for us is simple—use our brain and be bear aware. This means learning everything you can about bears and your designated route. Educate yourself about bears and bear behavior. Find out if grizzlies range anywhere along your route, what to do to avoid an encounter, and what to do if you don't. Quiz local land and wildlife managers about bears in the area: Any history of bear problems? Any trails or campsites closed because of bear trouble? Any garbage problems in the local area, such as open dumps?

Herrero spends so much time on this because he knows that knowledge of bears increases comfort levels, controls fear, and allows us to enjoy our trips to grizzly country. Enjoying grizzly country is, of course, another way of saying peacefully coexisting with the great bear.

Avoiding encounters might be easy compared to dealing with them.

On the critical (and very commonly asked) question "What do I do if a bear attacks me?," Herrero has changed his message in recent years. In the first edition of *Bear Attacks,* Herrero recommended dealing with black bears differently than grizzlies. Basically he recommended using passive resistance, or in the common vernacular, playing dead, when attacked by a grizzly bear and fighting back when attacked by a black bear.

One problem with this approach is, of course, identification. Many people can't tell the difference between the two species, especially during a sudden encounter. Even though most of the time, with a little research, it's easy to tell the difference, sometimes it's not. Even experts can't identify the species all of the time. There have been a few cases where they couldn't even do so when they had a dead bear and had to wait instead for laboratory analysis.

This problem, along with other factors such as his continued analyses of encounters and his own observations, has changed Herrero's advice in recent years. Now, instead of trying to identify the species, he separates bears into defensive and offensive, regardless of species. If you're attacked by an offensive bear (aggressive or, at the extreme, predatory), he advises you to fight back with all your might, with whatever weapon you can find, and don't play dead unless you want to be dead. With defensive bears (sudden encounters), he wants you to respond passively and submissively, and if the bear actually attacks, play dead unless the bear becomes predatory.

You might ask yourself, "If I have a hard time telling a black bear from a grizzly, how can I separate defensive from offensive?" But it's not that difficult.

Defensive bears cause most encounters as well as most injuries. These are surprise encounters where you suddenly come upon a bear, frequently a female with cubs, and the bear charges because it probably perceives you as a threat to itself, its offspring, or its food source, such as a carcass.

Offensive bears usually aren't surprised by your presence. Instead of fleeing or hiding, these bears (black or grizzly) come toward you and show signs of aggression. The offensive bear might come toward you in the open from a long distance or come into a camp during daylight. Herrero considers "offensive" a prelude to "predatory." An offensive bear might not intend to cause injury, but a predatory bear does. A predatory bear (a very rare occurrence) stalks you or comes into camp at night and tears into tents, probably looking for food, and may consider humans a food source. "Never play dead for any offensive bear," he strongly advises.

Curiosity is a well-known personality trait of the grizzly bear, and a curious grizzly could move toward you. This is probably not an offensive or predatory bear, but since you can't tell the difference, treat it like one.

There may be a third category, the so-called neutral bear. This bear would usually be visible and aware of your presence, but it continues doing what it's doing with no reaction to your presence. Nobody knows for sure what to do about this bear, but, for now, it seems best to take a good look and move on. Definitely do not move toward it for a better look.

In summary, and in Herrero's words, "read the behavior, not the species."

Another major development that has changed bear safety since he wrote *Bear Attacks* (1985) is the advent of bear pepper spray. Since Herrero's research for this book, capsaicin pepper–based spray has become a key element in bear management and surviving encounters.

Throughout the 1980s Herrero remained "skeptical but interested" in bear pepper spray. Now, however, after studying the details of sixty-six encounters involving the use of the spray, he's converted.

"While we do not know how these encounters would have ended in the absence of spray, the use of spray appears to have prevented injury in most, but not all, of these encounters, and I was surprised and impressed with these results," he wrote in his 2002 revision of his book. "I started regularly carrying pepper spray."

In the encounters he studied, Herrero found that bear pepper spray worked 94 percent of the time on "aggressive" grizzlies and 100 percent of the time on "curious" and "probably predacious" grizzlies.

Herrero cautions against considering bear pepper spray a cure-all and assures us that some injuries will still occur even if people carry bear pepper spray, but there would also be some injuries if they didn't. Nonetheless, he points out, it's much easier to aim and use bear pepper spray than firearms, and to his delight he couldn't find a single incident where spray appeared to increase the intensity of the attack. So, in summary, there's really no downside to carrying and using bear pepper spray.

"At the least," he wrote, "having pepper spray gives many people the confidence not to run from a bear, and this too will help decrease chances of injury in most cases."

The disadvantages of the spray, he notes, are the limited range (20 or 25 feet) and the interference from strong wind, dense vegetation, rain, cold temperature, and other environmental conditions, which can make the spray less effective.

One more thing Herrero likes about bear pepper spray is the impact. Unlike firearms, it doesn't hurt the bear.

A note of caution, though. Be careful how and where you use it. While studying bear pepper spray, Tom Smith found another use for it—as a powerful attractant!

Smith discovered that when you dispersed the bear pepper spray on objects like rocks, logs, or tents, it created a strong scent, which sometimes attracted bears. He also talked to some bush pilots who thought they could keep bears away from their airplanes by spraying it on their tires. But instead of acting as a repellent, it became an attractant. Bears rubbed and bit the tires, flattening them in a few cases.

The moral of this story is bear pepper spray can give you confidence (but hopefully not overconfidence) and probably deter an offensive bear, but never spray it around camp or get it on your clothing or tent. And, of course, it's no substitute for your brain. You must still follow the long-proven bear awareness rules for avoiding encounters, always the first priority. (See How Much Aversive is Enough.)

While researching the 1985 edition of *Bear Attacks*, Herrero discovered over and over that human food and garbage were the root cause of many injuries, mostly in or near national parks. Now, decades later, that's changed. The parks on both sides of the border have come as close to solving the garbage problem as possible. And the parks have also done an excellent job of educating visitors, especially those serious enough to go into the backcountry, about bears and bear awareness.

Improvements in keeping garbage away from bears and educating backcountry users have dramatically reduced the injury rates. The parks are much safer now than when Herrero did much of his early research, wrote the book, and made up the rules we live by in bear country.

So is this problem solved? Perhaps, but perhaps not.

Every summer day in the national parks of the northern Rockies, hundreds of encounters almost happen. Hundreds of hikers and other park visitors come within close proximity of a grizzly bear, and most of the time they don't even know it, thanks to the bear being one of the most incredibly stealthy creatures on Earth. Most of the time, though, the bear knows it. "Research clearly demonstrates that the normal response of grizzly bears is to avoid people," Herrero explains, "and not to act aggressively or to attack, even if a person suddenly appears nearby."

Perhaps all those grizzlies are learning they have nothing to fear from the hordes of humans hiking the trails of the parks. This message is currently getting drilled over and over, like a strobe light, into the bear's psyche. Will this stimulus change bear behavior and cause more encounters? Will grizzlies stop avoiding park visitors? With all these bears and all these people in the same spaces, the likelihood of more sudden encounters certainly increases, as well as the chance of a few bears getting human food or garbage and wanting more of it, possibly becoming predatory bears.

"The most dramatic change has been the cleaning up of the garbage," Herrero agrees. "Now it's reversed. Instead of two-thirds of the incidents being caused by food-conditioned bears, two-thirds or more are caused by sudden encounters."

Right now this isn't a big problem, as the number of encounters continues to decline, but what about ten years from now, or fifty years? What happens when national park grizzly populations become completely educated that they have nothing to fear from humankind? Herrero worries about it. "This is a serious problem for managers."

Assuming we can keep this potential problem at bay, it looks like Herrero and the hundreds of park managers, biologists, environmentalists, and writers who have helped him get the message out through the years may have actually won the war—and answered that pivotal question from 1967, the one that brought Steve Herrero his career. Are national parks with free-ranging grizzly populations too dangerous?

No.

The Bear Essentials of Hiking and Camping in Bear Country

The following is definitely not a complete checklist for traveling safely in bear country, but it's a good start. You can get more details from *Bear Aware: The Quick Reference Bear Country Survival Guide,* the source of this list.

- Knowledge is the best defense.
- There is no substitute for alertness.
- Hike with a large group and stay together.
- Don't hike alone.
- Stay on the trail.
- Hike in the middle of the day.
- Make lots of noise.
- Never approach a bear.
- Stay away from cubs.
- Stay away from carcasses.
- Know and adhere to regulations.
- Select a safe campsite.
- Camp below timberline.
- Separate cooking and sleeping areas.
- Sleep in a tent.
- Keep food odors out of the tent.
- Eat all the food you cook.
- Store food and garbage out of the reach of bears.
- Never let bears get food or garbage.
- Leave the campsite cleaner than you found it.

A Few Bears I've Met
and What I Learned from Them

Date: August 21, 1994
Place: Slough Creek Divide, Gallatin National Forest
Lesson: Bad things happen when you don't take your
        own advice.

By the time 1994 rolled around, the original edition of *Where the Grizzly Walks* had long gone out of print, and I had become much more educated in preventing surprise encounters with bears. I had even written a book on it, *Bear Aware,* and had given many talks to groups of hikers on how to safely travel in bear country. On this August day I learned what happens when you ignore good advice, especially your own.

That day I was researching my second hiking guide, *Hiking the Beartooths.* I had a full-time job as the publisher of Falcon Publishing, so I didn't really have time to hike every trail in the Beartooths that summer. Falcon required its authors to actually hike all trails they write about, so I had to set a good example. With this pressure on me, I resorted to running some routes in order to cover the 300 miles of trails before September snows buried the Beartooth Plateau.

On August 20 my partner at Falcon, Mike Sample, and I slept at the Box Canyon Trailhead at the end of the Boulder River Road south of Big Timber, Montana. The day before, we had met in Yellowstone Park and left my trusty Toyota pickup at the Slough Creek Trailhead. My plan was to leave Box Canyon at first light and cover 41 miles of trail up the East Boulder River, over the Slough Creek Divide, and all the way down Slough Creek in a single day. Normally this would be a five-day backpacking trip, but I didn't have five days.

I knew this plan was ambitious, but I'd done the same thing on other long routes.

To cover this much distance, I had to go light. I carried only a fanny pack with two water bottles and a straw filter, a lightweight raincoat, my emergency kit, polypropylene uppers and lowers in case the weather turned on me, and a few raisins and granola bars. I knew the trail passed through some serious bear country, especially along the last 11 miles, which followed Slough Creek through the park, so I had my smaller-than-recommended canister of bear pepper spray on my belt. In my infinite wisdom, I'd decided a large canister would be too heavy to carry while running. I'd also left my bear bell in the truck. I hated that bell clanging away and ruining my wilderness experience.

Mike was still sawing logs in his sleeping bag when I hit the trail a few minutes before first light.

During the first half of the trip, I saw some signs of bear, but not much. When I started down the south side of the Slough Creek Divide into the headwaters of Slough Creek, however, I started seeing bear tracks and scat everywhere. With a few exceptions like Big Game Ridge in Yellowstone and the Swiftcurrent Valley in Glacier, I'd never seen so much bear sign. I was still 10 miles from the park and 20 miles from my rig, so I kept jogging along and shouting "Hey bear!" every 50 or 100 yards.

Perhaps a half hour from the divide, I crested a gradual rise and dropped into a small gully with a trickle of a stream. Even though only a few seconds earlier I'd yelled "Hey bear!," I almost stepped on a grizzly, surprising the bear at a distance of about 15 feet.

At that point it was difficult to determine whether I was more startled than the bear. The bear bolted and ran off. I froze.

After running about 100 yards, the bear stopped, stood up on its hind legs, and swung its head from side to side. I remained frozen.

Then the bear charged back toward me so fast that I could hardly visualize it. The grizzly stopped about 15 feet away. It continued to shake its head from side to side and started making a "chop, chop" sound with its teeth, a frightening sound I hope I never hear again. This wasn't a huge bear, probably a subadult weighing less than three hundred pounds, but it was big enough. I didn't think much about it at the time, but it was a beautiful silvertip, and I remember how long its claws looked. But at that moment, I still had the mobility and awareness of an ice cube.

Now, you'd think that an experienced guy like me wouldn't freeze up in such a situation. But my brain went blank. Fortunately for me, doing nothing was the right thing to do in this case.

Finally I started to regain some control of my mental functions. The bear kept its distance, staring at me and continuing the "chop, chop" sound. It had its head down, and I could see the hairs standing up on the back of its neck.

I started to remember what to do, all the things I'd told people to do a hundred times but never had the chance to do myself, until now. I slowly took out my pepper spray and aimed it at the bear. I started talking slowly in monotone. "Please don't eat me, bear. It would really ruin my day, and I'm old and tough and pretty skinny, too, so you'll probably need another meal anyway."

I also slowly raised my arms and started moving them slowly over my head, trying to look bigger. I then started to slowly back away, still talking to the bear. To my surprise, the grizzly maintained the distance between us. As I backed away, it moved the same distance forward. I moved 10 feet; it moved 10 feet. I moved another 10 feet away; it moved another 10 feet toward me. Over and over. It seemed like an hour, but it was probably about two or three minutes.

I backed away at least 100 feet, but the bear was still 15 feet away, chopping and looking very menacing. The sensation I remember most about the moment was the extreme adrenaline rush I had. I've never used drugs, but this must have been what the ultimate high feels like.

I was scared, too, and I realized this could be it for me. I was alone, a bad idea for starters, and 20 miles from the nearest road on an infrequently used trail. Even if the bear didn't kill me, if I were injured this far back, I'd surely die before a search party found me or I crawled out.

My brain was racing a million miles an hour. What to do? The standard message I'd used in my book and in my seminars wasn't working. Just like at Camas Lake, the sound of a human voice wasn't doing the job. My voice hadn't alerted the bear of my advance, and it wasn't scaring it away now. I needed a metallic noise.

During my research over the years, I'd become convinced that metallic noise was much superior to shouting because it didn't sound like anything in nature and probably carried farther into the forest. This was an unscientific theory, of course, but I believed it. Ever since Camas Lake, I had developed a habit of clanging my aluminum fly rod case on rocks to alert any bears of my advance.

But I didn't have my fly rod case. In fact, I didn't have anything to make a metallic noise. I'd gone light. I only had fabric and plastic.

As I continued to back away and the bear continued to maintain the gap, I finally had an idea. I slowly put the pepper spray back in its holster, bent over and picked up two rocks from the trail, and clanged them together as hard as I could. The sound seemed dreadfully loud in the quiet of the forest—and it worked. The bear immediately spun around and ran with all its speed down the trail and out of sight.

It left behind a stunned trail runner overdosed on adrenaline. I felt so light, I almost had to hang onto a tree to keep from floating away.

After regaining my faculties, I continued down the trail. I gave up the idea of running. Instead I power-hiked, keeping two rocks in my hands and banging them together every few seconds until I broke out into the open meadows in lower Slough Creek, where the good visibility gave me enough confidence to pitch the rocks and run the rest of the way—and I didn't have much trouble keeping up a good pace. I arrived at my rig at six-thirty that evening—a wiser man indeed. And lucky, too.

9

How Much Aversive Is Enough?

Some courageous people in the parks have to make those tough calls. They could make the wrong call, and it could lead to somebody getting killed.
— Steve Herrero, chair, the Eastern Slopes Grizzly Bear Project Steering Committee

Gary Moses has a tough job. And he must do it just right because if he doesn't, people can die—bears, too—and society might have a new opinion about having grizzlies in our national parks.

Moses is in charge of the wildlife management committee at Montana's Glacier National Park, and wildlife management in Glacier often means grizzly bear management. He's been at it since 1989, and he worked in Yellowstone for six years before coming to Glacier. Moses is dedicated to saving the grizzly bear, but it can get frustrating. "Sometimes I really wonder if I'm making a difference," answered Moses when I asked him about it.

The walls of his office are covered with news clippings, editorial cartoons, and posters about bears. He even has the famous knick-knack of two bears breeding called "Bearly Making It in Montana." He's particularly proud of his collection of cheesy bear cartoons, which adorns one wall. After my trip to see Moses, I had to dig out a few of my old favorites about James Watt versus the grizzly bear and send them to him, but I don't know where he'll find space for them. Someday I'll go back and spend a whole day just reading his office.

Some bear scientists like Chuck Jonkel, president of the Great Bear Foundation, and environmentalists like the Sierra Club's Brian Peck think the National Park Service (NPS) should more aggressively pursue a policy of aversive conditioning. They worry about Glacier's bear population becoming more and more comfortable around humans. Basically, they think the bears may be getting tame.

On the surface it seems sort of simple. The park has a large and perhaps expanding population of grizzly bears (somewhere between 234 and 339) that has no reason to fear us. The bears haven't had a reason to fear us since 1910, when these heavenly mountains became a national park. Even though the grizzly bear probably has the slowest reproductive rate of any North American mammal, the Glacier grizzly population has gone through several generations of complete protection. That's several generations of an extraordinarily intelligent animal passing on wisdom to newborns, and one of those bits of wisdom must be something about being safe from men with guns inside the park boundaries, as well as the location of those invisible lines on the landscape.

Following that logical train of thought, the park's grizzlies would continue to get less and less concerned about coming closer and closer to the park's human visitors. Sooner or later the park has more encounters resulting in, most likely, both dead people and dead bears.

Critics liken it to a train wreck that hasn't happened—yet.

Not only does Glacier have a large population of grizzly bears, it also has a large population of hikers. Every summer day, hundreds of hikers probably come within close proximity to these bears and, in most cases, don't even realize it.

The park's backcountry camping permit system allows the NPS to control the number and influence the behavior of backpackers, and the number of backpackers has remained relatively stable. However, thousands of day hikers roam the backcountry every summer. Since no permit is required, the NPS has no way of controlling them or even calculating their numbers.

Backpackers must view a short video about hiking and camping in bear country, and they receive other information on bear awareness when they get their backcountry camping permit. But the NPS does not have these educational opportunities for day hikers.

The park's critics claim the best way to avoid the expected train wreck is more aversive conditioning. That means inflicting some type of pain or discomfort on the bears and making sure the bears associate that unpleasant experience with humans. This will, or so the theory goes, make bears afraid of us again.

Not only does this solidly fit into the easier-said-than-done category, but Gary Moses doesn't necessarily believe it. Like most biologists, he's cautious about agreeing with what others might consider obvious. Instead he looks at the facts, the track record of bear-human incidents in the park. This history tells a different story.

Over a twelve-year period from 1990 through 2001, the park had only nineteen injuries from grizzly bears, five from black bears, and seven from bears whose species was not determined. That's a total of thirty-one injuries, with an average of between two and three per year. During the same period grizzly bears caused two fatalities in the park, one in 1992 and one in 1998. The stats also show a downward trend, with no injuries at all in 2001.

What does Moses conclude from this? "Since there hasn't been a problem in recent years, perhaps we're building a body of evidence that what we're currently doing is working."

Steve Herrero, author of *Bear Attacks* and source of most of our bear awareness rules, tends to agree with Moses. "I don't think we'll ever see a year with double-digit bear-related mortalities."

But Chuck Jonkel draws a different conclusion from these statistics. "This is not really related to how much aversive conditioning they're doing," he says. "Aversive conditioning is more one-on-one with individual bears. The park has tight management of people and lots of other options, like closing trails, that might account for the low number of injuries."

In recent years, he adds, the park has really cleaned up the garbage situation and put forth a good educational effort. These actions may also account for the reduced number of bear-caused injuries.

Under Moses's guidance, the park does aversive conditioning on both grizzly and black bears and has been doing it for many years, mostly in frontcountry areas like campgrounds and along roads. Moses and his coworkers have written a detailed four-level document dictating who can do what, where, and when. For example, when a bear comes into the frontcountry and behaves like it's becoming "habituated" to humans, rangers blast it with rubber bullets or bean bags, scare it with exploding cracker shells, chase it with Karelian bear dogs, and do whatever they can to send the bear back to the backcountry with the fear of humankind. This will, hopefully, keep the bear from becoming "conditioned" (translate: worse than habituated), which sometimes means the bear must be "removed from the system." Not a good thing for a bear.

When a bear must be removed from the system, it's a sign of failure. "Before we ever touch a bear," Moses notes, "we do everything we can to prevent this from happening." That includes as much public education as possible.

Everybody agrees with prevention and education. Everybody believes that bears coming into the frontcountry are problems and must be dealt with forcibly. But what about bears still in the backcountry, bears that haven't become problems? How do you keep these bears wild?

That's the rub.

What do you do with a so-called neutral bear, peacefully grazing along the trail, aware of but seemingly unconcerned about legions of hikers gawking at it? This bear might not display any fear or any aggressiveness. Will this bear become a problem, coming closer and closer to the trail until there's a conflict ending in human injury and, probably, a dead bear?

Some people think so, and Chuck Jonkel is one.

Detractors such as Jonkel believe rangers should give a bear some type of negative stimulus every time it displays neutral behavior. Neutral is not good, they say. Neutral is one step from aggressive. And an aggressive bear is a problem bear and, in most cases, soon to be a dead bear.

Again, Moses isn't convinced. This bear might be a problem, he admits, but it might not be. "We have to take this on a case-by-case basis. We can't play the 'what if' game because there are so many what ifs."

Herrero agrees with Moses. In his work in Banff and other Canadian national parks, he lets neutral bears go without hazing. "There's no indication that a neutral bear will become more dangerous," he says. "It's a judgment call, but I'd let the bear go. Some courageous people in the parks have to make those tough calls. They could make the wrong call, and it could lead to somebody getting killed."

The goal of Glacier's bear management plan is to do whatever possible to prevent bears from becoming habituated. Aversive conditioning is one tool, but the park has others, like posting warning signs or closing trails.

"The first time we get a report of a bear in close proximity to hikers, we might not do anything," Moses says. "It would depend on the circumstances. But if the bear does it two or three times, then we're more likely to do something."

He also points out that the time of year and the availability of food sources influence the decision on what to do with the bear. "In general, we're trying to teach the bear to use habitat near trails only when people aren't around."

If the park decides a bear needs aversive conditioning, it has about forty employees trained and qualified to do it. Unfortunately the person on the scene usually isn't one of those trained in aversive conditioning methods. Moses could train more park personnel, but, realistically, there'd never be enough. The park often relies on reports from hikers, and there's a wide divergence of opinions among hikers on how close is too close.

Another problem is paranoia about what the park service would do to a bear. Some hikers don't report bear incidents because they're afraid the park service will harm or kill the bear. This is dangerously flawed thinking. The park needs all the information it can get on bear behavior, and a ranger might be able to blend together scattered pieces of information and spot—or, better yet, prevent—a dangerous situation. If a hiker fails to report an incident, he or she might actually increase the likelihood of injury or death, both human and bear.

When the right circumstances come together, the park has no problem aggressively using aversive conditioning. "When we decide to use aversive conditioning, our goal is to make sure the bear understands the source of the sound or pain," Moses emphasizes. "We need to send a message that this negative stimulus comes from humans."

However, he's hesitant to use aversive conditioning in all situations because of uncertain results. "There are so many things that can happen when we do aversive conditioning. I worry about what that bear will do. It could run over the ridge and right into a group of hikers." Moses frets about this bear being in a foul mood after getting shot in the behind with a rubber bullet and possibly injuring somebody.

Again, some people disagree. "I don't think the park does enough aversive conditioning," says Brian Peck. "In fact, I think we should blast every bear we can with pepper spray every chance we get. That'll keep them away from hikers. As far as I'm concerned, the park should require all hikers to carry pepper spray and use it on bears every chance they get."

The park does recommend hikers carry bear pepper spray, and most backpackers and day hikers do, but with no research on what might happen, Moses doesn't want hikers spraying neutral bears. He also worries about the bear pepper spray creating a false sense of security and allowing hikers to let down their guard in carefully dealing with food and garbage or getting generally nonchalant about trying to avoid encounters. And he doubts the park could legally require hikers to carry bear pepper spray, even if he agreed that it was a good idea.

"Basically we need to give bears a clear and consistent message to avoid people," Moses says, and one way the park does that right now is teaching bears they can't get food rewards from hikers. "Ninety percent of bear management is people management."

Moses has lots of help in this endeavor. In recent years hikers have been swamped with a multitude of bear awareness and zero-impact information. As a result, most experienced hikers have an elevated level of understanding about bears and bear awareness advice. "But," Moses worries out loud, "you always have new people who may not recognize the importance of this information."

Or haven't listened.

About a million people visit Glacier each year. Moses doesn't worry much about the seasoned backpacker, but he does worry about the person driving though the park who decides to take a short day hike on an impulse and doesn't pay much attention to the warning signs or the handouts received at the entrance station. Thousands of people hike the trails of the park every year with minimal, if any, knowledge of bear awareness. And there's little anybody can do about this.

"Aversive conditioning is an essential tool," Herrero notes. "It helps save the lives of lots of bears, but it doesn't address the root cause of the problem of why the bear is becoming habituated."

In the final analysis, let's all hope Moses is right. Let's hope Glacier's current aversive conditioning policy works. If it doesn't, the consequences could be catastrophic.

All bear experts agree that the existence of the grizzly depends on a tenuous level of social acceptance. One event that could cause a severe dip in that level of acceptance is an increased number of maulings. If the current trend changed, and we had several bear-caused fatalities in a single year, what would people think about that? Would support for the grizzly bear plummet? Would people even want grizzlies in Glacier?

Nobody is more concerned about this than Gary Moses. "More such incidents would obviously put an arrow in the quiver of those who think the only good bear is a dead bear."

Interagency Grizzly Bear Committee
Bear Pepper Spray Position Paper

The Interagency Grizzly Bear Committee (IGBC) produced this position paper in an effort to provide the public with recommendations on how to select an adequate bear pepper spray. The IGBC does not promote or endorse any particular commercial product. The following are only recommendations, and the IGBC does not guarantee the effectiveness of any product. However, the IGBC does recommend the use of bear pepper spray in addition to following proper bear avoidance safety techniques.

Selecting a bear pepper spray:

- Purchase products that are clearly labeled "for deterring attacks by bears."
- Spray concentration should be 1.0 to 2.0% capsaicin and related capsaicinoids.
- Spray should be at least 225 grams or 7.9 ounces of net weight.
- Spray should be derived from Oleoresin of Capsicum.
- Spray should be in a shotgun-cloud pattern.
- Spray should be delivered at a minimum range of 25 feet.
- Spray should last at least 6 seconds.
- Spray should be registered by the EPA.

When to use bear pepper spray:

- Bear pepper spray should be used as a deterrent only in an aggressive or attacking confrontation with a bear.
- Bear pepper spray is only effective when used as an airborne deterrent sprayed as a cloud at an aggressive animal. It should not be applied to people, tents, packs, other equipment, or surrounding area as a repellent.

How to use bear pepper spray:

- Each person should carry a can of bear pepper spray when working or recreating in bear habitat. Spray should be carried in a quick, accessible fashion such as in a hip or chest holster. In your tent, keep bear pepper spray readily available next to your flashlight. You should also keep a can available in your cooking area. Spray should be tested once a year. Do not test spray in or near camping area. Be sure to check the expiration date on your can of bear pepper spray.
- Remove safety clip.
- Aim slightly down and towards the approaching bear. If necessary, adjust for crosswind.
- Spray a brief shot when the bear is about 50 feet away.
- Spray again if the bear continues to approach.
- Once the animal has retreated or is busy cleaning itself, leave the area as quickly as possible (don't run) or go to an immediate area of safety, such as a car, tree, or building. Do not chase or pursue the animal.

No deterrent is 100 percent effective, but compared to all others, including firearms, bear pepper spray has demonstrated the most success in fending off threatening and attacking bears and preventing injury to the person and animal involved. The proper use of bear pepper spray will reduce the number of grizzly bears killed in self-defense, reduce human injuries caused by bears, and help promote the recovery and survival of the grizzly bear.

Remember: Bear pepper spray is not a substitute for following proper bear avoidance safety techniques.

A Few Bears I've Met
and What I Learned from Them

Date: August 10, 1967
Place: Apgar Mountain, Glacier National Park
Lesson: Just when you think you're in control, something reminds you that you aren't.

That year everything changed for the grizzly and the people who manage it.

On August 13, 1967, two grizzly bears killed two young women in two separate locations on the same night in Glacier National Park, the first bear-caused fatalities since this Montana park was created in 1910. This single night not only changed bear management forever, but also burned a new perception of the grizzly so deeply into the public consciousness that it will probably never fade away. Jack Olsen was primarily responsible for that lasting impression by chronicling the two deaths in an expertly written, megaselling book called *Night of the Grizzlies*.

There was another bear incident in 1967. Nobody was hurt, it wasn't newsworthy, and Olsen didn't consider writing a book on it. In fact, until this book came out, only Dave Stanley and I even knew about it. It had no impact on the public consciousness, but it certainly did on my consciousness.

In 1967 I worked on Glacier's trail crew. My primary job was clearing trails, but in those days, before the widespread use of smoke jumpers in the park, the trail crew were considered "hot shots" and were dispatched as a first response to forest fires, usually caused by lightning strikes. That was a bad fire year, so bad that the National Park Service ended up closing the entire park. By the time August 10 rolled around, I had already spent about three solid weeks fighting fires, joyfully racking up the overtime to cover next semester's tuition, with a little left over for beer.

There were so many fires that the park divided up the trail crew into two-man teams (no female trail crew members in those days) and put each team on one of the fires in charge of a twenty-five-man crew of "drafted" fire fighters, usually unemployed men who answered the urgent call at the local job service office. Dave Stanley and I were in charge of a crew from Great Falls.

I haven't heard from Dave since 1967, but if he happens to read this book, I'm sure he'll remember what happened that morning. We'd gone ahead of the crew to scout out the fire line to make sure the mostly contained fire hadn't flared up anywhere along it. The terrain was very rugged, straight up and down, some of it on cat trails gouged out of the surface of Apgar Mountain, courtesy of a fleet of D-9 bulldozers the park service set loose on it. You can still see those scars today, thirty-six years later.

One section of cat trail plunged steeply into a gully of unburned brush and just as steeply climbed out of it. When Dave and I passed through the bottom of the ravine, we heard a small rustling in the brush. It was enough to make us stop and look around, but not enough to alarm us. "Just a squirrel," I remember thinking. Actually, to be honest, I wouldn't remember it at all if it weren't for what happened next.

After Dave and I climbed to the top of the ridge above the ravine, we stopped for a short breather. As we quietly sat and looked down at where we'd just walked, a huge grizzly stepped out on the cat trail exactly where we had been two or three minutes earlier. The bear looked around for a moment, but I don't think it knew we were up there on the ridge watching it as it slowly melted into the brush on the other side of the cat trail.

Why is this so significant? To me, it tells the story of what happens a hundred times a day in Glacier, Yellowstone, Banff, Denali, and other parks that have large populations of grizzlies and hikers. When Dave and I passed through that gully, we no doubt passed less than 20 feet from that hiding bear. Obviously it could easily have had us for breakfast. We had our trusty Pulaskis (a combination hoe and axe) with us, but we wouldn't have had time to use them. We probably wouldn't even have had time to blink. Bear pepper spray hadn't been invented yet, but it would have been useless because we wouldn't have had two seconds to get it out.

We were obviously within what some biologists call the defensive perimeter of that bear, i.e., close enough to prompt an attack. Amazingly even a large bear like this could completely conceal itself in brush only a few feet away from us.

Without a doubt, we were completely at this bear's mercy. The year 1967 was a bad berry year, and fires and fire fighters were running amuck throughout the park, upsetting the normal behavior of bears and all other wildlife. It certainly seems like such circumstances could make a bear hungry and cranky.

But on that day nothing happened. The bear chose not to attack us, and undoubtedly this happens many times every summer day in the park.

To me, this is the real story of bear-human interactions—what doesn't happen. You'll never see, of course, a headline on the front page of the *New York Times* that says anything like Grizzly Bears Refuse to Attack Millions of Hikers in Glacier Park, no more than you'd see the headline A Hundred Million People Drove to Work Today Without Having an Accident.

Think about it. Society has the deep-seated perception of grizzlies as man-eating beasts, yet only one in a million or perhaps many millions of these situations results in human injury.

The reason I remember this so clearly is because three days later, while listening to my fire radio, I heard the panicked reports from the Granite Park Chalet, only about 10 air miles away from Apgar Mountain, about a bear attack in the nearby campground. I later read the dramatic news accounts and Olsen's book, and all I could think was that it could've been me, but it wasn't. Maybe someday I'll know why.

10
Killing Trout
to Save Bears

*The grizzly bear is a living symbol of the American West, a
wilderness icon, and the essence of what makes Yellowstone
Yellowstone, an ecological canary in the coal mine, whose well-
being indicates health for many other wildlife species, as well as
human communities which rely upon the land.*

—Aldo Leopold, *A Sand County Almanac*

Imagine this. You're on a big boat in Yellowstone Lake in the middle
of Yellowstone National Park, which is, of course, an enduring monument to our efforts to preserve wild nature. You're with a group of
dedicated National Park Service (NPS) employees, and you ask yourself, What are we doing here?

The answer: Killing trout, as many as possible.

Sound a little strange? Well, it sure seemed like it when I spent a
day on the *Freedom* doing just that.

"We originally called it *Trout Slayer,*" explains Steve Gale, who
was in charge of the trout-killing crew on that day, "but we decided
we should put a little more positive spin on it and call it *Freedom.*"

That name reveals the ultimate goal, freedom from the evil lake trout, which threatens one of the grizzly's prime food sources, the cutthroat trout.

Gale is referring to a massive metal boat, with the physique of a tug boat, custom designed for gillnetting the lake trout from Yellowstone Lake, the so-called Inland Ocean, with 14.6 square miles of surface area, 110 miles of shoreline, an average depth of 140 feet (maximum 320 plus in West Thumb), and a chilly average temperature of 42°F (never gets above 66°F even on hot summer days). The *Freedom* has advanced GPS electronics that allow it to efficiently plot locations of gill nets and direct routes between them.

This huge expanse of freshwater provides an ideal habitat for the largest population of cutthroat trout in North America, about 2.5 million. The NPS calls this "the last great refuge for the once-widespread Yellowstone cutthroat trout." But now, regrettably, there's a new fish in town, a threat to the cutthroat's dominance, a bigger, meaner predator with a voracious appetite—the lake trout. And the lake trout's primary food source is none other than the slower, less aggressive, easier-to-catch cutthroat trout.

Unlike the indigenous cutthroat, the lake trout is a nonnative species, and only native species are welcome in Yellowstone Park. Nobody knows how the lake trout came to Yellowstone Lake. It's actually possible this could have occurred naturally by fish swimming over the Continental Divide on the Two Ocean Plateau from the Snake River drainage where Heart, Lewis, and Shoshone Lakes host mature lake trout populations. Fisheries experts, however, consider this quite unlikely. More likely, in their opinion, somebody referred to in the fisheries business as a "bucket biologist" illegally introduced the lake trout into Yellowstone Lake, probably into West Thumb, which has more of the fish than the rest of the lake. Probably unknown to this person at the time, the bucket biologist set in motion a gradually unfolding ecological disaster that could seriously affect the grizzly bear's ability to survive in the Greater Yellowstone Ecosystem.

My day on the *Freedom* wasn't an interview. It was work. We spent eight hours hauling in gill nets, removing fish, cutting off fish heads, puncturing air bladders, carefully stacking nets, and then resetting them. This goes on for eight hours a day, seven days a week, from early July through October on the *Freedom* and a companion craft. The folks who do this day after day definitely earn their paychecks (which probably aren't big enough to fit the work).

"It's so huge," Gale sighs. "It's hard to know whether we're making a difference."

In July 2002, when I took my shift, the *Freedom* was targeting smaller fish in deep water, about 150 feet down. The goal is to reduce lake trout numbers as much as possible without netting cutthroat trout, which usually don't venture down to that depth. Nonetheless, we caught one cutthroat for every five or six lakers. Some were still alive, and the crew worked hard to revive them by putting them in a live well to recover and then burping their air bladders before gently releasing them. Regardless of the effort, though, most probably died anyway, just like a large percentage of trout caught and released by anglers.

"We try not to catch cutthroats," Gale emphasizes. "But we do and some die. You could say it's for their own good."

The cutthroats found dead in gill nets serve a useful purpose. We cut off their heads and stored them in carefully marked zip-locked bags for use in another research project that is looking for a cure for whirling disease, another threat to the cutthroats in the park.

Lakers, however, get no such royal treatment. The crew sometimes cuts the net to untangle a struggling cutthroat, but not so for the lakers. We ripped them out of the net, whacked their heads on the edge of the metal table, and threw them into a plastic tray. Later we measured them before spearing their air bladders and dumping them overboard in deep water.

In the fall the government trout slayers target known lake trout spawning grounds in shallow water and net larger fish, hopefully before they can spawn. Gale notes that the average size of the spawners has been going down, a good sign that the gill netting might be putting a dent in the lake trout population. The largest spawner they had caught so far in the project weighed twenty-four pounds, but the biggest caught in 2002 was a paltry eight pounds. Since prespawn females can reach over sixty pounds (the world record is sixty-six pounds, eight ounces, caught in Great Bear Lake, Northwest Territories), this should be good news.

The bad news is that they haven't found most of the lake trout spawning areas. "There might be a hundred spawning areas in Yellowstone Lake," Gale notes, "and we only know the location of three or four of them."

Although lake trout are successfully reproducing in Yellowstone Lake, as witnessed by the presence of several age classes, the smaller size of the fish might mean the population hasn't matured yet, and there's still time to minimize the impact on the cutthroat population.

You gotta have hope, right?

Yes, but let's call it temporary hope or a strategic delay of the inevitable because, right now, there's no cure.

This ambitious gillnetting operation, funded by a new park fishing license fee, has been criticized as a waste of money. Nonetheless, it has the potential to reduce the lake trout population, or at least keep it from growing. The problem is that the gillnetting operation isn't like a surgical operation that removes a tumor—you can't physically remove the lake trout from Yellowstone Lake. Instead, it's like putting an ecosystem on kidney dialysis—you can never stop. You must keep doing it over and over and over. If the park service ever lets down its guard, if politicians ever decide to divert that money for a few years to another purpose like paving highways or thinning forests or building smart bombs, the lake trout will take over Yellowstone Lake.

To this, Chuck Schwartz, leader of the Interagency Grizzly Bear Study Team, wholeheartedly agrees. "The NPS is on a treadmill right now. As long as they keep gillnetting, they can keep ahead of the lake trout. If they ever lose their funding, we're in big trouble."

What does killing lake trout have to do with saving the grizzly bear? More than you might think.

Most people have seen pictures of bears feeding on salmon in Alaskan rivers. In Alaska salmon are an essential component of the bear's diet. On the other hand, few people have seen pictures of bears feeding on cutthroat trout in Yellowstone Park, but trout may be as important to the grizzlies here as salmon are to the bears of Alaska.

This worries NPS scientists like Kerry Gunther, the park's chief bear biologist. If the lake trout flourishes in Yellowstone Lake, the cutthroat population could decline to "10–20 percent of current abundance," according to a special report written for the director of the NPS. In real numbers, that translates into 2.5 million cutthroats becoming 250,000.

Right now, however, Gunther believes the grizzly is doing "just fine." He bases his opinion primarily on the number of bear sightings, particularly females with cubs, which has noticeably increased. "It used to be rare to see a grizzly. Now, you see them everywhere," he says confidently.

But with the specter of the lake trout coupled with other threats to the Yellowstone grizzly, will it always be so? It certainly wasn't in the recent past.

In the early days of the park, the NPS allowed open garbage dumps. At first the dumps doubled as sanctioned bear-watching sites, complete with bleachers and a schedule of garbage dumpings so bears and people could arrive at the same time. The NPS also allowed road-side bear feeding, and the bears quickly learned they could get free handouts on demand. Consequently, during the 1940s, 1950s, and 1960s, watching the bears of Yellowstone was a national pastime.

It soon became obvious to the NPS that this wildlife folly couldn't continue. Step by step, the park moved back to the policy of letting natural systems operate without our help.

First, the NPS closed the dumps to public viewing. Second, the park moved to a policy of discouraging visitors from feeding bears or any other wildlife. And then, in the early 1970s, the NPS made an ultracontroversial decision, strongly opposed by famous bear researchers Frank and John Craighead, to abruptly close all of the park's garbage dumps and start hauling garbage out of the park to commercial landfills.

The end result of these actions, Gunther explains, was the loss of a key food source for bears, human food and garbage, and shortly thereafter, a sharp decline in the Yellowstone grizzly population. Since the majority of the park's bears had been conditioned to depend on this reliable food source, the closure resulted in hordes of hungry bears, then problem bears, then dead bears. Some bears may have died from undernourishment, but most died because they were involved in encounters while frantically searching for new food sources. Some bears obviously couldn't give up the taste for human food and garbage and wandered far and wide to get it. They found it at campgrounds and rural homes around the park and hence became "problem bears," the kind of animals that biologists "remove from the population."

So, for about fifteen years, not only biologists like Gunther but also twenty or thirty million park visitors didn't see many bears. The roadside bears were gone, and the wild bears that survived the bloodshed kept themselves unseen. This obviously disappointed most visitors. A recent survey by the park found that visitors hoped to see "bears" or " grizzly bears" as much as "waterfalls" or "Old Faithful," and much more than things like "scenery" or "wildlife."

In the early 1980s, according to Gunther, the population decline ended, and the Yellowstone grizzly started to recover and expand its range outside the park. He calculates that the grizzly has increased its range about 40 to 45 percent since the 1970s. By "expansion," he means "consistent occupation," not incidental sightings.

This history lesson helps to make Gunther especially concerned about the lake trout situation. It took about fifteen years for the grizzly population to adjust and stabilize after the dump closures. Some bear experts, like the Craigheads, had speculated the Yellowstone grizzly wouldn't make it at all. Fortunately they were wrong, but it's certainly possible the population came precariously close to the invisible point of no return.

The famous bears of Yellowstone were eventually able to adapt to life without the dumps and find alternative food sources, and in some cases that new menu item was cutthroat trout. If the cutthroat dramatically declines, will the bears be able to do it again? What food source will replace the cutthroat? How hard will it be to find a replacement in the likely event of declines in the abundance and reliability of other key food sources such as army cutworm moths, whitebark pine nuts, and winter-killed elk?

These questions plague Gunther and other bear managers and environmentalists. Gunther's current research indicates that about 21 percent of the Yellowstone grizzly population, at least seventy-five bears, use the cutthroat streams regularly, "but it could be as much as 30 to 40 percent," he notes. He isn't sure all of the grizzlies observed on the streams are feeding on trout, but he speculates that most of them are.

During May, June, and July, as many as a million cutthroat trout from Yellowstone Lake travel up most of its 140 tributaries to spawn. This exposes them to predation, and there is no shortage of predators—eagle, otter, osprey, coyote, mink, black bear, raccoon, and the biggest of them all, the grizzly. In fact, the NPS has a list of forty-two mammals or birds that use cutthroat trout as a food source.

If lake trout did the same thing as the cutthroat, the invader might not pose a major threat to the grizzly. Actually, it might be better because the much larger lake trout would be a bigger meal. Regrettably, though, lake trout don't venture into the shallow streams. They spawn in shallow water on reefs and rocky points in the lake where grizzlies couldn't possibly catch them.

Looks like the lake trout is not only bigger and meaner and faster than the cutthroat, but smarter, too.

John Varley, dean of the park's scientists, also believes the Yellowstone bear population has at least "stabilized" in recent years, and he thinks prospects for the next ten years are bright, but he's not so sure about "thirty years from now."

Varley serves as director of the Yellowstone Center for Resources, which coordinates all scientific research in the park. He's been around a long time—at Yellowstone for twenty-eight years but "in the business longer than that." His tenure includes a ten-year stint as chief of fisheries in the park, so he's intensely interested in the lake trout situation, a colossal challenge for his scientific team.

In 1994, when the NPS confirmed the presence of lake trout in Yellowstone Lake, Varley's operation quickly made it a priority. After assessing all of the options, park scientists concluded that gillnetting was the only possible way to control the spread of the lake trout. The task ahead was daunting, to say the least—and expensive, too. Fortunately the park had recently solved the money problem by implementing a fee for fishing licenses. All money raised by the license fees must be spent on the conservation of fisheries and aquatic systems, and a huge chunk of it goes to killing lake trout.

Previously fishing was free in the park, but anglers supported the need for the fee to fund fisheries operations. Not only was there no uproar, as there often is when license fees go up, but many anglers thought the park didn't go far enough because the new license fee was lower than nonresident permits in neighboring states. "The feedback we received was that it was too low," Varley recalls.

With the money secured, the gillnetting operation went into overdrive in 1995 and has stayed there ever since. But has it worked?

Varley is cautiously optimistic. "We're at the cusp of knowing if we can accomplish what we set out to do," he says. "In 1995 we caught one cutthroat for each lake trout we caught. Now we catch 270 lake trout for each cutthroat. We can really mow them down on the spawning grounds."

"This year (2002) we had two signs that it's working," Varley reports. "First, there's no more big fish. We're taking the top off the population. Second, we've doubled the gillnetting effort and ended up with a lower catch. In fisheries science, when you increase the effort and get a lower catch, that means the population is declining."

At the same time, Varley is realistic and admits there's really no cure. He says the park is constantly exploring new options that are sort of "way out there," such as releasing sterile male lake trout to curb reproduction or introducing a lake trout–specific disease or parasite into the lake, but "right now, it looks like gillnetting forever."

Sport anglers already helped the park when they willingly accepted license fees to fund the anti-lake trout effort, and now Varley is looking to them again for help. "Right now," he notes, "anglers are responsible for about 25 percent of the lake trout catch." So the park is looking at ways to increase this by encouraging anglers to target lake trout—and kill them, of course. No catch-and-release fishing allowed for lake trout. No limit either.

You could never get a park ranger to give you a specific spot to go cutthroat fishing, but they'll tell anglers precisely where to go lake trout fishing and help in any other way possible to encourage it. One rather wild idea the park is currently considering is placing a bounty on lake trout. "What would happen if we had a $5.00-per-fish bounty?" Varley asks.

Bounties are generally considered outdated wildlife management, but in this case, think about it. Anglers might do it. They'd be helping the fishery, having fun doing it, and making money on top of that— with no limit on the fun or the money.

One reason to consider a bounty is the park's failure to attract the people who really know how to catch lake trout because, as Varley says, "We don't have the big fish."

Interestingly, Varley points out that the Craigheads didn't find any significant use of the cutthroat by the grizzly in their studies in the 1950s and 1960s. Grizzlies didn't start showing up on the cutthroat streams until the early 1970s. Varley theorizes that there were two reasons for this. First, the dumps provided plenty of quality food until they closed in the early 1970s. Second, in the 1960s the cutthroat population collapsed to the point of "commercial extinction," which means more effort won't catch more fish.

"We needed to turn around this fishery," he recalls. And they did.

In 1975, when Varley was chief of fisheries, he instituted innovative fishing regulations calling for catch-and-release in most park waters and a 13-inch size limit (anglers could only keep fish that were 13 inches or smaller) to keep cutthroats in Yellowstone Lake. The results were stunningly successful. In fact, Varley says proudly, the new regulations, particularly the 13-inch size limit, "worked better than any regulations we've ever tried."

With the new regs in effect, the cutthroat population blossomed— ironically at about the same time the park closed the dumps and the bears desperately needed food. "We like to think that there is a correlation between the dump situation and the grizzly switching food sources," says Varley.

Sometimes it's better to be lucky than good.

The Original

He saw his first grizzly bear in 1958. In fact, he saw thirty or forty of them that day, at a garbage dump in the Hayden Valley, deep inside Yellowstone National Park. That prompted John Craighead and his brother, Frank Jr., to launch a twelve-year research project to learn more about the grizzlies of Yellowstone. Now in his late eighties, John Craighead hasn't been closely following recent research in Yellowstone, but he still has a few opinions on what should be done.

For close to fifty years, Craighead has lived in a modest house on the edge of Missoula, Montana—or at least it used to be the edge of town. Because of runaway growth, he now lives closer to the middle of town. He keeps two golden eagles in his backyard, one of them an incredible thirty-five years old. Inside the house, he has a parrot named Papaya and a Steller's jay named Stella, of course. When I got there, the first thing Papaya did was fly up on my shoulder and take a hunk of flesh out of my neck because, I suppose, I invaded his territory. Stella didn't bite, but she playfully dive-bombed me a few times during the interview.

Craighead's life has always been about wild animals, and it always will be. He may be one of the most famous scientists in the United States, because of his work with the National Geographic Society on the Yellowstone grizzlies. You could consider him the original model for bear researchers.

So what does this man, a scientist extraordinaire who studied grizzly bears for over forty years, think about the future of the great bear?

"The grizzly bear will have a hard time making it over time," he predicts, "but there is no immediate threat. With the world's population doubling in the next fifty years, there's going to be tremendous pressure for more extractive industry, and that's going to weigh on the grizzly bear. The first thing we need to do is protect the public lands and maintain biodiversity. That's going to be difficult under the present administration."

The last thing we need to do, according to Craighead, is take the Yellowstone grizzly off the threatened species list.

"I think it would be a mistake to delist the grizzly bear," he says. "Wyoming wants to have a hunting season—I think this would also be a big mistake. With more and more intrusions into the grizzly bear's habitat and with the president we have now (George W. Bush), there's going to be lots of resource development, so we should give the grizzly bears all the protection they can get."

Asked about the purported increases in the bear population, Craighead expresses his doubts. "I've heard about increases in the number of grizzly bears, but I don't know if I believe it. Bears in Yellowstone now require more territory, so it would be easy to mistake expanding range for increasing population."

Since he lives in Missoula, Craighead has closely followed efforts to reintroduce the grizzly into the nearby Selway-Bitterroot Wilderness. He strongly believes that grizzly bears should have stable populations in multiple ecosystems, including the Bitterroots, with enough protection for travel corridors between them to allow movement. "It doesn't have to be a lot of movement, but enough to maintain genetic transfer."

The proposed Bitterroot reintroduction has become so controversial and political, however, that now Craighead isn't convinced it would benefit the bear. "Putting grizzly bears where they aren't wanted doesn't help the bear in the long run." But he admits the only real alternative, natural repopulation, would be "a very slow process."

Like several other scientists and environmentalists, he opposes the concept of citizen management, the basis for the reintroduction proposal. "I don't think it would work to put the decisions in the hands of political people instead of biologists."

During the last years of his Yellowstone project, his findings and opinions became quite controversial. He strongly recommended that if the dumps (which he called "eco-centers") must be eliminated, they should be slowly phased out instead of abruptly closed. Nonetheless, the National Park Service opted for abrupt closure.

Politics may have played a role in the dump closures, but most of the people involved disliked the basic idea of the noble grizzly getting fat on discarded hot dogs and disposable diapers. Regardless, the dump closures caused a split in the scientific and environmental communities, with some scientists and most environmentalists siding with Craighead's go-slow recommendation, but with the decision-makers taking the position that the Yellowstone grizzly must be quickly converted to natural foods.

In the aftermath of the dump closures, the Yellowstone grizzly population (about 309 strong, according to Craighead) took a nosedive. Nobody disagrees that this happened, but the debate continues as to the severity of the population decline. Park bear managers estimate the population went down to 183 to 209 animals, but Craighead thinks it dropped to 140 to 150 bears.

Craighead claimed this post-dump mortality brought the Yellowstone grizzly dangerously close to extinction. Now, thirty years later, he still has an unusual take on the situation. "Grizzly bears will use much less territory when an eco-center is established," he explains. "Grizzlies do a lot better when they can feed collectively when they have a lot of food in a small area, like the salmon streams in Alaska."

Establishing an eco-center is easy, according to Craighead. "You simply provide food in a small locale, like we did with the dumps. I don't think we're ready for that right now, but down the line we'll come to this. The downside is that if you get the bears concentrated, people will want to develop more country because the grizzly doesn't need as much land."

This doesn't mean Craighead recommends opening garbage dumps for grizzly bears, because he doesn't, but he presents an interesting prospect of using the eco-center as a backup plan. If our efforts to preserve enough quality habitat fail, the eco-center approach might help maintain a larger population with less protected land. We wouldn't have to use a garbage dump to create an eco-center, of course; we could use an alternative food source. In any case, though, any such plan would likely be ultracontroversial.

But, then, it seems everything about the grizzly bear is ultracontroversial.

A Few Bears I've Met
and What I Learned from Them

Date: August 9, 1999
Place: Coyote Creek, Yellowstone National Park
Lesson: Never depend on a bear to do what a bear is supposed to do.

One thing everybody agrees on is that you can't generalize about grizzly bears. As soon as you start believing bears will behave in a certain way, a bear comes along and proves you wrong.

I proved that again on Coyote Creek.

My wife, Marnie, and I were on a two-night backpacking trip in the Hellroaring area. The trail starts in Yellowstone and goes north outside the park into the Absaroka Mountains. We had hiked in along Hellroaring Creek and spent our two nights near the Hellroaring Guard Station. On our second day we took a long day hike up to Carpenter Lake, and on this day we were making a loop by hiking out on the Coyote Creek Trail, which joins up with the Hellroaring Trail about a mile from the trailhead.

By this time in my life, I was a very bear aware sort of guy. After writing *Bear Aware* in 1996, I gave many lectures on bear awareness, and before that I taught classes on how to hike in grizzly country for twelve years at the Yellowstone Institute. One question I received in all of my classes and lectures was "What should I do if I see a bear on the trail ahead?" I always answered it by saying something like this: "If you don't want to see a bear (or any other wildlife), stay on the trails where bears expect to find humans. Hike in the middle of the day when it's hot because bears should be tucked away in a cool, comfortable day bed. If you do see a bear ahead on or near the trail, don't panic. Don't run. Calmly assess the situation, and do the right thing. If the bear is a long way off, at a safe distance, make noise. It should run away because it might not have known you were there, and, of course, bears want to avoid people. If it won't move, abandon your trip if you can. If you can't abandon, take a long detour around the bear."

Well, I should say that my wife isn't like me at all. She doesn't live to see grizzly bears like I do, so when we're out hiking, we do what we can to avoid seeing them. That day was no exception. It was hot, scorching hot in fact, and we were hiking in the middle of the day through dry, open country, common in the northern section of Yellowstone Park. The sun was cooking us, and I was putting out a big sweat—and after three days without a shower, I suspect you wouldn't have needed to be a bear to smell me.

At about 11:30 A.M. we rounded a big, sweeping bend in the trail where it bowed off to the east to stay on the contour and cross an intermittent stream that runs into Coyote Creek. On the other side of the drainage, about 500 or 600 yards away, we saw a huge grizzly, probably an old boar, and it was coming down the trail towards us. It was at a safe distance, but if it continued on the trail and we did, too, we'd be smelling its breath in five or ten minutes.

So what to do?

This had never happened to me before, but from all I'd read, I knew we should remain calm, which we did (or at least I did), and make sure the bear knew we were there. The bear seemed quite content, unconcerned about anything, and possibly unaware of us. So we yelled at the top of our voices, "Hey, bear, hey bear! Get off our trail!"

But the bear just kept sauntering along, not even breaking stride, not even stopping for a second to look our way.

I put dents in my aluminum fly rod case banging it against rocks, putting out the type of disgustingly loud noise you don't want to hear in a pristine wilderness.

Nothing happened. The bear kept coming.

At this point my wife was getting agitated. Calm was not the word I'd use to describe her demeanor. And I became increasingly concerned about this bear that wasn't doing what it was supposed to do.

So I yelled at the bear again and at the same time banged my rod case so hard that I broke it. Finally the bear stopped, but did it run off? Hardly. Instead it looked our way for a few seconds and stepped off the trail about 5 feet and lay down.

Right by the trail! It was still about 400 yards away, but we could see it lying there as clear as day. It just lay there, 5 feet from our way home.

So what to do?

This bear was obviously aware of us. It was, as they say, a "neutral" bear that, in this case, obviously wanted this trail. We were in its way, and it had decided to wait until we moved on. And we were more than anxious to accommodate it. This was no time for playing chicken. We gave up the trail.

Off the trail we went, down into the steep ravine, increasing our distance from the bear, then through an open area where we could keep our eye on it, which we did about halfway down to the stream bottom. It was tough-going with overnight packs. We got really tired and sweaty and scratched up our bare legs climbing over jumbled downfall. As we neared the riparian zone, we entered a stand of scattered aspens and junipers and lost sight of the bear—not a pacifying turn of events for my dearly beloved.

Fifteen minutes passed before we climbed up the other side of the creek bed into the open where we could see the trail again, and what did we see? We saw that big bear slowly sauntering along on the trail exactly where we'd been making all that noise. It wasn't scared. It wasn't aggressive. It just wanted to get somewhere, and the trail was its path of least resistance.

We watched the bear for a long time. A superb sight, no doubt—a creature completely in control of its environment, definitely the top of the food chain that day at Coyote Creek. We sweated our way for another half hour up to the trail and headed home. Along the way I noticed my wife had an awfully fast pace for that last 3 miles back to the trailhead. We'd been hiking together for thirty years, and that was the first wild grizzly she'd ever seen, a fact that made me happier than it did her.

I don't want to anthropomorphize animals, but I've always thought about what might have been going through that big bear's brain. It must have been something about those annoying hikers getting in its way. Maybe it was smart enough to be patient and know neutral bears stay alive, aggressive bears don't. I always wondered what would've happened if we'd been on a similar big bend in the trail where you could only see 20 yards away, instead of the fortuitous high-visibility situation we were in where we could see that ol' silvertip at such a safe distance.

I'll always wonder, but I'll never know.

11

Ecosystem Thinking in Touristland

The bears love it here. They know we love them.

—Andy Russell

I first met Beth Russell-Towe back in 1989 at the Governor's Conference on Tourism in Missoula, Montana. She was sitting behind a table on the trade show floor under a small banner labeled Trail of the Great Bear with a steady stream of people lined up waiting to talk to her, most of them with the same question I had: "What's the Trail of the Great Bear?" After a long talk with her that day, I realized that she was really on to something. This could be the rudimentary beginning of a new approach to ensuring a future for the grizzly bear. It might even be the ultimate answer to the question "Why do we need grizzly bears?"

Because we can't afford to lose them.

Or at least the tourism industry can't.

Russell-Towe certainly didn't invent the concept of ecotourism. It has been around for decades. She was, however, among the first, if not the first, to focus on the all-important and mutually beneficial relationship between the tourism industry and the grizzly bear—and the fact that at least in the northern Rockies, on both sides of the border, the future of the great bear and the tourism industry is linked. They depend on each other, but neither knows it. In this part of the world, the tourism industry depends on great scenery, open space, wild country, and clean water and air—in general, a quality outdoor environment. Interestingly enough, that's what the grizzly bear depends on, too.

"We need to marry tourism and conservation," Russell-Towe insists, and she has pretty much devoted her life to making it happen.

Before starting Trail of the Great Bear, she worked for another nonprofit organization, the Southern Alberta Tourism Association. Prior to that she lived and worked on a cattle ranch on the east edge of Alberta's Waterton Lakes National Park with her famous father-in-law, Andy Russell, author of the classic book *Grizzly Country* and a dozen other books and three feature-length films on grizzlies, wilderness, and ranching. She now lives in and runs Trail of the Great Bear from crammed offices above a gift shop with the same name in the tiny town of Waterton. This gateway community is packed into the only flat spot on the shores of massive Waterton Lake.

Trail of the Great Bear began by promoting environmentally sound tourism development in a corridor linking Canada's first national parks, Banff and Jasper, with America's first national park, Yellowstone. In later years Grand Teton National Park and Jackson Hole were added. A map of the Trail of the Great Bear ecotourism corridor generally coincides with a map of the last remaining range of its namesake.

"We're taking the ecosystem approach," she explains. "We're striving to be the ecotourism model and give definition to what the word really means."

Russell-Towe describes the organization's progress as "fabulous," even though she admits to early delays in developing key relationships with government agencies in the United States. She diplomatically describes it as the agencies having difficulty "thinking Canada."

Another problem the organization faces is changing normal travel thinking, which she describes as east-west and countrycentric. It's an uphill battle to get people to think north-south or transboundary when travel planning. "Lots of people will always go to Las Vegas," she concedes, "but a growing segment is going for learning vacations. We're starting to see more ecosystem thinking."

In addition, the conservation side of her proposed marriage still faces challenges. "The grizzly bears certainly aren't out of the woods yet," she says. "They're still vulnerable. The climate has turned so prodevelopment, and we're seeing more pressure for energy development. The 9-11 attack and the poor economy have created a bad political climate."

Nonetheless, she forges ahead, always wearing a smile. "In the long run, we'll be okay. I have faith in human nature."

Talking with Beth Russell-Towe, you can't help having a blush of enthusiasm that the great environmental battle will actually be won. After agreeing on that point, we drove out through a late spring snowstorm to Hawk's Rest, her father-in-law's ranch.

Andy Russell, now in his late eighties, is close to what you'd expect after reading a few of his books—a crusty old cowboy with a wit as keen as a skinning blade. Russell has been a bronc buster, hunting guide, outfitter, naturalist, trapper, wildlife photographer, and filmmaker, in addition to running a cattle ranch on the east edge of the national park. He hasn't had much formal education but has had a whole lot of the "Rocky Mountain variety" in his words. And it's easy to speculate how daughter-in-law Beth developed her unwavering optimism.

"I'm optimistic," he answers when I ask what he thinks about the future of the grizzly bear. "We definitely have a lot more grizzly bears than we had in the 1930s, more than there ever have been, in fact. We have better protection now. The grizzly bear isn't hunted anymore."

"We have grizzlies all over our ranch right now," he reports. "I've had three of them right in my driveway. The bears love it here. They know we love them."

"The grizzly bears gotta eat. If they can find good food sources, they'll be fine. They don't eat as many cattle as they used to. We've never had a cow killed by a grizzly, and I always question if that's true all over this country," he wonders, and proceeds to tell of a neighbor who had a cow hit by lightning but claimed a grizzly killed it.

To make sure Hawk's Rest is always a safe home for the grizzly, even after his death, Russell has placed a conservation easement on the ranch. This means it can never be subdivided and used for anything except ranching. "There's a few ranchers who don't feel the way we do, but I'm not going to worry about them."

One reason for Russell's optimism (and Beth's, too) is a proposal to significantly expand Waterton Lakes National Park. "The park itself is not enough," Russell says, "but there's a million acres over there, and it's all good bear habitat. I know this because I hunted there."

Russell refers to a huge chunk of wild country west of the Continental Divide and Waterton Lakes National Park that straddles the international border and Montana's Glacier National Park. Regrettably, only about 100,000 acres (40,500 hectares) of it will become part of the proposed Flathead National Park. The size of the new park has been greatly reduced to avoid including known coalfields.

That's the bad news. The good news is a companion proposal to partially protect a vital wildlife corridor (about 925,000 acres, or 350,000 hectares) along the Continental Divide between Waterton-Glacier International Peace Park and Height of the Rockies Provincial Park and the Banff-Kootenay-Yoho National Park complex. This "special management zone" won't provide protection comparable to a designated national park, but it sets the tone for any future development to be as environmentally friendly as possible. The primary purpose of the zone is to provide an enduring travel corridor for large animals like the grizzly bear.

"In the zone nothing will be disallowed but we have to be kind to nature," explains Bob Peart of the Canadian Parks and Wilderness Society. "The criteria for new development will be to protect nature."

"We need both areas," he emphasizes. "Both need to get done. They go hand in hand."

Not surprisingly, Peart's organization and other environmental groups are going to extraordinary lengths to make both happen. They are, for example, raising money to upgrade a privately owned lumber mill in exchange for the company giving up timber leases in the forests that are due to become part of the new national park.

New special management zones and national parks certainly help make the Canadian Rockies more livable for grizzly bears and people, including the tourists. The designation and management of these areas are an example of conservationists and the tourism industry working together to benefit both parties as well as the grizzly bear.

Bob Sandford of Canmore, Alberta, coordinates the Heritage Tourism Strategy, a unique alliance of tourist industry representatives and conservation groups working together to map out the future of the Canadian Rockies. Each year the organization emphasizes one aspect of the local landscape. In 2001 it was the Year of the Great Bear. In 2002 it was the Year of the Mountain. But the ultimate goal stays the same—creating new ways to approach tourism development.

"We have to rethink what we are and accept that we have to do things differently," Sandford explains. "We have to learn why wildlife is so important to our economy. All the things that make this place special are threatened. Bears are powerful icons that get right to the heart of what's happening here, but it's not just the grizzly bear that's threatened here."

His implication is, of course, that the tourism industry itself is also threatened if it destroys the environment that attracts a steady stream of people.

"We must have an alignment between the tourism industry and ecosystem understanding," he continues. "We have many issues with the tourism industry, such as the islandization of Banff National Park."

That "alignment" is what the Heritage Tourism Strategy is attempting to accomplish, a Herculean challenge indeed. And he knows this challenge can only be met through peaceful consensus-building. "We had to get rid of this adversarial relationship."

Sandford has been working on this a long time, going at least back to 1977 when he was a naturalist for Parks Canada. But now he's in a position where he can really make a difference—and create a completely new approach to attracting tourists. "We need to make the ecosystem a tourist attraction. If we can, we can preserve the legacy of the grizzly bear permanently."

What works best for Sandford and his coworkers is getting senior tourist industry officials involved in these discussions, which apparently has never really happened before. "They've been used to fighting," he points out. Now, however, they're starting to discuss and think ecosystems. One example of this new spirit of peaceful cooperation is free distribution of vital bear awareness information to tourists.

"I'm not sure this is working yet," he admits, "but we can learn to live with bears. All we have to do is want to do it."

Banff, Alberta, is the gateway community for Banff National Park. It's a condensed collection of gift shops, hotels, and pubs on the outskirts of the park that attracts large numbers of well-heeled tourists. Elk roam the streets at night, and wolves and grizzlies follow them through the freeway underpass under the veil of darkness and take them down in the town square or in backyards.

Canada Highway 1 is a high-speed, four-lane road that follows the famous Bow River as it flows east out of the park. The superhighway, the major east-west route in Canada and consequently often choked with traffic, essentially divides Banff into two smaller parks. To put it bluntly, this is about the last thing you ever want to see in a wildlife-rich national park. Underpasses and overpasses have been built to provide some wildlife movement, but the highway still serves as an effective barrier to grizzly bears, especially females.

"Females aren't making it across the highway," notes Steve Herrero, leader of the Eastern Slopes Grizzly Bear Project. "This is an early sign of what happened in Yellowstone (i.e., islandization and genetic isolation). The end result is habitat fragmentation."

"We probably have about 25,000 grizzly bears in Canada," he says, "so it's tempting to say (the United States) can always get bears from Canada, but the population along the border is the most threatened."

Colleen Campbell, a local naturalist, works with Bob Sandford and the park on trying to control the speed and minimize the impact of the freeway. She has a tough job. Most people going through the park aren't interesting in much except getting through it—fast. They aren't ecosystem thinking.

"Human-caused mortality is the greatest threat to the grizzly here," she believes. "Almost all of the quality habitat in the Bow River Valley is along roads."

Some bears get hit trying to cross the road. Others refuse to cross, but they might need to reach key food sources or pioneer new territory. Some get food rewards from unthinking tourists and eventually become casualties of the fed-bear-is-a-dead-bear syndrome.

"We need better ways to get the message out," Campbell insists. "Here in Canada, we're a little soft about how we get information out."

She and her coworkers do what they can. They talk to as many people as possible. They have agreements with some resorts and tour operators to give out vital information on bears and other wildlife, but she considers the impact of their current efforts insufficient.

"I'm not that optimistic because the targets for education are constantly moving targets," Campbell explains. "When you're back in New York City and we have to shoot a bear," she wants to tell tourists who feed bears, "I hope you remember that your fingerprint is on the bullet."

But she admits that might not be the biggest problem. "We have to change the way people think. I don't know what to do. Some of these people are my neighbors. We have to get them to slow down."

Good luck on that one, Colleen.

How Would We Notice?

People living in Colorado, California, Oregon, and many other states and provinces don't live with grizzlies anymore. But they still enjoy a quality environment and great scenery. People living in Alberta, British Columbia, Idaho, and Montana still live with grizzlies. If these states and provinces lost their last grizzly bears, what would the difference be? Would we notice the difference? I asked that question to most bear experts interviewed while researching this book, and here are their answers:

"It's important to understand how much we have already altered the biogeography of the West. Losing the bear would be a final step over the threshold to where the landscape loses its essential integrity. People are not going to travel across the continent or over the oceans to visit a landscape that has been compromised as much as the one they have at home. The grizzly is a symbol of what's unique about this place. Without it we're just like any other place."

—BOB SANDFORD, coordinator, Heritage
Tourism Strategy

"Without the grizzly, there would be no way we could walk around in Yellowstone without thinking the sound of a twig breaking is different, a lot different than it sounds in Colorado. The grizzly bear transforms the landscape for us."

—LOUISA WILLCOX, former project coordinator,
Sierra Club Grizzly Bear Ecosystems Project,
now with National Resources Defense Council

"When out in the backcountry, we would no longer have that fear—the same feeling I get when walking home from dinner in Washington, D.C. You hear a noise behind you and say, 'Is this it for me?' When I have that fear, when I'm watching every twist in the trail ahead, I have a different attitude. It's like what the mountain men must have felt. It adds authenticity to the wilderness experience."

—JOHN VARLEY, director, Yellowstone Center
for Resources

"Our whole world is one of controls. Yet, in grizzly habitat, it is uncontrolled. There, we are not the dominant force. We'd notice because the grizzly bear forces us to be more aware of our environment."

— CHRIS SERVHEEN, coordinator, Interagency
Grizzly Bear Committee

"One of the first things we'd notice is how we think and feel when camping out in the wilderness, but I'm not sure that's a positive thing for the grizzly."

— KATE KENDALL, bear scientist, Glacier
National Park

"To really tell the difference, you'd need to be there before and after the grizzly bear. I find it amusing that people say that when they are up here in Montana visiting Glacier it's because we have grizzly bears here."

—BRIAN PECK, consultant, Sierra Club Grizzly
Bear Ecosystems Project

"Without the grizzly bear, we wouldn't have a biologically complete ecosystem, just like we don't out on the plains without the bison. Actually, it's like your car. If you keep taking pieces out of it and throwing them away, sooner or later it won't function."

—GARY MOSES, chair, Wildlife Management
Committee, Glacier National Park

"If they'd ever hiked in Yellowstone and had seen a grizzly, they'd notice the difference. There is just something about hiking on a mountain that has an animal that can kill and eat you."

—KERRY GUNTHER, bear management specialist,
Yellowstone National Park

"If you take enough nature away, you'll notice the difference."
—STEVE HERRERO, professor emeritus of
environmental science at the University of
Calgary and chair, Eastern Slopes
Grizzly Bear Project Steering Committee

"If they're staying in a tent up at Oldman Lake (in Glacier National Park), it's not the same as sleeping out in the West Elk Wilderness in Colorado. I've done both, and there's a big difference. It's the feeling you get when you're camping in grizzly country, or even just hiking through it."
—DAN CARNEY, director of wildlife research,
Blackfeet Reservation

12
Nibbled to Death

*Right now (2001), a tragedy of extinction is indeed playing out
in the Selkirks and the Cabinet-Yaak ecosystems. Of particular
concern is the Cabinet-Yaak with perhaps no more than 11
bears, which suffered the loss of an adult female and cubs and
yielded no reproduction this year. When you're this close to
zero, every animal can be the difference between population
survival and extinction.*

—Sierra Club brochure

Caesar Hernandez isn't the typical environmentalist, and, hopefully,
he isn't alone in his beliefs. Like many other enviros, he works long
days to save habitat for grizzly bears and many other animals, including *Homo sapiens,* so I understood why he got fighting mad when he
saw the bumper sticker telling motorists to "Honk If You Bitch
Slapped an Environmentalist Today." That's a groin shot for somebody who has dedicated his life to preserving wild nature and who has
his own bumper sticker saying "If You Love the Creator, You Have to
Love the Creation."

Fortunately he didn't jump out at the stoplight and start a discussion with the man in the rusty pickup just ahead. In Montana's Flathead Valley—home to ultraconservative politicians, wise users, meth
labs, and militia camps—you never know what would happen, and I

didn't want to find out. I wanted to spend the day talking with Hernandez about saving grizzly bears, not cleaning up after a street fight.

We had planned a day hike in West Fisher Creek to discuss a rapidly shrinking grizzly habitat otherwise known as the Cabinet-Yaak Ecosystem. However, that little incident diverted our conversation to politics. The polarized political debate is definitely one reason the grizzly bear is still a threatened species.

Why, I asked, would the Flathead Valley—a mecca for outdoor recreation, home of fabulous Flathead Lake and the crown of the continent, Glacier National Park, along with many wild rivers and wilderness areas, a place where virtually everybody enjoyed the great outdoors—have such a prevalent negative attitude towards environmentalists? You'd think that a community with an economy that heavily depends on outdoor recreation and that "eats the scenery" every day would welcome people like Hernandez who sacrifice themselves economically, socially, and potentially physically to save it for the rest of us.

"Enviros are partly to blame for it," Hernandez concedes. "We've gone too far in some cases."

He went on to explain how northwestern Montana used to have a bustling logging- and mining-based economy, rich with good-paying union jobs, but then economic conditions changed and many of those jobs disappeared—just like much of the forest disappeared during the 1970s and 1980s. Environmentalists aren't really responsible for this economic downturn, he insists, but their behavior gives that perception.

But that perception might be closer to reality than some environmentalists would like to believe. The Flathead National Forest offers somewhere between six and ten new timber sales per year. Since 1996 all of them (a total of about fifty timber sales) have been delayed or canceled because of appeals (and most of them before 1996, too). For the past six years, not one single sale has gone through without an appeal. That's reality.

Nonetheless, instead of environmentalists ruining the local economy, Hernandez believes it was the timber industry itself, with its long history of short-term thinking, overcutting, and lack of sustained-yield forest management. "If we'd only practiced sustainable forestry up here, we wouldn't have a problem."

What does a guy who works more than full-time for the Montana Wilderness Association know about the sustainable forestry and timber biz? Well, as it turns out, quite a bit. Hernandez spent most of his adult life as a timber worker—four years working in a lumber mill and twelve years as a high-lead faller for logging operations.

At the same time Hernandez was paying union dues as a sawyer, he was volunteering his time on nights and weekends, trying to save wilderness and grizzly bears. "You can't really understand your adversary until you've been there," he believes. "And I walked a mile in their boots."

This demeanor puts him at odds with some of his environmental friends. To illustrate, he told me about his recent work on a nearby timber sale, which seemed reasonably well planned to him and would provide needed timber for local mills. "I told them 'don't appeal, please don't appeal this sale,' but they did it anyway," he recalls. "Sometimes, they (environmentalists) just don't realize that these are people trying to survive in a changing economy."

Public perceptions of environmentalists and grizzly bears is a big issue in the Flathead Valley. Go to the breakfast bars in the early morning or the saloons at night, and you'll hear about it. A growing number of rather extreme people blame environmentalists for most of their troubles and often focus on the grizzly bear as little more than a tool of conservation groups to stop resource development. This perspective has, at times, sunk to outright hatred for the grizzly—the type of sentiment that prompts somebody to grab his rifle from the gun rack and illegally shoot any grizzly unwise enough to show its face along a logging road, which for a bear is difficult to avoid since there are so many logging roads in the Flathead and Kootenai National Forests.

A local radio personality has fanned the flames of this controversy by popularizing the term "Green Nazis" to describe environmentalists, thereby perpetuating polarization in the debate over preserving what wilderness remains in northwestern Montana. This characterization obviously insults hard-working, low-paid environmentalists like Hernandez, but it clearly also intensifies their resolve to carry on the fight.

And the fight over keeping the last roadless land roadless is critical to the grizzly bear, especially in the beleaguered Cabinet-Yaak Ecosystem, one of the six key ecosystems identified by the U.S. Fish and Wildlife Service (FWS) as essential to the great bear's future. This ecosystem, the wettest and most productive in the region, not only provides high-quality habitat for grizzlies, but it also provides a major linkage zone to get grizzlies from expanding populations in the Northern Continental Divide Ecosystem into the Bitterroot Ecosystem, fifteen million acres of wild country, mostly in Idaho, which needs a viable population of grizzly bears to convince environmentalists the species has really recovered.

It might be repulsive to some to consider the majestic grizzly bear a political animal, but in the Flathead, the name fits. The end result is near-violent debates over every mine or timber sale or rural subdivision, without much talk of compromise. Actually there's not much talk, period. Hernandez, along with a few other enviros, and some moderates on "the other side" have discussed compromises, but the vocal fringes on both sides often drown out the voice of reason.

This type of polarization hardly builds much-needed social acceptance for the grizzly, which will be necessary for the bear's survival. The negative atmosphere has prevailed as the Cabinet-Yaak grizzly population has dipped down to only fifteen to twenty-five animals, with possibly as few as three reproducing females. Habitat disturbance is probably the leading cause of this decline, but authorities suspect human-caused mortality could cause the population to dip below the point of no return—if it hasn't already. They know of at least three illegal shootings of grizzlies within a three-year period (1999 to 2001) but suspect there may be at least one unknown incident for every one they know about. Included in that list is Christy, a locally known three-year-old female in the Yaak found dead of multiple gunshot wounds.

Losing any female in a beleaguered population is an ominous event. Female grizzlies don't reach sexual maturity until five or six years old and don't replace themselves in the population for ten years. Most reproduction occurs after they're twenty years old, a narrow window since they usually only live to their early thirties at best.

In a population ranging as low as fifteen grizzlies, according to the Sierra Club, or as high as thirty bears, according to the FWS, twelve bears were killed in three years (1999 to 2001), all human-caused and all three years exceeding mortality limits established by the FWS. That's why Louisa Willcox formerly of the Sierra Club calls this "an extinction story in progress."

You hate to think that this could all be about politics.

When I called Hernandez to talk about grizzlies and habitat preservation in the Flathead, he said, "You up for a day hike?," which for me is like asking a fish if it likes water. He had to get water quality samples from some old mine adits on the east face of the Cabinets, so I readily agreed to tag along. I especially appreciated getting out on the trail and away from the bumper stickers before a fight broke out.

We made it to the trailhead in his completely broken-in Suburu wagon (252,000 miles and going strong), picking up his daughter, Hannah, along the way. She also had an old Subaru with more bumper stickers than I had ever seen on a car, ranging from "Tree-Hugger" to "Wild Women Never Get the Blues."

Hernandez carefully parked his trusty chariot at the end of the road, facing it downhill, just in case, and we headed up an old jeep road, which was supposed to have a closed gate because of mining mitigation agreements, but the USDA Forest Service (FS) had left it open nonetheless.

Along the way we talked mostly about mining, the most serious threat to grizzly habitat in the Cabinets (it's logging over in the Yaak, according to Hernandez). Three massive silver-copper mines had been proposed for the area: two already had operating permits (but not operating yet), and the third, the Rock Creek Mine, was currently under a controversial permitting process and was called by the Sierra Club "the last nail in a bear-tight coffin" for the Cabinet-Yaak grizzly population.

Hernandez and his daughter talked of mining company ploys and secret side deals for land exchanges, buying up penny stocks to get control of mining companies, and the challenging complexities of bankruptcy proceedings, Class I air litigation, and the bane of all environmentalists, the ancient Mining Law of 1872, which is still on the books and giving away public land to miners, making it impossible for land-managing agencies or environmentalists to get any real control over mining activity. They tried to explain the tangled web of federal and state agencies, lawsuits, mitigation agreements, and multinational mining conglomerates and their elusive subsidiaries. It's enough to confuse an entire think tank, but the punch line is clear enough: Mining threatens the last grizzlies in the Cabinet Mountains.

"It's not just the big mines," Hernandez points out. "It's all these hobby mines."

He is referring to hundreds of small mining companies, ranging all the way from fairly significant operations with a dozen workers to weekend gold prospectors with portable sluice boxes bought through a per inquiry ad on the Outdoor Life Channel. These small-timers don't need permits, and the 1872 law gives them its blessing to run roughshod over public land and essentially claim it as private property forever. Many of these so-called mining claims now have little to do with mining, but instead serve as sites for second homes and hunting cabins, most with roads across public land to reach them. In historic irony, Congress also passed a bill in 1872 to create our first national park, Yellowstone.

"Every drainage on the east side of the Cabinets has inholdings that are patented mining claims," Hernandez explains, "and most of the time the miner wants roads built into his claim."

That's where we went that day, to an inholding within a stone's throw of the already much-restricted wilderness boundary.

I shouldn't give the impression that it's all work and no play for environmentalists. They definitely enjoy their work, especially those few days when they get out in the mountains. Some wise users might not believe this, but enviros are basically normal folks. You know, the type of people who put one shoe on at a time, pay taxes, and hope for grandchildren.

At lunch Hernandez wolfs down a ham sandwich and talks about filling his cow (elk) permit, getting some of the standing dead larch he saw on the way in for firewood, and Hannah's recently earned degree in geology and current job search, the same kind of stuff you hear down at the Redneck Saloon on Friday night. It makes you think that if the two sides of this debate sat down and really talked it out, they'd find plenty of common ground.

It's also clear that Hernandez is a worthy opponent for any conglomerate, a perfect example of how one person can make a difference in America. He's been doing this for nearly thirty years, after growing up on the streets of Chicago, and he's no shrinking violet. I witnessed that later when he crawled into mine adits to look for water samples, places I thought only animals walking on four legs would dare venture.

On the way out we ate huckleberries until our fingers were purple. Farther down the trail Hernandez pointed out the little medal markers on trees signaling the presence of even more mining claims and keyed them to ominous gray blocks on the FS map. He talked about finding millions of dollars to buy the claims, but concluded there's little chance of that kind of cash coming along to save grizzly bears in the Cabinets.

While driving down West Fisher Creek Road on the way back to Kalispell, Hernandez points out checker-boarded sections of land owned by the Plum Creek Lumber Company, all recently logged. "They clear off all the trees on their sections," he points out. "You can't log the entire drainage, so the forest service can't log its land, and now there's no lumber for the mill."

Actually, you can tell that Plum Creek is sort of a sore spot for Hernandez. The company owns huge tracts of timberland in the Flathead Valley, most of it already clear-cut.

"And wait until they start subdividing it," he warns, even though he knows this process is already underway. Plum Creek is splitting up some of its land in the nearby Swan Valley into ranchettes and marketing them nationally as trophy-home sites. Hernandez worries that such residential development, coupled with the already prevalent mining and logging activity in the Cabinet-Yaak, might mean taps for the area's grizzly population.

"They (Plum Creek) are getting by paying low taxes by declaring this as timberland, and now they're going to make it residential land." For this, he thinks Plum Creek should have to pay back taxes at the higher rate for at least five years on land they subdivide and sell for residential purposes. He concludes there's little chance of this happening, but I couldn't keep from thinking that the guy down in the saloon grousing about his tax bill might just agree with Hernandez. Maybe they should get together and talk about it.

The 94,000-acre Cabinet Wilderness Area was part of the original wilderness preservation system designated in 1964 when Congress passed the Wilderness Act, but now the Wilderness Society has it on its "most threatened" list. The wilderness is less than a mile wide at one point because the FS drew the boundary to avoid including mining claims and significant timber resources, creating a ridiculous hourglass-shaped Cabinet Wilderness. Congress used this suggested boundary to provide wilderness protection only for this narrow strip of rock-and-ice landscape, ignoring the lush, lower-elevation country that not only provides better habitat for grizzly bears, but also contains the oldest living cedars in America.

The Cabinets, along with the even-more-threatened Scotchman Peaks Wilderness Study Area (officially not part of the Cabinet-Yaak Ecosystem) across the Bull River Valley on the Idaho-Montana border, are the last remaining roadless areas of any significant size in both the Kootenai and the western half of the Flathead National Forest.

The nearby Yaak Mountains are 97 percent public land, but not a single acre has been protected from development, and from the air the maze of logging roads looks like split spaghetti. More than 17 percent of the last roadless lands in the Yaak have been roaded since the FWS listed the grizzly as a threatened species in 1975. Since 1987 the

Kootenai National Forest has allowed logging on 237,000 acres, 68,000 of which are within the grizzly recovery zone.

And the grizzlies in the Cabinet-Yaak Ecosystem are the most threatened of them all. The situation is so dire, in fact, that the Sierra Club calls them "the walking dead." To this, the FWS almost agrees, calling the population "not viable" and proposing "uplisting" the Cabinet-Yaak grizzly population's legal status from threatened to endangered.

Together with the nearby Selkirk Ecosystem, these two huge areas optimistically support as many as seventy grizzly bears. Bear managers have studied the linkage between the two areas and found a small "fractured" link, currently open to resource development. The Sierra Club calls the partially developed corridor a "mortality sink."

"The Yaak has been hacked, almost to death, by logging," according to the Sierra Club. "If we are to protect the unique wildness of the Yaak, we must take decisive and immediate action to not only protect what wild country remains, but also begin to restore those lands that have been abused by industrial development."

So what's the solution to this problem?

Steve Herrero, leader of the Eastern Slopes Grizzly Bear Project, has one. "When the habitat is stressed, the mortality goes up. You can't have grizzly bears without quality habitat. You need to control mortality *and* protect habitat."

The Sierra Club has one, too, but don't expect the FS or the timber industry to agree. "Curtailing and ultimately stopping the commercial logging in the national forests of the Yaak is necessary," the environmental group insists. "Because the Yaak Valley has been so heavily impacted by logging, an extensive agency restoration plan is essential. But it must be a true restoration plan, not an excuse for more logging under the guise of cleanup."

When discussing the future of grizzly habitat in a place like the Cabinet-Yaak, the debate commonly turns to the oft-asked question, "How much is enough?" The answer is predictable. Anybody speaking from the mining, timber, real estate, or motorized recreation industries likes the idea of the Greater Yellowstone and Northern Continental Divide Ecosystems being enough, primarily because the majority of the land base in these areas is designated national parks or wildernesses already and therefore not available for development. This makes the presence of the threatened grizzly politically correct, but to be biologically correct, the range of the grizzly must be expanded beyond these two already protected areas.

These two ecosystems, in spite of their immense magnificence, aren't enough, at least according to just about every bear expert on Earth. Interestingly, during the only-good-bear-is-a-dead-bear atmosphere of the early 1900s, the grizzly survived in these two large (over 4,000 square miles each) ecosystems. But the big bear didn't survive in many smaller wild areas, which could foretell its future in the 2,600-square-mile Cabinet-Yaak Ecosystem.

To achieve scientific recovery, bear managers somehow need to stop the "islandizing" of ecosystems, which greatly increases any species' vulnerability to the forces of extinction. Most authorities insist we should have a viable grizzly population in the Bitterroot Ecosystem, and the Cabinet-Yaak provides the best linkage zone to reestablish a Bitterroot population, but if erosion of habitat continues at the present rate, Cabinet-Yaak will be the missing link.

Extinction is a hard word. Nobody likes using it, but in the not-too-distant future, we might have to when referring to the grizzly population in the Cabinet-Yaak.

Cumulative impacts, not any single development, pile up and become the trapdoor to extinction. However, in an already heavily developed habitat, such as the Cabinet-Yaak, one development can come along that finally pushes a population of endangered animals over the edge and onto an irreversible path to extinction, or as Herrero calls it, "death by a thousand blows."

Such is the case with the massive Rock Creek Mine that is proposed on the western side of the narrowest section of the Cabinet Wilderness.

"The cumulative effects caused by other proposed actions in the area (i.e., other mines, large and small, more roads, a proposed ski resort, omnipresent logging, second-home subdivisions, etc.) will continue to erode the grizzly's already shrinking habitat," notes the Rock Creek Alliance, a broad-based group fighting the Rock Creek Mine. "The (FWS) repeatedly suggests that the Rock Creek Mine could very well drive the grizzly out of the area . . . thus eliminating them from the Rock Creek drainage entirely. This action, coupled with the Noranda Mine (another large mine in the Cabinets), could drive a wedge between the grizzlies in the southernmost one-third of the Cabinet Mountains and those in the rest of the Cabinet-Yaak.

"The Rock Creek Alliance believes the only reasonable and prudent alternative that will allow the Cabinet-Yaak population of grizzly bears to recover would be to expand the recovery area for the species, excluding industrial development such as large-scale hard-rock mining. Construction of the Rock Creek Mine, especially in combination with other proposed and permitted mines in the area, would surely sound the death knell for grizzly bears in the Cabinet Mountains."

The FWS, ultimately in charge of recovering threatened species, has changed its stance on the subject several times. In July 2002 FWS released this revised opinion: "After reviewing the current status of the grizzly bear, the environmental baseline for the action area, the effects of the proposed Rock Creek Project and the cumulative effects, it is the Service's biological opinion that approval of the Rock Creek Project on the Kootenai as proposed is likely to jeopardize the continued existence of the grizzly bear in the Cabinet-Yaak Ecosystem."

Two years earlier, the agency had released an opinion favoring the mine, but howls of protest and threatened litigation prompted a change in heart. Then, in May 2003, the pendulum swung away from conservation and back to development when the FWS re-reissued its biological opinion of the Rock Creek Mine, going back to the original position (from 2000) that the mine wouldn't jeopardize the continued existence of the grizzly bear in the Cabinet-Yaak Ecosystem.

"We are very well aware of the significance of any impacts on such a small population of grizzly bears," FWS regional director Ralph Morgenweck explains. "However, we believe the proposed activities and significant mitigation plan . . . will not substantially degrade the baseline habitat conditions for bears and will provide some beneficial effects for bears throughout the Cabinet-Yaak Ecosystem."

So why all the waffling? Who knows, but it's hard to believe politics didn't have some influence. And a few people don't mind saying it out loud.

"This whole thing appears to be driven far more by what is politically acceptable to the administration than by science," claims Lee Metzger, a bear population expert and retired director of biology at the University of Montana. "In my view, the grizzly population in the Cabinets is being managed for extinction."

The FWS based its most recent opinion on the belief that the Noranda Mine wouldn't actually be developed, but that seems like wishful thinking. This mine already has an operating permit, and even though mining rights have been sold, the new owner is only waiting for silver prices to go up before opting for development. The FWS also expects that significant mitigation activities such as making the mining company pay for two bear management specialists, "bearproofing" nearby campgrounds, and requiring the FS to close several logging roads in the area will cancel out any negative impacts of the mine.

As you might expect, environmentalists were aghast at the FWS reversal. "I don't think there is any amount of mitigation they can do to protect the small population of grizzly bears from the mine," counters Mary Mitchell from the Rock Creek Alliance. She strongly disagrees that the Noranda Mine is "out of the picture." Instead, she points out, it has a valid operating permit and a new owner that's "actively marketing" the project.

Brian Peck of the Sierra Club is a little more pointed in his criticism. "Surprise, surprise!" he blasts. "Unable to find its missing spinal column, the FWS has rubber-stamped the Rock Creek Mine, again."

In a press release, the Sierra Club summed up the situation like this: "With too few bears and a declining trend, insufficient secure habitat, tenuous and shrinking linkages, excessive mortalities and woefully inadequate regulations, the last thing grizzlies need is the Rock Creek Mine."

Appeals and lawsuits will likely delay the mine for years. Hopefully the grizzly bear will still haunt the Cabinet-Yaak Ecosystem when the fight is finally over.

How does habitat disappear? Well, technically, it doesn't. But bears do.

Instead of vanishing, the habitat becomes unusable by grizzly bears. They go elsewhere, if there is an elsewhere, or they die—and they rarely die of old age. Several scientific studies have shown that grizzlies avoid roads and that increased motorized access contributes to more human-caused bear mortality, including those killed by poachers.

Nobody, not even a person with a serious bent for resource development, ever stands up on a soapbox and suggests developing an entire ecosystem. Instead that person stands up and says that this is only one mile of new road, only one small mine, only one wilderness cabin, or only one tiny timber sale, and it won't make the species go extinct.

They're almost always right, of course. That road or mine or cabin or timber sale often doesn't have a measurable impact on the big bear's future—by itself.

What no developer ever says, however, and what environmentalists say over and over is that the incremental impact must be considered. And not just in the Cabinet-Yaak, although it serves as a perfect example of how cumulative impacts shrink grizzly habitats. This micro vanishing act is happening everywhere in every ecosystem and in every linkage corridor between them, all ever-so-gradually becoming less usable by the great bear, so slowly it would take time-lapse photography from a satellite to see it. But there's no doubt that inch by inch, cabin by cabin, log by log, mine by mine, the last grizzly habitat is disappearing. It's being nibbled to death.

Management by Elimination

After a long chat with Clarence Tabor, it's obvious the USDA Forest Service (FS) is doing a perfectly good job of managing grizzly habitat in the national forests. Or a perfectly lousy job because, somehow, the federal land-managing agency in control of most of our remaining grizzly habitat south of Canada has managed to alienate everybody.

When you talk to environmentalists, you hear a constant stream of criticism about how the FS is controlled by resource-extractive industries, plagued with "timber beasts" in key administrative positions, and wasting most of its budget destroying the last vestiges of roadless forestland, otherwise known as grizzly habitat.

But when you talk to concerned citizens like Tabor, president of Montanans for Multiple Use, a person referred to as "a wise user" by environmentalists, you definitely get the opposite perspective.

Tabor, along with the 300-odd members of the rapidly growing organization, believe environmental groups have taken control of the FS and have *their* disciples in key administrative positions, busily undoing decades of progress—and not helping the grizzly bear.

Retired after thirty-four years as an engineer for the FS, Tabor really hates to see what's happening to the agency, which, in his opinion, has become an extension of the environmental movement.

"The FS changed because the preservationists came in and took charge. They believe the national forests are the world's playgrounds," Tabor complains. "The FS now manages not for what they remove, but for what they leave. I believe there are people in the FS who attend Earth First functions."

In talking to environmentalists, it's easy to get the impression that people like Tabor are an evil force of mean-spirited thugs. But at least in this case, the opposite is true. Tabor is soft-spoken and as passionate about his views as any environmentalist—and he has a more gracious demeanor than most environmentalists I know. He has, in fact, as much affection for the landscape as any environmentalist, and he wants to see it filled with wildlife, including grizzly bears.

"I like grizzly bears and elk and deer and all the rest," he says rather defensively. "When I was younger I used to enjoy riding about 6,000 miles a year on my trail bike on forest roads."

Recently the main focus of Montanans for Multiple Use has been the forest plan for the Flathead National Forest in northwestern Montana, and the main concern has been road closures. Tabor is not happy about the FS's "campaign to destroy the roads," as he describes it. "They (the FS) say this is insignificant even as they're ripping out trailheads and thousands of miles of roads and claiming it's all for the benefit of the grizzly bear." He calls this new policy "management by elimination."

Figures provided in 2003 by Allen Rowley of the Flathead National Forest show the total miles of roads decreasing from 3,927 in 1986 to 3,790 in 2002, a reduction of only 136 miles. Of those 3,790 miles, however, most (2,147 miles) have travel restrictions. Some restrictions are seasonal, usually during early spring when grizzly bears tend to be at lower elevations near roads or during the fall hunting seasons, but most travel restrictions are yearlong (1,735 miles of roads).

"It's all politics," Tabor claims. "The environmentalists are using the grizzly bear to close the roads. In vast areas they're closing all the roads. And it's not only the environmentalists. The FS is doing it, too. I take this personally because I missed family reunions to get these roads built."

Tabor thinks the grizzly bear did just fine during the time the forest had all those roads. Back in the 1950s, he notes, you never saw a grizzly, "even from Going to the Sun Road." Now, he claims, you see them everywhere. "The problem now is that there are too many of them," he states. "The grizzly bear has definitely recovered. Biologists have been saying that for twenty years." Several scientific studies have found that more logging roads mean fewer grizzlies, but Tabor doesn't believe it.

"The roads have some impact on the grizzly bear in the early spring by increasing access for black bear hunters, and there are a few mistakes," he admits, and because of this, he thinks some spring closures might make sense—but that's as far as he goes. "When we had a big network of roads, it diluted the pressure. Now it's too concentrated."

Tabor thinks more roads result in more wildlife. "What we end up doing by closing all the roads is protecting the predators, which reduces the number of deer and elk." He thinks deer and elk tend to stay close to the roads because they know they're safer from predators there, so when there are fewer roads, the big-game animals have less security from predators like grizzly bears. He also favors planting favored deer and elk foods along roads to further benefit both the deer and elk and the bears that prey on them.

All these road closures also affect people, according to Tabor. "The cut is way down, and now we hear about no harvesting of timber at all and a couple of thousand jobs lost. They've reduced the cut from 100 million board feet to 54 million, but we're not even close to that. There's no flexibility for the logging company because they've used up all the backlog (of timber available for harvest).

"We see all this blamed on the grizzly bear, but I fault the forest service, not the grizzly bear."

What Is the Greatest Threat to the Grizzly Bear?

During the course of writing this book, I asked everybody the same question: "What do you think is the greatest threat to the grizzly bear?" Here are some of their answers:

"People and their consciences. It's ultimately the people who make the difference. That's how we got down to the last 2 percent. The good news is the grizzly bear is still here. It's here because people care. We can make peace with this animal if we want to do it."

> —LOUISA WILLCOX, former project coordinator,
> Sierra Club Grizzly Bear Ecosystems Project,
> now with National Resources Defense Council

"Habitat destruction. We're losing grizzly habitat. It's going down, down, down. Not as fast as it once was, but still down. Once the grizzly bear starts a dive toward extinction, we can't stop it even though you still have a few bears out there. You could have three old males out there at the end of a cirque, but what good does that do?"

> —CHUCK JONKEL, bear scientist and president of
> the Great Bear Foundation

"It's not just the loss of habitat. It's how it is lost. If you build houses there, that's the worst thing that can happen to the grizzly bear."

> —KEVIN FREY, grizzly bear management
> specialist, Montana Department of Fish,
> Wildlife & Parks

"Man is the biggest threat. He can both deplete the population and destroy the habitat. Nothing else kills grizzly bears."

> —JOHN CRAIGHEAD, chairman,
> Wildlife-Wildlands Institute

"Private land development. It puts more people into grizzly bear habitat and increases conflicts and mortalities."

—CHRIS SERVHEEN, coordinator, Interagency
Grizzly Bear Committee

"Not enough space, not enough habitat. And not just habitat, but not enough quality habitat."

—HANK FISCHER, former Northern Rockies
representative for Defenders of Wildlife

"Habitat loss and fragmentation from encroachment and development. The parks are not enough."

—KATE KENDALL, project leader, Northern
Continental Divide DNA Monitoring Project

"Compromised habitat and habitat security. We have less habitat and less secure habitat in each ecosystem in the recovery zone. We are creating island ecosystems, and there is very little movement between them, and now we're circling them with development. The Selkirk, Yaak, and Cabinet populations will definitely be gone soon unless something happens. And we wonder why the grizzly bear is in trouble."

—BRIAN PECK, consultant, Sierra Club Grizzly
Bear Ecosystems Project

"Habitat fragmentation and development in the already limited range of the grizzly bear. I'm worried about genetic isolation. We need a linked system of grizzly habitat."

—GARY MOSES, chair, Wildlife Management
Committee, Glacier National Park

"Loss of habitat through development. But it's also true that you can have a lot of human use in grizzly habitat and still have bears if you just don't shoot them."

> —KERRY GUNTHER, bear management specialist, Yellowstone National Park

"Bad management that lacks recognition of the grizzly bear's requirements."

> —ANDY RUSSELL, outdoorsman, author, conservationist and filmmaker

"Our human greed. We're nice people, basically, but greedy. We have too much short-term thinking. We are also, fortunately, an enlightened species, so we can see how the grizzly bear can be perpetuated and how we can coinhabit with it."

> —BETH RUSSELL-TOWE, founder and executive director, Trail of the Great Bear

"The cumulative impact on the habitat and increased mortality. We know that grizzly bears just can't stand excessive mortality."

> —STEVE HERRERO, professor emeritus of environmental science at the University of Calgary and chair, Eastern Slopes Grizzly Bear Project Steering Committee

13

The Bear Medicine

If we're going to survive as a species, we need to learn to live with nature. I'm optimistic we can learn to live with the grizzly, but it will be a great struggle. People are willing to accept the increased risk, but they won't change their behavior.

—Steve Herrero, chair, Eastern Slopes
Grizzly Bear Project Steering Committee

It was nice to finally meet the man who helped plug the black hole.

I had read about Dan Carney, and other biologists and environmental leaders had been singing his praises. Carney is director of wildlife research on the Blackfeet Reservation, a huge tract of land that shares its western boundary with the eastern edge of Glacier National Park.

Carney worked with Chuck Jonkel on the Border Grizzly Project from 1978 to 1982 before he went to Virginia for a master's degree from Virginia Tech and a five-year stint studying black bears in Shenandoah National Park. Then in 1987 he moved to the Blackfeet Reservation for a wildlife biologist job, and like the other bear people featured in this book, he's been at it ever since. "I had opportunities to go elsewhere and do other things," he says proudly, "but this seemed to be the place I could make the most difference."

Sound familiar?

In recent years, partly because of Carney's work, the previously unstable political relationship between the tribal council and "outsiders" like the National Park Service and U.S. Fish and Wildlife Service has become increasingly cooperative. And apparently the grizzly is making a comeback on the reservation.

"The Blackfeet Reservation used to be a black hole," Carney admits. "Grizzly bears came onto the reservation but they never left, or as they say around here, they got smoked up."

But now the reservation has a healthy population of grizzly bears that travel freely back and forth across the park/reservation boundary. "The grizzly population has definitely increased," says Carney. "This is no longer a black hole."

Grizzly hunting is prohibited on the reservation, but Carney hasn't really noticed much interest in hunting bears among tribal members. The tribal council gives out free black bear permits to tribal members, but most don't even bother to pick one up. Tribal members rarely, if ever, eat bear meat, and they aren't trophy hunters, so why waste the time and energy hunting bears?

During his tenure on the reservation, he has helped put radio collars on more than a hundred grizzlies. "The first year I was here, we really had to work to catch any grizzly bears. It took us all season, probably close to 200 trapping nights, to catch five. Now we could easily catch that many in a month."

The Blackfeet Reservation is an important part of the Northern Continental Divide Ecosystem, about half of it within the official grizzly recovery zone. "The Endangered Species Act applies here, just like everywhere else," Carney notes.

It's a good thing it does, because Old Ephraim pays no attention to the boundary between the reservation and the park. Almost all of the grizzlies Carney monitored with telemetry moved freely back and forth over the park/reservation boundary. As a population, the grizzlies spent about half of their time in the reservation and half in the park, but he found both extremes. Some bears lived all year on the reservation and went into the park to den, but others spent almost all their time in the park and only occasionally ventured onto the reservation.

In recent years Carney's emphasis has switched from research to management. "Our research told us we needed more management of problem bears. Now more than half my time goes to dealing with problem bears, but everything we do is sanctioned by the IGBC, just like in Glacier Park." In short, he does almost exactly the same thing the B Team does.

Carney serves as a diplomatic bridge between the neighboring national park and the tribal council, a partnership that in the past has gotten stormy at times. Some park policies differ slightly from those on the reservation, he notes, and some park rangers may be a bit more "sensitive" to bears than he is, but, in general, the relationship has been excellent.

Carney's biggest problem is money. He has one or two wildlife technicians to help him, depending on the season, but he and his helpers had to unexpectedly take off two months without pay in early 2002 because of tribal budgetary problems. "My technicians couldn't take being laid off for months, so they moved on."

With the exception of monetary problems, however, Carney is quite happy with the tribal council. He's not a member of the Blackfeet tribe himself, but he assures me that this has never been a problem for him.

The grizzly population is doing fine, if not better than fine, and not one person has ever been killed by a bear on the reservation. "Around here they joke that bears don't eat Indians, but I don't think that has anything to do with it." Sound wildlife management and healthy interagency cooperation have been responsible for the good track record. For example, Carney uses the same type of aversive conditioning methods rangers use in the park. He also works closely with the park on management actions such as relocating problem bears.

And it's working. "Actually, I'm optimistic about the future," Carney says, "as long as we can keep up with management needs (translate: as long as he has enough money), and the public starts to realize they're living in grizzly country and accept this. If that happens, I think we'll have bears here for a long time."

But will they accept it? Carney's biggest bear problem is people. "We need more than education. Some people really need to change their attitudes."

He worries about the pace of rural development. More and more people are moving out of the cities and into grizzly country, sometimes right next to the park boundary. "Most of them have three dogs and lots of garbage, and they don't have a clue they're even moving into grizzly country. This increases mortality and displaces bears."

"Garbage is a big problem on the reservation," he says. "You'd think we could have solved this problem by now." To help solve it, however, Carney and his technicians spend part of their time educating people on how to keep garbage away from bears, along with the other basics of living in grizzly country. During the winter months when the bears are tucked away under 5 feet of snow for a six-month snooze, Carney spends his time talking to kids in schools and working with ranchers on how to peacefully coexist with the grizzly. "People yell and scream about having to do some extra work in dealing with their garbage, but I'm afraid somebody will get hurt by a bear. Then they'll take care of their garbage, won't they?"

Listening to Carney, you could easily start thinking that the bear management situation on the Blackfeet Reservation isn't any different than anywhere else. That's not completely true, at least in two ways.

First, Carney is mystified as to why environmentalists don't seem to get excited about resource issues on the reservation. If there's any threat to Glacier Park or the revered Badger–Two Medicine roadless area adjoining the southern boundary of the reservation, environmental groups marshal the troops and send out legal warriors to strongly oppose these developments. But on the reservation, at least according to Carney, enviros mostly just look the other way.

"We have the entire Rocky Mountain Front section of the reservation, right next to the park, leased for oil and gas development," he points out, "and there was no opposition to it." The process for appeal and opposition is basically the same as outside the reservation, Carney claims, yet environmental groups don't even seem to notice this threat.

"It's mainly because all the environmental groups are stretched so thin," explains Brian Peck of the Sierra Club. "We're all underfunded and underpeopled. For some reason, the reservation is below our radar line. There are lots of reasons but no excuses."

Peck doesn't completely agree with Carney on options. He believes it's more difficult to appeal and oppose projects on the reservation. "But this is a big problem. The reservation is 1.5 million acres. That's bigger than Glacier Park, and lots of it is prime grizzly habitat. There's a big sanitation problem, and we're already losing five or six bears each year there."

He cites one more problem, usually unspoken. "Some environmental groups think Native Americans are automatically allies in conservation and that they have gone through enough already, so they don't want to take them on over an environmental issue."

True, perhaps, but this only contributes to the problem. Peck loses sleep over the specter of "full-field development" of oil and gas reserves on the reservation. "No grizzly bear population has ever survived full-field development. It's going to be difficult to recover the grizzly bear without building up good populations on the Rocky Mountain Front, and not just the southern half but the northern half, too (i.e., the reservation)."

This means that having bears on the reservation is as important as down around Choteau, but it gets much less attention from environmentalists. And the truth is, nobody knows why.

Could unbridled energy or tourism development happen on the Blackfeet Reservation? Possibly, and definitely more likely than on adjoining federal lands, and if it did, it would likely reopen that proverbial black hole.

A second bear management difference might be Native American culture and tradition, which isn't an issue for bear managers on nonreservation land. The Blackfeet Reservation (along with the Flathead

Reservation north of Missoula) can make a big difference in the recovery of the grizzly bear, and Native American culture can be a significant part of modern bear management.

Many native people consider the Bear Mother the creator of all life and view the bear as a sacred animal. But on the Blackfeet Reservation, this is apparently not as significant as you might think, at least according to Carney. "Blackfeet culture has not really been a problem in managing bears on the reservation. Bears are not as revered as you'd think. Actually most people on the reservation don't seem that interested in bears."

The Blackfeet Nation consists of three tribes (Pikuni, Blood, and Peigan) with differing views on bears, and due to the passing of years and intertribal and interracial marriages, religious attachment to the bear has weakened. But it hasn't disappeared.

Marvin Leatherwax, who teaches native studies at Blackfeet Community College in Browning, agrees that the bear has become less significant in Blackfeet culture and religion, but he also knows the bear is still powerful medicine for some Blackfeet people.

Long ago, according to Leatherwax, the spirits of the Blackfeet and the spirits of the bear made a treaty with each other to peacefully coexist. This meant, in essence, not killing each other.

However, if a bear violated the treaty, it had to be killed. The warriors of the tribe would organize a hunt, using their dogs. The Blackfeet and their dogs would try to trap the grizzly on the edge of a cliff or against a steep wall where the bear couldn't escape. Then one very courageous brave would step forward for the final act.

When the Blackfeet warrior thrust his spear into the heart of the bear, he received the spirit of the bear. It was important to use a spear so there would be actual physical contact with the bear, which allowed the spirit to transfer from the dying animal to its Blackfeet slayer, who from that point on had the bear medicine and a bear medicine bundle to go with it. Having the bear medicine made him a healer, or medicine man.

To this day the bear medicine continues to be passed on from generation to generation. Leatherwax, in fact, has the bear medicine, which has been passed on since the 1700s, when a grizzly was killed by one of his ancestors more than three hundred years ago. He received it from his grandmother long ago, and before he dies he, too, will pass it on.

The process of passing on the bear medicine is partly sacred and secret, but, in general, it goes like this: A young person expresses interest in having the bear medicine and shows signs that he or she believes in the old ways of the Blackfeet, including holding and revering the bear medicine bundle. This courtship commonly starts with a vision quest, in which the young person sees himself or herself having the bear medicine. Then, he or she re-expresses interest in having the bear medicine and sometimes offers a gift to the current holder. In the old days this gift would be an offer to build a lodge or write a special bear song or prayer. Nowadays the gift can be anything that might be considered special to the current holder of the bear medicine.

In the final stages of the process, the young person offers the bear medicine holder a pipe to smoke. If he or she accepts the pipe and smokes it, this signifies agreement to pass along the bear medicine to the young person. Then, at some future date, a secret ceremony is held to transfer the bear medicine and bundle. The details of the ceremony are sacred and not for publication.

All of this still happens on the Blackfeet Reservation, but apparently it has no impact on modern bear management, according to Carney. The culture of the bear became an issue once in the late 1990s when Carney's team had to kill a few bears for management reasons. Tribal members asked to say prayers over the bears after they were killed, but the interest in doing even this has faded away.

In the late 1990s, Gayle Skunk Cap Jr., a wildlife technician working for Carney, interviewed tribal members on attitudes towards bears, mainly because the reservation's bear management plan called for incorporation of Blackfeet culture and tradition. He discovered that tribal members held many different beliefs concerning bears, depending on personal experiences and exposure to traditional ways. Skunk Cap's survey didn't discover much, except confirming that opinions varied widely. Some comments helped Carney and his team in handling bears by attempting to prevent the bad luck some tribal members believe comes from improper handling. With the help of this survey, bear management on the reservation is now deemed sensitive to the culture and traditions of the Blackfeet people.

As a footnote, when Blackfeet legends mention the bear, they usually refer to the "Real Bear," which is the grizzly bear. The black bear is considered the grizzly's poor cousin and is referred to, more simply and less affectionately, as the "Bear."

In any case, it appears real-life bear management is going well on the Blackfeet Reservation, relatively unaffected by tribal culture. A day in Dan Carney's life seems no different than a day in the life of Gary Moses or Mike Madel or Tim Manley. They all go about their work (and it is work!) each day and manage people and bears (usually in that order) using the same policies, saying the same things, and, quite remarkably, having the same strong underpinning of pure dedication to saving the grandest of all the creatures on Earth.

The Legend of the Medicine Grizzly

Long, long ago, a Blackfeet war chief named Mad Wolf was camped with several other chiefs near Cut Bank Pass, not far from Pitamakan Pass. He was in one of the lodges talking to the other chiefs about the battle he had recently won with a Kutenai war party. While telling his story, Mad Wolf's wife came running into the tipi and told the chiefs she had just seen a Gros Ventre chief come out of the woods and hang his war bonnet on a big fir tree.

The chiefs hurried to the big fir tree just as an entire Gros Ventre war party emerged from the forest. The Blackfeet fired on the Gros Ventre, killing all of them except their leader who took refuge in the forest. The Blackfeet clipped all the branches off the trees around him with their bullets, but they couldn't hit him.

He yelled at the Blackfeet, "Come on. I am not afraid. My name is *A-koeh-kit-ope,* and my medicine is powerful."

The Blackfeet warriors charged him, but the chief fought savagely with his knife, all the time roaring like a grizzly bear.

As the night came to an end, the fighting continued. The Blackfeet chiefs began to think the Gros Ventre chief had supernatural powers, so they decided to let him go, but the Blackfeet said they would scalp the Gros Ventre warriors they had killed. To this, the chief replied, "No, they are my brothers. I will not leave them."

So the Blackfeet finally killed him in hand-to-hand combat. Then, they discovered that the grizzly bear was his medicine. He had a grizzly claw tied in his front hair. The Blackfeet were so afraid that his power would escape that they built a big fire and burned his body. If even a small spark escaped the blaze, they retrieved it and put it back into the fire.

When the fire went out, the Blackfeet quickly moved camp. But *A-koeh-kit-ope,* which stands for Medicine Grizzly, came back to life and transformed into a huge grizzly bear and followed the Blackfeet. *A-koeh-kit-ope* came upon the Blackfeet as they were making their new camp and killed many of them, and the rest escaped by fleeing into the forest.

A year later, when the Blackfeet camped again by the big fir tree to cut new lodgepoles, an enormous grizzly came into the camp at night, killing some of the Blackfeet and some of their dogs and chasing away the horses.

From that point on, whenever the Blackfeet camped near the big fir tree, they saw the Medicine Grizzly. *A-koeh-kit-ope* only came in the night and disappeared before daybreak. The Blackfeet knew his medicine was strong, so they did not try to shoot him. Years later, when the Blackfeet made peace with the Gros Ventre, the Gros Ventre told the Blackfeet that *A-koeh-kit-ope* was a great medicine man who could never be killed.

—from Walter McClintock, *The Old North Trail*, 1910.

14
Running the Trapline

Simply put, the great bear has all the strikes against recovery that the creator could have bestowed upon it, including finding its last refuge in the well-armed West that looks to John Wayne for a role model. It is still true today that very few bears die a natural death; almost all die because we kill them.

— Louisa Willcox, former project coordinator, Sierra Club Grizzly Bear Ecosystems Project, now with the National Resources Defense Council

If you aren't a hunter, you might not understand why they do it. If you are a hunter, you know why Timothy Hilston was up early on October 30, 2001. He left Great Falls, Montana, around 4:00 A.M. and drove 110 miles to the Blackfoot-Clearwater Game Range. He wanted to be there before sunrise because he'd been lucky enough to draw a coveted cow permit, and he planned on filling his freezer with a year-long supply of elk meat.

Hilston probably reached the game range at about 6:00 A.M., drove about a mile north of U.S. Highway 200, and parked his truck at the trailhead. He'd only walked a short distance from the trailhead before he shot his elk, probably around 6:30 A.M.

For elk hunters, the shot signals the end of the fun and the beginning of the work. He laid down his rifle with the bolt open (indicating he was done hunting for the day), put on surgical gloves, and started gutting the elk. Somewhere during the field-dressing, he remembered he hadn't tagged his elk, so he stopped to cut the notch out of his tag. Later, investigators theorized that after Hilston notched the tag, but before he had time to attach it to the elk, he saw the bears, a female grizzly and two cubs, coming toward him.

That was the last thing Timothy Hilston saw.

After studying the evidence at the scene, investigators speculated that Hilston had backed away from the elk carcass about 20 feet upon seeing the bears. At this point at least one of the bears attacked him, and he received numerous bites on the chest, back, head, neck, thighs, and buttocks. After the bears abandoned the wounded hunter, he struggled back toward his pickup truck, but he only made it about 400 feet from the scene of the attack before he collapsed and died.

Late that night Hilston's relatives reported him missing, and at about 11:30 A.M. the next morning, the Powell County search and rescue team found his body and immediately contacted the local game warden, who, in turn, alerted Jamie Jonkel of the Montana Department of Fish, Wildlife & Parks (MDFWD) and Chris Servheen of the Interagency Grizzly Bear Committee (IGBC). Servheen and Jonkel, along with several coworkers, went to the scene and set three snares and two culvert traps, hoping to catch the killer bears.

When the search and rescue team made its discovery, it noticed the bears had not fed on the elk carcass, except for a few small mouthfuls out of one of the hams, nor had they consumed Hilston's body, which was removed a short time later. The bears had, however, attempted to cache the elk carcass by partially covering it with debris.

At some point between the time the body was removed and the bear management team arrived on scene, the bears had returned to feed on the elk carcass. Investigators theorized that the presence of the body had served as a deterrent and kept the bears from returning to feed on the elk carcass. However, the bears had obviously been hanging around this prime food source, waiting for opportunities to feed, so the bear managers left the elk carcass at the site, hoping it would lure the bears back to the scene and into their traps.

It worked. When they returned early the following morning, the female grizzly and one cub were snared, and the other cub was nearby. Servheen, officially in charge, gave the order to shoot all three bears.

Servheen had made a tough decision, and he knew it might be controversial. And sure enough, some people disagreed with the decision to kill all three bears. Witness this comment from the Great Bear Foundation: "The GBF supports the killing of the female, but not the two cubs. A minimal aversive conditioning program keyed to the cubs as they 'learned how to be a grizzly' could have reduced the deaths to two (the hunter and the mother bear). When a murderer kills someone, even in Texas, they don't kill the murderer's kids!"

In the official report on the incident, Servheen explained his rationale for killing all three bears: "The evidence available indicates an act of unnatural aggression rather than an act of natural aggression. Natural aggression involves defensive behavior associated with the defense of a food source, defense of young, or a surprise encounter. Unnatural aggression involves aggressive behavior associated with approach toward humans aggressively to attack or seize food sources. The fact that this attack occurred in daylight in an area with good visibility and the fact that the hunter was in possession of an elk make this an unnatural aggression. The hunter would have been visible for 20-plus yards if the bears were approaching along the blood trail of the wounded elk. Bears involved in unnatural aggression are removed as dangerous to humans because such bears are very likely to continue such behavior. As management agencies we have responsibilities to the public as well as to the recovery of bears, and removal of unnaturally aggressive bears is a public safety issue."

Concerning the controversial killing of the cubs, Servheen explained it as follows: "Cubs reflect the behaviors taught to them by their mothers. To a great degree, their mothers teach cub bears how to behave, where and how to seek food, what places and activities are associated with foods, and what to eat and how and where to seek things to eat. These cubs were being taught to seek food at human elk kill sites. In the case of Mr. Hilston, they were taught to be aggressive to people at such sites. Such behavior would likely lead these young bears to continue to seek food at human elk kills. There is a possibility that these cubs could have learned that being aggressive to people at such sites results in obtaining the elk. Based on what we know about bear behavior, it is reasonable to assume such behavior would lead these young bears into further conflicts with humans as they grew up."

In a later interview, he added: "The possibility of those cubs surviving was zero or less. We count all cubs of the year as dead, but not yearlings. They can survive."

Grizzly mothers spend two or three years raising their cubs and teaching them what they need to know to survive. Cubs orphaned during their first year aren't big or educated enough to make it, but after a year or more they have a chance.

Serveheen certainly didn't enjoy killing the bears, particularly not the cubs. After all, he likes bears more than most people, and he has spent his entire professional life trying to preserve the grizzly bear. It's his job to make tough decisions, and he did it. In some cases it's obviously necessary to kill bears in order to save bears.

Timothy Hilston's death was a tragedy, but the incident also caused the death of three grizzly bears. This story is played out way too often to suit environmentalists, agency bear managers, and just about everybody else. Bear mortality related to hunting has soared in recent years. At the very least, this increased mortality slows the progress toward recovery and eventual delisting.

In the Northern Continental Divide Ecosystem (NCDE), for example, wildlife officials recorded nineteen human-caused mortalities in 2001. At least eight of these were caused by hunters or related to hunting. This exceeds the IGBC's goal for human-caused mortalities of 4 percent of the minimum estimated population, which would be about fifteen bears. In the previous year, 2000, there were twenty human-caused deaths, also exceeding the IGBC goal. In the Wyoming section of the Greater Yellowstone Ecosystem, outside the national park, hunters or hunting guides have been responsible for the deaths of at least twenty-seven grizzlies since 1994, five in 1999. And game wardens commonly believe that for every known illegal kill, another goes unreported.

"If the great bear is ever to recover from its threatened status," predicts Liz Howell of the Wyoming chapter of the Sierra Club, "hunters have to learn proper behavior." Organized hunting organizations hate to agree with the Sierra Club, but in this case, they do.

Will there be more such bloody fights between hunters and grizzlies? Most likely. At least that's the opinion of Jamie Jonkel, MDFWP bear biologist for the Blackfoot Valley. In fact, it may have already happened. He recalls a hunter who disappeared in the mid-1990s on Huckleberry Pass, which isn't far from the Blackfoot-Clearwater Game Range.

The Blackfoot Valley is not only productive ranching country, but also prime habitat for big game. "There's more hunting going on here than most places," according to Jonkel.

He doesn't think bears keying in on hunters and their kills is anything new. "It's ancient," he says. "It's been going on for hundreds of years. A lot of this is about learned behavior. Grizzly bears have been getting carcasses from hunters for a long time."

Jonkel thinks bears follow hunters because they've learned to equate hunters with food, as do wolves and mountain lions. They also listen for ravens because the raucous birds signal the presence of a downed animal.

Jonkel's counterpart at MDFWP in south-central Montana, Kevin Frey, agrees. "I think it's been going on for a long time, more than ten years at least, but as the bear numbers have increased, it's gotten worse. It's not in all areas, mainly the areas that are heavily hunted."

Frey likens the beginning of the September big-game seasons to the beginning of the berry crop ripening or the salmon spawn in Alaska, noting that bears are historically keyed on these phenological events. "I've had hunters following a blood trail and a bear was, too, and the bear passes them up and gets the elk first. Then you have an encounter. I have a friend who had a grizzly follow him all day while he was hunting, waiting for him to knock something down."

"We actually did a project on this," Frey notes. "We had marked bears, and we could see the distribution change. The bears moved right into the heavily hunted areas as soon as the hunting camps went up and the activity started, even before the first elk went down. The bears knew that when the people started coming, it was dinnertime."

After studying grizzlies in the Blackfoot Valley for several years, Jonkel has noticed a pattern. In the early spring, shortly after the bears emerge from their dens, they head for the big-game winter ranges looking for winter-killed animals. Then they work the elk calving grounds looking for easy-to-catch newborns. In the fall they move to the game range and other heavily hunted areas looking for gut piles and downed animals. They listen for gunshots, check tree stands, and follow blood trails to dead or dying game.

And then there is Molly. Jonkel likes to tell about the exploits of this female grizzly he radio-collared and tracked for years. Molly learned to follow bow hunters and remember their tree stands. She'd regularly check them out, like "running a trapline." She got so good at it, "she was getting the deer or elk before the hunter got out of his stand to look for it."

Hunters normally wait for twenty or thirty minutes after shooting a deer or elk to let it die before trying to retrieve it. This common practice apparently played right into Molly's plans.

Think about hunters for a minute, especially bow hunters. They travel off-trail through grizzly country in the predawn darkness, commonly alone, as quietly as possible. They use artificial calls that sound like distressed or injured animals. They rattle antlers together to sound like two bucks fighting—and not thinking about bears. They mask human smell with "buck scent," or elk urine. If they have a successful hunt, they leave the smell of high-quality grizzly food to permeate the woods and seduce bears.

Is it a miracle there aren't many more confrontations?

Perhaps, but the reason for the great track record could be twofold. First, hunters are extremely aware of their surroundings. Their training and built-in alertness may prevent many encounters. Second, the grizzly deserves praise for being so incredibly aware of its surroundings that it can detect and avoid even the most stealthy hunter stalking through the night, making no noise—and smelling like stale elk pee.

Have grizzlies learned to equate rifle shots with their next meal? Jonkel thinks so. Frey thinks so, too. Jonkel tells of a research project he worked on in the Thorofare south of Yellowstone Park. He and his coworkers were having a hard time catching bears, so they tried firing rifles around the traps to see if it would attract more of them, but the results were inconclusive. "This may have worked, but we weren't sure."

Frey is a little more certain, saying he has brought grizzlies into traps by firing rifle shots. "I don't know if bears come right to the rifle shots," he theorizes, "but they'll come to the area looking for gut piles and carcasses."

Going to rifle shots is one thing, but what if grizzlies are attracted by elk bugles, even the amateurish imitations of the real thing blasted out by thousands of elk hunters every September, when elk are in the rut and grizzlies are panicked to fatten up for their long winter fast.

During the rut, starting in late August and going through early October, bull elk try to gather the largest possible harem. As a warning to other bulls to stay clear of their cows, they send out a long, eerie squeal terminated with a series of grunts. It's called a bugle. The sound of the elk bugle increases a hunter's heartbeat and gives him trigger itch, but it might also bring in the bears. The bull elk doing the bugling is thinking about sex, not predators. Consequently the elk might be more vulnerable to attack. It's a rare grizzly that tries to take down a herd bull, but when the bull is distracted and exhausted from weeks of combat with other bulls to keep his harem, the odds swing in the bear's favor.

Early-season hunters use artificial devices to emulate the elk's bugle, hoping to lure a big bull close enough for a good shot. Unfortunately the grizzly might not know the difference between the imitation and the real thing.

Frey regularly sees this happen. "It's sure not abnormal down here (south-central Montana). Every year I talk to two or three hunters about a bear coming in to their elk bugles. In one case, in Slough Creek, two bears came in at the same time from different directions. We also had one situation in Slough Creek where a grizzly jumped a hunter in his stand and bit him a couple of times, but then I guess the bear realized it wasn't an elk, so it took off."

Frey is certainly qualified to comment on grizzlies coming in to elk bugling stands. It happened to him.

"I had the same thing happen myself while I was archery hunting," he recalls. "I was moving through a stand of whitebark pine and stopping here and there to bugle. Then I saw him, a fairly large grizzly running through the trees. He ran right into a squirrel midden about 70 or 80 yards away from where I'd just bugled. Then he stopped and charged right at me. I was all camoed up, so he couldn't see me. He got real close, close enough that I could see his eyelashes. I stood up, and he stopped and ran off."

Frey had early tracking snow, so he could backtrack the bear and get the rest of the story. He found that the grizzly had essentially stalked him for a long way, from bugle to bugle, even to where he had his horses.

Frey sees some grizzlies getting "pretty bold" and recalls an infamous big boar in the Slough Creek area that routinely tracked hunters and hung around hunting camps and elk kills. "But he got too bold. One night he stuck his head into a tent and got shot."

They say there's no such thing as an old bold pilot, or mountain climber, and I guess that's true with grizzlies, too.

"Last year (2001), we had a good whitebark pine year," Frey

reports, "so we didn't have much conflict with hunters. If there's another food source (e.g., pine seeds), they'll go there, but if it is a poor food year, they'll interact with us to get food. The bears are pretty tolerant of hunters, but you can't fool around anymore. You've got to do things right."

For example, Frey notes, "I always tell people to separate the gut pile from the carcass if they can. The gut pile has a stronger smell. Bears like bloody meat, of course, but they'll go to the gut pile first."

"This is definitely on our radar screen," says Steve Wagner of the Rocky Mountain Elk Foundation (RMEF), referring to both the problem of hunting-related bear deaths and the theory of grizzlies being lured in by rifle shots and elk bugles. "We're concerned about it and are starting to discuss it." He also said the RMEF, a leading national prohunting conservation group, is working on a position paper on this issue, but right now the organization has no official position on it.

"There's no definitive science on this," says Chris Smith, chief of staff for MDFWP, "but there's certainly anecdotal evidence from Alaska and some sections of the Yellowstone and NCDE that indicates grizzly bears are keying into gut piles and rifle shots. As far as elk bugles go, bears are effective predators, and it wouldn't surprise me if bears have been responding to elk bugles forever. They certainly respond to deer distress calls in southern Alaska."

Smith doesn't, however, consider this a priority in an era of declining wildlife funding. "If we proved that this happens, what difference would that make?," he asks. "We'd still have the same recommendations we do now concerning making hunters more aware of bears."

Ditto for bear mortality. "We haven't seen the need to make any adjustments in hunting regulations to address bear mortality. If the mortality increased to a point where it affected the population, then we'd probably do something. Current mortality levels may be slowing recovery, but it certainly isn't preventing recovery.

"I'd be much more concerned about the border populations like the Cabinet-Yaak and Selkirks," he notes. "These populations are hanging on by one claw, but populations in Yellowstone and the NCDE are doing well. One reason we're seeing more mortality is that there's simply more bears, and they're moving farther from the parks.

"Our major concern is mistaken identity by black bear hunters," he explains. "We've taken special steps there."

Smith refers to new educational efforts and a required bear identification test that black bear hunters must take before they can buy a black bear license. "The FWS determined that the existing level of incidental take by black bear hunters did not jeopardize the grizzly population," Smith notes. "If it did increase, the FWS might see some need for additional regulations."

In Montana concern over the safety of bears and hunters led to new recommendations for hunters in occupied bear country (see Thinking Grizzly). These recommendations were published in the brochure *How to Hunt Safely in Grizzly Country* and in the big-game hunting regulations. Other states and provinces are adopting similar regulations and recommendations.

The big-game regs are only one way to educate hunters about bear awareness. The B Team spends a lot of time on educational programs such as preparing a new twenty-minute segment on bear awareness for hunter education classes, putting up trailhead signs, and talking to the media. "I think we can win this educational battle," Jamie Jonkel predicts.

One group of people that completely understands all of this is the hunting outfitters—and they're doing something about it. For example, professional outfitters are working with Dick Clark, a professor at the University of Montana–Dillon, on a special course to train outfitters to be more bear aware. "Since we've been doing the course," Clark assures, "there has been a growing awareness of the bear situation."

Clark predicts the next step in this educational project is making the same information available to the hunting public. "Our outfitters can become instructors in their local communities."

"Most outfitters understand the problem and realize that things need to change," agrees Jonkel. "They're getting meat out the same day, hanging it high, boning out the animal right away and getting it out of there ASAP, and separating the gut pile from the carcass."

Jack Rich of Seeley Lake, Montana, is a good example. He lives and hunts only 3 miles from where Timothy Hilston met his untimely death, and he has been a leading advocate among outfitters for adjusting time-worn practices to a new world mandating the preservation of grizzly bears. "We've had several encounters through the years," he says, "but fortunately nobody has been hurt."

Rich took the time to tell me about one of those encounters. Early one morning a client of his shot an elk. Rich helped him with the initial field-dressing, then left the hunter to finish the job and went back to camp, about a half mile away, for the mules. While the hunter continued his work, a large grizzly came within 75 feet, but the hunter held his ground, and, according to Rich, they had "a Mexican standoff" for a few minutes. Then the bear moved away and lay down to watch the hunter butcher the elk. Another hunter and his guide joined in to help quarter the elk, and again the bear moved towards the hunters and then retreated. When Rich arrived with the mules to pack away the meat, he also saw the bear, but it didn't come any closer. After he and the successful hunter left, the other hunter and his guide moved away from the gut pile to have lunch. Within a few minutes the grizzly, along with a cub that had been hidden until then, were on the scene cleaning up the gut pile. Because of situations like this, "We almost never leave a hunter alone anymore," he says.

He has had grizzlies try to claim downed game left in the backcountry overnight, but he has never had a serious confrontation. Perhaps that's because he takes special care to avoid this situation. "Once you have an animal down, your risk increases. Our policy is that from the time we shoot the elk, we want it to be at the meat processor within twenty-four hours."

That's a tall order since Rich's hunting camp is 10 miles from the nearest road. About half of his downed elk stay out overnight. When this is necessary, he and his guides leave as much human scent on the carcass as possible. They hang dirty clothing on the antlers, and before they leave they urinate in a circle around the downed animal. "It's a little crude," he admits, "but it has worked for us."

"My family has been outfitting in this area for sixty years," Rich notes, "and we've always believed it's important to show the bear we're in charge."

Rich's policies put him at odds with some agency recommendations. In particular, he disagrees with the agency recommendation calling for separating food 100 feet from camp. "We need to establish a line in the sand that the bear can't cross," he explains, "and people in the camp is the best deterrent. We put food in bear-resistant containers, but we leave them in camp. I don't want people going out 100 feet from camp before dawn to get our food cache. Leaving the food out there creates a big liability. The agencies are sending out the wrong message. I think it's bad policy." He also points out that organizations representing professional hunting outfitters agree with his position on leaving food in camps.

Another policy he questions is the agency recommendation to give up an elk if a grizzly displays aggressive behavior. "Don't give up the elk. If you do, you're telling the bear that it's tougher than you are. It's like the class bully. Once you back down, you're in trouble. It's a recipe for disaster. You stand your ground. Don't tell the bear that this is his elk. Tell him it's yours. We're not quiet and subdued like some people recommend. We fire rifle shots into the air and yell and scream. I don't believe in acting submissive."

However, agency bear managers, including Kevin Frey, disagree with Rich on this point. "Getting injured or shooting a bear over an elk carcass isn't worth it," Frey contends. "If a guy leaves a carcass all day and night and a bear claims it, that's the hunter's fault, not the bear's. You can't just leave the meat out there like you used to. I'm not going to tell the average hunter to go out there and reason with a grizzly bear over an elk. An outfitter might have three or four people and horses. That's intimidating to a bear, much more than one guy out there by himself."

Rich has started outfitting his hunters and guides with bear pepper spray and follows other recommendations, but he believes there should be two different sets of regulations for hunters and hikers. "I didn't go to college, but I have a Ph.D. in dealing with bears and hunters."

As to whether rifle shots double as dinner bells, Rich thinks it could be happening. "That's a tough question," he says. "I think some older bears are starting to make the connection between hunters and gut piles, but not just rifle shots. That's why we need to let the bear know we're still at the top of the food chain."

On October 9, 1995, two hunters in British Columbia found out what it means to not be on top of the food chain.

Scott McMillion eloquently wrote about this incident in his best-selling book, *Mark of the Grizzly,* in a chapter devoted to what he called "dinner bell grizzlies."

William Caspell and Shane Fumerton had mountain-biked and hiked 3,000 feet up Mount Soderholm, which is near the Continental Divide and the Alberta-British Columbia border. They were hunting elk and mountain goats in a wild area that also supported a large population of grizzly bears.

Sometime that day they shot a trophy bull elk. A time-delayed snapshot taken from a stump showed two happy hunters with their prize. But that happiness was obviously short-lived, because soon after the photo was taken, they were both dead.

That night, back at camp, Fumerton's wife was waiting with their seven-week-old baby. When the hunters didn't return, she called for help. Regrettably it took two days to locate the scene, and weather kept searchers from investigating for two additional days.

On October 11 a helicopter search team spotted a female grizzly, along with two cubs, on an elk carcass and buzzed her. Even when hazed by the helicopter, she refused to give up the carcass. While trying to scare her off, the chopper's prop wash kicked up debris, including what looked like a hunting license, so authorities knew they had big trouble.

Mother Nature stepped in to make matters worse. An early-season snowstorm swept through the area, making flying impossible and dumping 3 feet of snow on the scene. All told four days had passed before authorities were finally able to fly back to the scene. They shot the bears from the helicopter then did their best to determine what happened by searching for evidence buried beneath the snow.

This incident casts some doubt as to which creature is on top of the food chain. In this case, it wasn't men with guns, even men trained to use them—it was a smallish, 255-pound mother grizzly.

Searchers found both men dead of massive head injuries in separate locations 450 feet and 1,200 feet from the dead elk. They found the rifles, too—one about 65 feet away from the elk, unloaded and leaning against a rock, and the other about 50 feet from Caspell's body, containing a live cartridge partly chambered. The local coroner believed the injuries were consistent with a bear attack, but the truth is, nobody will ever know for sure what happened on Mount Soderholm.

A logical theory, however, is that the bear attacked the hunters as they started field-dressing the elk. Either the men died fighting and the bear dragged them from the scene, or they fled and were individually chased down and killed.

Grizzlies spend around six months in the den and often a month or so in the spring involved in mating activities. This leaves about four or five months for putting on enough fat to make it through the next winter buried under snow somewhere on a north-facing slope. If the bear can't bulk up enough, it may die in the den. This creates a physiological panic called "hyperphagia" that begins in August and lasts through October. Perhaps that undersized, hyperphagic mother desperately needed that elk carcass for her and her cubs to survive—and subsequently became the top of the food chain.

The Mount Soderholm and Blackfoot-Clearwater incidents spotlight both sides of the debate over the impact of bear hunting on the grizzly's psyche. There is a theory that hunting grizzlies makes them more wary, which reduces the number of encounters and, in general, makes the wilderness safer.

Frey, for one, believes it. "I know this is a hot button for environmentalists," he says, "but it might be just what the grizzly population needs. Hunting grizzly bears is good for grizzly bears."

However, Frey emphasizes that we all should get one thing straight. "Bears don't watch TV. They have no association with gunshots. They don't know what they are. We assume bears think gunshots are dangerous, but they have no way of knowing this. Maybe it used to be that way, but that's not passed on through the generations anymore. This is a different bear here now."

Frey deals increasingly with backcountry encounters because he has so much big-game hunting in his region (north of Yellowstone Park). Grizzlies keep coming into hunting camps and having conflicts with hunters—and "getting killed, some reported and some not."

"Any hunting season we'd ever have would be very limited," Frey assures environmentalists. "We'd probably kill fewer bears than we do now, and it would put some fear back in the grizzly population."

Mike Madel, Frey's counterpart in Choteau, agrees. "It would increase wariness among bears and could reduce problems during years with poor berry production, when bears move down into farms and ranches to find food. If we held hunts on private land where we didn't want bears habituated, then it would be the boldest and least wary bears that would be killed."

And, of course, Madel and Frey would argue that these are the bears that get killed anyway—and probably should be.

The Blackfoot-Clearwater tragedy may support the idea that a grizzly hunting season could keep the woods safer. Grizzlies haven't been hunted for more than a decade in the area, and very lightly for two decades prior. In the Blackfoot-Clearwater area, grizzlies have become quite bold and arguably unwary of hunters, possibly even tracking them in search of their next meal. Timothy Hilston was only the second hunter ever killed by a grizzly in Montana, but some people think this incident signals the likelihood of more such encounters in the future as the bears get less wary.

On the other hand, the Mount Soderholm incident may help

debunk the theory. Grizzlies are hunted in this area, and have been for many decades, but the bear that killed William Caspell and Shane Fumerton was obviously not afraid of humans.

In Alaska from 1990 through 1997, bears killed or seriously injured 144 people. Of this total, 59 were hunters. Alaska has a large and growing grizzly population that has always been heavily hunted. Yet, in Alaska it doesn't appear as if bear hunting has made the grizzly population more wary or reduced the number of bloody confrontations.

In Montana and Wyoming grizzly hunting has been banned or severely limited for about thirty years, ending completely in 1991 when a national animal rights group, Fund for Animals, successfully sued to stop the already-restricted Montana season. Since then, have grizzlies become so unwary that the number of encounters has increased? No. Instead, in both states, the number of serious encounters and deaths has gone down by roughly 30 percent.

With such conflicting information, it's hard to know whether grizzly bear hunting—or the absence thereof—has any real impact on the number of encounters. We do know, however, that there will be a few more fights to claim the coveted spot on top of the food chain.

Thinking Grizzly

The Montana Department of Fish, Wildlife & Parks (MDFWP) includes these precautions for hunters in the general big-game hunting regulations.

- If you hunt alone, let someone know your detailed plans and have a way to periodically check in. Consider hunting with a partner.
- Hunting partners should share details of their hunt plans and have a check-in or communications system.
- Carry bear pepper spray and know how to use it.
- After a kill, get the animal out of the woods as soon as possible. The longer a carcass remains lying on the ground, hung up in a hunting camp, or in the back of a truck, the more likely it is to be discovered by a grizzly. Be aware that some grizzly bears have learned that a rifle shot means a gut pile or animal carcass.
- Carcasses left in the mountains overnight should be covered and made to be visible from a distance. Locate an observation point and clear the brush in that direction. Mark it with a piece of clothing or flagging. Drag the gut pile away from the carcass and cover it with brush. Before leaving, walk to the observation point and memorize the site.
- Next morning, approach the downed animal carefully. Yell or whistle repeatedly. With binoculars, study the scene from the observation point and scan the area for movement. Grizzly bears often drag the carcass a short distance before covering it under a pile of dirt and debris.
- If a grizzly bear is at the site and refuses to leave or the meat has been cached and is not salvageable, report the incident to FWP. Hunters who have lost an animal to a grizzly may be eligible for another license.
- Never push a grizzly exhibiting aggressive behavior off a carcass.
- If you live in grizzly country, it is best not to hang carcasses behind the house or in the garage for extended periods. Big-game carcasses

stored outside should be hung from a stout 15-foot pole at least 25–30 feet off the ground. The elk or deer should be suspended from the center of the pole and well above a bear's reach. Grizzly bears have been known to climb trees and stand on objects in order to reach carcasses.

- Some grizzly bears are opportunists and change their behavior in order to take advantage of new food sources. So if you are hunting or living in grizzly country, always assume that grizzlies are in the area and make sure your camps, cabins, and homes are bear-proof, and that all bear attractants are contained or removed.

- Report encounters with grizzly bears to FWP (1–800–TIP–MONT), USDA Forest Service, or in an actual emergency, contact 911. Seeing a grizzly is not necessarily an encounter or an emergency. Report encounters where the bear displayed aggressive or defensive behavior toward people, livestock, or pets.

With these recommended precautions, the MDFWP includes a map titled "General Distribution of the Grizzly Bear in Montana," which ironically includes many areas not officially listed as occupied grizzly habitat.

Epilogue:
Reflections of Pages Past—
What We Need to Do to Save
the Grizzly Bear

*There was, in fact, only one place from which you did not see
Escudilla on the skyline; that was the top of Escudilla itself. Up
there you could not see the mountain, but you could feel it. The
reason was the big bear.*

—Aldo Leopold, *A Sand County Almanac*

After researching and writing this book, talking to many bear experts,
and personally studying grizzly bear conservation issues for thirty
years, I have come to this conclusion: Several decades will pass before
we know where the grizzly will walk, but the decisions we make today
will promise or deny a future for the great bear. Only our children and
grandchildren will know if we did the right thing.

Nobody knows what the future holds, of course, but I've developed a few opinions about what we need to do to make sure the grizzly has one. Most match the opinions of the "bear people" I've interviewed, but some are my own take on what we should do to guarantee a dignified future for the majestic grizzly.

The real enemy of the grizzly bear . . .

You've probably heard that it's hard to plan for draining the swamp when you're up to your butt in alligators. A version of this old saw might be the grizzly's biggest problem. If we fail to plan, we plan to fail.

It's hard to concentrate on something that might happen a hundred years from now when we can't afford to pay the second mortgage or fill up the Suburban. We have to struggle to consider the distant future when the here-and-now involves worrying about terrorism or whether our kids can find good jobs. It's our nature to concentrate on the short term.

As for our political leaders, the people we elected to represent us and make tough decisions, well, let's have a reality check on this one. They'll always be thinking about the next election, not the next generation.

That's why cumulative impacts are so serious. Most bear experts rant and rave about habitat destruction being the great enemy of the grizzly bear, but it's hard to fight an enemy you can't see. This slow nibbling away of habitat is almost impossible to stop because we only see it in minute, seemingly harmless pieces, not as a whole. Nobody ever climbs up on a soapbox and says, "let's destroy an ecosystem."

We can focus on the big hard-rock mine, and frequently defeat or delay it, but that's not the real enemy. It's the wilderness cabin with apple trees and bird feeders, the hobby mine, or the half-mile road extension. When we build a cabin, another one doesn't burn down. When we pinch off a tree, another one doesn't automatically grow to maturity. When we build another mile of road, another mile doesn't disappear off the map.

Compounding this problem is the often-forgotten fact that much of this cumulative impact happens on private land. People in the northern Rockies protect their private property rights like trained guard dogs. We may have enough public land to provide a secure habitat base for a viable grizzly population, but we may not. Much of the private land is surrounded by public land and is located in low-lying riparian zones, which often provide key seasonal habitat and important travel routes for grizzly bears and other large wildlife such as elk and bighorn sheep. Grizzly bears do not pay attention to NO TRESPASSING signs. Regrettably but understandably, *Ursus arctos horribilis* and *Homo sapiens* both like the most fertile places.

Somehow, we need to focus on this incremental erosion of the habitat base on public and private land. If we don't, decades from now the habitat base might slip imperceptibly below the level where it can support a viable grizzly population. How sad it would be if we didn't even notice the day the grizzly bear went extinct.

. . . Or is this the real enemy?

Most bear experts and even the environmental doomsayers buy this worst-case scenario: We'll have grizzlies for a long time even if the population gradually becomes smaller and smaller and eventually extinct in the wild a hundred years or more from now. However, we have a short-term threat that we definitely don't think about enough. If we lost the currently high level of social acceptance for the grizzly bear, it could disappear from the western landscape in a few years.

Let's have another reality check. We don't have grizzly bears in the northern Rockies because of the Endangered Species Act, or because we still have large wilderness areas and national parks, or because Canada augments U.S. populations, or because the Sierra Club watchdogs federal and state agencies, or because EarthJustice sues them a lot. We have grizzlies in the northern Rockies because we want to have grizzlies in the northern Rockies. We want our parks and wildernesses to be complete and provide a home for the big bear. We want the mountains to feel higher, and the wildflowers to look brighter. Today, as I write this, we accept the grizzly as it is, where it is, and we might even accept it in a few places it isn't.

But that could change suddenly.

It wouldn't be the first time. In the early 1900s we didn't accept the grizzly—anywhere—so we killed every bear we could find. We eliminated the grizzly from all but 2 or 3 percent of its historic range in the course of a few years. A hundred years ago we wanted this species to go extinct, along with the wolf, mountain lion, coyote, and most other predators. Eradication was the goal. The coyote might be too smart and elusive to eradicate, but not the grizzly. We could easily kill every last one.

Fortunately in the mid-1900s, we started to understand the role of predators in the natural world and developed a higher level of social acceptance for the grizzly a few years before we killed them all. Maybe the bear won't be so lucky next time.

Nowadays we're actually letting the grizzly expand its range into mountain ranges long devoid of the big bear—the Wind River, Tobacco Roots, Gros Ventre, Gravellies, and Spanish Peaks, even the expansive Bitterroots. At the rate we're going right now, we might gain public support for having grizzly bears in the Gospel Hump, Sawtooths, Great Burn, Pintlers, Pioneers, and Wyoming Range. The grizzly bear could repopulate the Missouri Breaks and Charles M. Russell Wildlife Refuge (CMR), if we allow it to. We even hear talk about making a home for the grizzly in Utah, Colorado, and California. Only a few years ago, such talk would have been laughable.

You could argue, Yes, it's a good time for the grizzly, but what could change this trend of gradually improving acceptance of the bear? I see some even worse worst-case scenarios than incremental habitat destruction.

First, and I believe foremost, we must be religiously bear aware and constantly educating ourselves about living with bears. Right now this is another improving trend, and may it always be so. Through government agency educational programs supported by private enterprise with some great documentary videos plus a plethora of hyperactive writers like myself, most people have learned how to hike, camp, hunt, fish, mountain bike, and otherwise travel in grizzly country safely. The result has been a constantly shrinking number of bloody encounters, and subsequently, fewer bloody descriptions of maulings in *Reader's Digest* and less anxiety over grizzly bears in the public's collective consciousness.

What worries me is how easily this trend could reverse. Even one particularly newsworthy incident could reverse decades of progress towards accepting the grizzly as part of our ecosystem. The ultracompetitive media has a "piling-on" tendency and often overplays a story. A single dramatic incident in a rural community where the grizzly is expanding its range could erase all tolerance for this expansion.

Secondly, and however improbable it might be, it's still possible that a predatory bear could emerge, the stuff of gore flicks like *Claws* and *Grizzly*. There probably wouldn't be more than two or three attacks before we hunted the killer bears down, but nonetheless, the media would have a big one. The story would be told a thousand times, which is not a good thing for the grizzly bear.

Even if a single bear doesn't go crazy and start looking at us for its next meal, there's still a chance for a public relations disaster. Consider this: Thousands of hikers, hunters, and other recreationists travel to every corner of the northern Rockies, into every blank spot on the map, looking for wild solitude, thereby creating many opportunities for encounters. The grizzly population as a whole may be getting less and less afraid of us. Simply because of the sheer number of opportunities, the number of people injured could increase.

Over the past fifteen years, we have had a steadily decreasing number of maulings, but we can only be so bear aware. We can't escape the fact that more and more often we share a remarkably small slice of landscape with a creature that could take its turn at the top of the food chain. Either a bear or a hiker makes a small mistake, and you have an encounter—and another front-page headline. Right now we're looking at the statistics and feeling good about our progress, but we could easily be at a statistical low point with nowhere to go but up.

What will happen when we have more encounters? How will we react to our favorite hiking trail or hunting area being frequently closed because of "bear activity"? Once or twice, we're okay with it, but more often or permanently—and in more and more places—well, maybe we aren't okay with it. Maybe then our level of social acceptance will slip.

That's one way it could happen, but there's another way social acceptance for the grizzly could plummet—even without an increase in the number of encounters. The political winds could turn against the grizzly.

An animal rights group could construct a plausible argument that big-game hunting in occupied grizzly habitat violates the Endangered Species Act (ESA) because it creates circumstances that result in dead bears. That group could file a lawsuit to prevent this "illegal take" (as defined in the ESA) and point to many documented cases where hunters or guides have shot grizzlies in camps, during the hunt, or over debates about the ownership of downed game. The same group could—and perhaps more easily—argue that black bear hunting in grizzly country results in dead grizzlies because of mistaken identity. They would have some hard evidence to back up this claim. We've worked hard on getting hunters to avoid mistaking grizzlies for black bears, but have we done enough?

Such litigation could result in stiff restrictions or closure of black bear seasons and possibly the same for elk and other big-game seasons in certain heavily hunted areas such as north and south of Yellowstone National Park. With this action, the animal rights group would drop a political bombshell that would have the opposite impact the plaintiff hoped for, i.e., helping the grizzly. It could rapidly reduce our tolerance for the grizzly—at least in the northern Rockies where hunting is popular and politics is local.

Fortunately, large environmental groups clearly see the likelihood of an extreme political backlash, so big-game hunters have a few best friends they don't know about like the Sierra Club and Defenders of Wildlife. We can depend on the national groups to not drag hunting into court in a misguided attempt to save the grizzly. However, there are dozens of smaller, possibly more extreme, organizations, and who knows what they'll do. Even a one-person-band group could severely hurt the grizzly's chances for survival with a poorly conceived lawsuit. Keep your fingers crossed on this one!

So perhaps the real enemy of the grizzly bear, in the short term at least, is not habitat destruction. Instead it might be an unexpected downturn in social acceptance. It doesn't make any difference how much habitat we have if we don't want grizzly bears.

Canada won't save us

In the past, people trying to keep the northern Rockies south of Canada a viable home for the grizzly had a safety net. Bears coming down from Canada through linkage zones have augmented grizzly populations in Idaho, Montana, and Washington. Now, those links are almost gone, and east-west highway corridors have become serious barriers to bear movement.

It's hard to overplay the significance of linkage zones to recovery efforts, and it isn't only linkage with Canadian bear populations. Recovery may, in fact, depend on our ability to preserve minimally developed safe zones where bears can travel between the Northern Continental Divide Ecosystem (NCDE) and the Cabinet-Yaak, Selkirks, and Greater Yellowstone Ecosystems, and perhaps the most important, the expansive Bitterroot Ecosystem, fifteen million acres of it, all missing the spirit of the great bear.

Right now these linkage zones are on the brink of becoming unusable by the grizzly, if they aren't already. If this happens, we are left with "islandized" populations, which are doomed to genetic isolation if not extinction.

No agency in any state or country decided to destroy a linkage zone, nor does any single development stand out as the culprit. Like grizzly habitat in general, the zones are nibbled to death one acre or one cabin at a time, a destructive but familiar trend.

PC bears

All bear scientists want biological correctness, not political correctness, to determine where the grizzly walks, but they should brace themselves for the inevitable. Politicians will have their day.

It might be biologically correct to allow grizzlies to live in Sun Valley or the Crazy Mountains or Jackson Hole, but is it politically correct? Not likely. It might be biologically correct to allow a population of grizzly bears to establish itself on the prairie habitat east of the Rocky Mountain Front, even as far east as the Charles M. Russell National Wildlife Refuge, but is it realistic, politically, to have grizzly bears in these areas? I think we know the answer to this question.

Our system is set up to make decisions based on election cycles, not life cycles, and that's one trend unlikely to change. That's politics, doing what needs to be done to get elected every two years, not doing what needs to be done to make sure a big hairy animal survives into the twenty-second century.

Spending money wisely

Optimism not backed up by science should not dictate decisions. It takes a long time to see the impact of any decision on a slow-reproducing species like the grizzly bear. At some point in time, probably about fifty years from now, it'll become clear whether the grizzly bear has been saved or doomed by the decisions we make today—such as delisting in a political atmosphere that makes relisting nearly impossible.

That's why we need to be so careful. Doing nothing might be the best option in many cases—for example, not delisting, not uplisting, not approving the Rock Creek Mine, not reopening hunting seasons, not building a road, not allowing trophy home development in key linkage zones, etc, etc.

When we don't know what to do, we need to study the situation and find out. That takes money. Lots of it, in fact, much more than bear scientists could ever expect to receive.

Sometimes, however, it's not a matter of money. It's more a matter of priorities. We don't need to spend any more money, for example, to determine that we need a secure, linked base of quality, roadless habitat to have a viable grizzly population, regardless of the number of bears in that population. Perhaps some of the research money we have available now should go to protecting key habitat and linkage corridors, by doing real, on-the-ground things that obviously make a difference, such as obliterating unused logging roads (as opposed to putting up a gate or Kelly hump that can be removed later) or retiring mining and grazing leases.

We already know that bears are moving into the ever-growing "urban interface," getting into garbage and then getting killed, a trend no bear manager expects to end anytime soon. Perhaps educating rural residents to remove or lock up bear attractants or teaching schoolchildren how to grow up in bear country, or organizing neighborhood watch groups in rural valleys to self-police residents should become priority uses of our limited funds—a higher priority, than getting a better (and possibly very expensive) estimate of the number of bears we *might* have.

We certainly need scientists to help us make the right decisions. However, scientists need to really think about how they spend their funding. Decade-long research projects to count bears might not be the best way to spend our money. Buying easements or bear-proof dumpsters, beefing up the number of state bear management specialists, or increasing school educational programs might all be much better uses for this money.

Everybody agrees we need a good foundation of science, but can some research wait while we address more immediate needs? Does it really matter whether we have 800 or 900 grizzly bears when we haven't learned to live with them? Does it matter how many grizzlies inhabit the Cabinet-Yaak if we allow this beleaguered ecosystem to become unlivable for the species? Should we spend money on education and habitat protection first, and then later try to determine population size and dynamics?

Tough questions, and I don't have the answers, but I hope scientists will ask them when allocating the shrinking pot of money available for any type of wildlife research and management.

Media bashing

Most bear people routinely blame the media for giving the grizzly the image of a bloodthirsty beast. And it's true the media has dramatized maulings to the detriment of the bear. Bashing the media, however, gets us nowhere. Instead we need to work with the press and change the message.

Here's one more reality check. Reporters aren't going to write what bear biologists want them to write. Instead they're going to give readers and viewers what they want. That's their job. Maulings make the front pages because editors know readers have an intense interest in bears. I personally doubt this will ever change. The grizzly will always be hot copy.

Instead of blaming the media and Hollywood for irresponsibile journalism, bear managers and environmentalists should help educate reporters. Instead of trying to convince the media to underplay or not cover bear maulings, we should try to change the message to make it less destructive to the grizzly's image.

The last thing bear scientists or managers should do is avoid reporters or snipe at the media from afar. Instead, they should view every incident (and every call from a reporter) as an opportunity to educate the public and improve—instead of worsen—the grizzly's public image.

United we stand, divided we fail

Visualize this: All stakeholders in the future of the grizzly bear (state and federal agencies, environmentalists, timber companies, miners, outfitters, ranchers, hunters, hikers, community leaders, local residents—even governors and U.S. senators—et al) in a room with a big clock in the middle of the table, like labor negotiators with a midnight deadline. They are there to decide the future of the grizzly bear.

Unrealistic? I don't think so, not if everybody really wanted to find the common ground. It's done all the time, and I see no reason why it couldn't happen here. The resulting compromise could come in something like this.

Environmentalists, for starters, need to agree with each other— and collectively seek a compromise and give up the strategy of endlessly delaying development long enough to let the next generation save the day. In addition, they would have to fold the "bear card," now used so frequently and effectively to trump resource development. A cessation of litigation—or at least a cease-fire—would likely be essential to any deal. Let's call it an out-of-court settlement.

The enviros would also have to give up some suitable habitat. They'd have to settle for enough habitat to guarantee an adequate population. This would likely turn out to be an expansion of current recovery zones (which were too small in the first place) and strict limitations on development in key linkage areas between them.

The grizzly bear is, of course, also a stakeholder. We don't need an expensive scientific study to tell us that the big bear will take everything it can get. It will continue to expand its range and conceivably could reclaim most of its historic range, if we'd allow it. So we need to draw some lines on the map. The bears can't see them, but we can.

When grizzly populations in the protected zones reach carrying capacity and bears start pioneering new—and unprotected—habitat, enviros need to take a deep breath and accept the eventuality that these bears probably will—and should—die an early death, even, perhaps, during carefully managed grizzly hunting seasons.

Enviros need to accept the biological fact that when a population of any species grows to a certain size and reaches carrying capacity, there must be controls. We can't have grizzly bears everywhere, and we can only have so many in designated habitats. Perhaps the best way to limit the population size of large animals is legal sport hunting, a bitter pill for some environmentalists, but certainly a key element of any compromise. State wildlife agencies won't sign on to any deal that doesn't include the option of grizzly hunting seasons.

Grizzly hunting appears to be the ultimate hot button for some environmentalists, but these strong emotions lack perspective. Carefully controlled hunting, certain to be limited by eco-politics (e.g., strict quotas, no shooting of females with cubs), would likely have a minor impact on grizzly populations. In fact, hunters might end up getting the habituated bears that would—and should—be killed anyway. No hunting would—or should—be allowed without strong science to back up recommendations. Yet any talk of grizzly hunting keeps enviros away from this negotiating table. I'll never understand why.

Many people who accept deer hunting consider bear hunting barbaric. Yet, is a deer so different from a bear? Is it because bears resemble humans when skinned? Is it because we rarely eat bear meat? Or is it an irrational emotion?

People who accept goose hunting loathe swan hunting, even though the swan is little more than an oversized snow goose. People might accept pheasant hunting, but not dove hunting. Is it because they coo in the morning? Swans and doves are elegant and beautiful, but are they more elegant and beautiful than a ring-necked pheasant or green-winged teal? I wonder.

Environmentalists should take a rational and unemotional look at hunting and approach it scientifically, like they do most issues. Hunting is just one piece, and a small piece at that, in a grand compromise to save the grizzly bear.

On the other hand, habitat protection would be a major part of any settlement. Resource developers and politicians would simply have to give up any hope of digging or cutting or drilling on large tracts of public land. They need to look in the mirror and say, "Okay, it has been a good fight, but it's over. Let's call it a game and be satisfied with 97 percent of the continental United States and take the other 3 percent off the table, forever."

This set-aside would encompass most existing roadless lands in the northern Rockies south of Canada. These last blank spots on the map wouldn't need to be "Big W" wilderness. They could have a less restrictive (and less politically volatile) designation—as long as it was enduring and prevented road building. Such a designation could, for example, allow such activities as semipermanent outfitter camps, aerial logging, or mountain biking and still provide the security the grizzly needs.

This wouldn't pass the litmus test for "balance" from an environmentalist's point of view, but if they could accept it, perhaps resource developers would follow suit. We all should. There was never a social contract between federal agencies and local communities to keep the recovery zones at their current size, and expanding them must be part of any compromise. Environmentalists will never accept—nor should they—only the PC areas (translate: national parks and wilderness areas) for the enduring home of the grizzly bear.

Local communities, including many that don't have grizzlies right now, would have to accept the fact that they'll have a big bear in their backyard. People living in semirural communities absolutely must learn and comply with the rules of living with bears. We shouldn't try to reach this goal through enforcement because there'd never be enough government money to achieve adequate compliance, and the enforcers would only foster "Big Brother" resentment among westerners. Instead we need an intense social intolerance for anybody not properly handling garbage or other bear attractants. Leaving garbage out for bears should have the same level of acceptance as spanking your child in public or smoking in church.

With a combination of quality education and peer pressure, rural residents can learn to live with bears. If we do our part, the bears will probably stay out of trouble and maybe even die of old age.

Hikers, hunters, mountain bikers, anglers, and other recreationists must religiously follow the rules of bear awareness to continue to reduce the number of encounters. Each mauling worsens the grizzly's persona and makes recovery efforts more difficult. Recreationists must also accept the additional risk, however small, they take when entering the grizzly's domain as part of the deal—or, in my humble opinion, consider it an added attraction.

Wildlife agencies need to get over the endless state vs. federal debate and work together. States should have control of wildlife management, but we can't let this age-old debate overshadow the goal of doing what's best for the bear. State control of wildlife with some federal oversight solves this problem. Meanwhile, environmentalists need to overcome their paranoia that state wildlife agencies only want to unleash legions of trophy hunters.

That's it. That's all it would take to stand united and end the controversy over saving the grizzly bear. Am I dreaming when I think this could happen? I hope not.

Extinction?

I hate to say this word out loud because it's profane. Nobody likes to think about it, but nobody can deny that it's one of the grizzly's future options. Biologically, the grizzly will probably always exist in zoos and drive-through wildlife parks. In my mind, however, the day the wild grizzly population declined to a point where it couldn't recover would mark the day the species went extinct. After the last grizzly is gone, the mountains might look the same, but you wouldn't be able to "feel" them the way you can when you share them with the big bear. Those mountains in Glacier or the Absaroka or the Bob or Yellowstone or the Cabinets, well, they'd just be plain, ordinary mountains.

More than a bear

The grizzly is an umbrella species. Protecting grizzly habitat protects habitat for many other species. It's tempting for those who favor resource development over preservation to say we would do just fine without the grizzly. As far as we know, no other species depends on the grizzly bear to survive. And people get by nicely in California and Colorado without grizzly bears, even though they used to have them. That could prove to be true in Montana and Wyoming, too, but the states certainly wouldn't be the same—livable, even pleasant, but not the same, because the wild heart of the land will have been ripped out.

While working for a resolution to the seemingly never-ending controversy over grizzly bears, we should understand what we're doing. We aren't merely saving grizzly bears. We're saving habitat for many species along with the last of wild North America.

Where will the grizzly walk?

Unless we have a dramatic downturn in social acceptance, we'll have grizzlies in designated national parks and wildernesses for a long time. It's not only biologically but also politically correct to have grizzlies in these protected areas.

But bear experts say that's not enough. To achieve recovery the grizzly population must expand into surrounding habitat that's not so politically correct—onto private land or more of the public domain, some already roaded, some de facto wilderness, and all on the menu of private enterprise.

People aren't going to stay out of this unprotected public domain. Instead, we'll have to somehow share it with the silver-tipped bear, like we do in the national parks and wilderness areas, and we'll continue hiking, hunting, and mountain biking with no chance of this ever changing.

And the privately owned grizzly habitat? This private land is usually scenic and semiremote, so rest assured that we aren't going to stop building roads and homes in these rural valleys. Some environmentalists think zoning or other regulation can control development of key private-land habitat, but I see that as unfounded optimism. This is, after all, the West where the frontier spirit never dies and private property rights remain sacred. Others think private land can become public land, but there's no political support for this, let alone enough money.

Predictably, bears won't stop coming into rural communities. Perhaps they're hyperphagic females with cubs lured there by an uncontrolled substance called garbage (translate: bear drugs) or apple trees, bird feeders, dog food, and horse pellets. Or perhaps they're adventuresome subadults, like the Ninemile Grizzly, pioneering new territory. Regardless of the reason, bears will move into these privately owned valleys just as certainly as people will move there.

The point is, we can't keep bears and people apart—not in rural communities on private land, not on unprotected public land, not even in the deepest wilderness. This brings me to the punch line. Assuming we can learn to live with grizzlies around our second homes and wilderness campsites as well as learn to accept grizzlies on the mountains in our backyards and then peacefully coexist with them, well, then, the answer to that question—where will the grizzly walk— is simple. The grizzly will walk where we allow it.

A Few Bears I've Met
and What I Learned from Them

Date: May 15, 1973
Place: Behind my office, Helena, Montana
Lesson: I heard the requiem sound.

In the spring of 1973, a female grizzly and her two cubs wandered into a campground in Glacier National Park. They were tranquilized and moved to the park's interior, far away from campgrounds and "safe," or so everybody thought.

Twelve days later, a stockman shot the female near Bigfork, Montana, about 75 air miles away, after she killed a sheep. What compelled the mother bear to take her cubs and flee the park's safety, swim the Middle Fork of the Flathead River, climb the Great Northern Mountains, swim either the Hungry Horse Reservoir or the South Fork of the Flathead River, cross the Swan Range, and enter the heavily populated Flathead Valley remains a mystery. But it meant the end for this matriarch. For her crime of killing one sheep, she was executed.

After the shooting, game wardens found the two cubs huddled helplessly nearby. Too young to survive without a mother, the orphans were brought to the fish and game department's Helena office. Their new home was an 8-foot-square concrete-floored cubicle in the department's shelter for orphaned wildlife. Their cage was only a stone's throw from my office, and I could hear them bawling as people filed past their pen, exclaiming how "cute" they were but missing the significance of what they saw.

Others from my office regularly visited the shelter, but I could muster the courage only once or twice. As I looked through the chain-link fence and the cubs stared back, I could only think of the grizzlies I'd seen in earlier years, especially the two cubs crossing Starvation Creek. Those cubs were exactly in the right place, and these cubs were exactly in the wrong place. Just as I'll always remember those few seconds when I was mesmerized by the majestic mother and her family at Starvation Creek, I'll never forget these stare-downs with the two orphans.

This was hard on me. These two newborns, which seemed so synonymous with wildness, would have to give up their wild birthright to survive, even if it meant a lifetime of exile. There would be no going back to their proper place, the splendor of Glacier's wilderness. I actually considered bringing my hunting rifle and finishing them right there. It would've been better for them.

I didn't, though, and the zookeeper came and carried the cubs away to mature in a big-city zoo. Certainly this must be a fate worse than death for a grizzly bear. After enjoying a few brief months of wildness, the cubs were condemned to a cage where they must endure hordes of humans trooping by, gawking across the moat, tossing in peanuts, but not understanding. I only hoped that the reminiscence of their momentary freedom was etched too dimly on their memories as to not haunt them for the decades to come.

These two cubs taught me that if the mighty grizzly, the symbol of the wilderness, our most magnificent mammal, ever becomes extinct, this will be the final curtain call—the requiem sound will be the merciful whimper of a homeless, caged cub.

*Escudilla still hangs on the horizon, but when you see it, you
no longer think of the bear. It's only a mountain now.*
—Aldo Leopold, *A Sand County Almanac*

Bibliography

Books

Bailey, Vernon. *Biological Survey of Texas*. U.S. Department of Agriculture, Biological Survey. Washington D.C.: Government Printing Office, 1905.

———. *Mammals of North Dakota*. U.S. Department of Agriculture, Biological Survey. Washington, D.C.: Government Printing Office, 1926.

———. *Mammals of New Mexico*. U.S. Department of Agriculture, Biological Survey. Washington, D.C.: Government Printing Office, 1931.

Bell, Major Horace. *On the Old West Coast*. Edited by Lanier Bartlett. New York: William Morrow, 1930.

Brown, Gary. *Great Bear Almanac*. New York: Lyons & Burford, 1993.

Busch, Robert. *The Grizzly Almanac*. Guilford, Conn.: Lyons Press, 2000.

Chadwick, Douglas H. *Yellowstone to Yukon*. Washington, D.C.: National Geographic Society, 2000.

Cockrum, E. L. *Mammals of Kansas*. Vol. 7. Lawrence, Kans.: University of Kansas Publications, Museum of Natural History, 1952.

DeVoto, Bernard, ed. *The Journals of Lewis and Clark*. Boston: Houghton Mifflin, 1953.

Fischer, Hank. *Wolf Wars*. Helena, Mont.: Falcon, 1995.

Frome, Michael. *Battle for the Wilderness*. New York: Praeger, 1974.

Haynes, Bessie, and Edgar Haynes. *The Grizzly Bear*. Norman, Okla.: University of Oklahoma Press, 1966.

Herrero, Stephen. *Bear Attacks: Their Causes and Avoidance*. New York: Lyons & Burford, 1985.

———. *Bear Attacks: Their Causes and Avoidance*. 2d edition. Guilford, Conn.: Lyons Press, 2002.

Kaniut, Larry. *Alaska Bear Tales*. Anchorage, Alaska: Alaska Northwest Books, 1983.

————. *More Alaska Bear Tales*. Issaquah, Wash.: Sammamish Press, 1989.

Leopold, Aldo. *A Sand County Almanac*. New York: Oxford University Press, 1949.

Leopold, A. Starker. *Wildlife in Mexico: The Game Birds and Mammals*. Berkeley and Los Angeles: University of California Press; London: Cambridge University Press, 1959.

McClintock, Walter. *The Old North Trail*. London: Macmillan, 1910.

McCracken, Harold. *The Beast That Walks Like a Man*. Garden City, N.Y.: Hanover House, 1955.

McMillion, Scott. *Mark of the Grizzly*. Helena, Mont.: Falcon, 1998.

Mills, Enos A. *The Grizzly: Our Greatest Wild Animal*. Boston: Houghton Mifflin, 1919.

Muir, Jean. *The Adventures of Grizzly Adams*. New York: Putman, 1969.

Olsen, Jack. *Night of the Grizzlies*. New York: Putman, 1969.

Prodgers, Jeanette. *The Only Good Bear Is a Dead Bear: A Collection of the West's Best Bear Stories*. Helena, Mont.: Falcon, 1986.

Robinson, Doane. *Encyclopedia of South Dakota: Pierre*. Published by the author, 1925.

Russell, Andy. *Grizzly Country*. New York: Alfred Knopf, 1968.

Sandford, Robert William. *Year of the Great Bear*. Canmore, Alberta: Year of the Great Bear Steering Committee, 2001.

Schneider, Bill. *Where the Grizzly Walks*. Missoula, Mont.: Mountain Press, 1977.

————. *Bear Aware: The Quick Reference Bear Country Survival Guide*. Guilford, Conn.: The Globe Pequot Press, 2001.

Schoonmaker, Walter. *The World of the Grizzly Bear*. Philadelphia: J. B. Limmincott Company, 1968.

Schullery, Paul. *The Bears of Yellowstone*. Boulder, Colo.: Roberts Rinehardt, Inc., 1986.

Stevens, Montague. *Meet Mr. Grizzly*. Albuquerque, N.M.: University of New Mexico Press, 1944.

Storer, Tracy I., and Lloyd P. Trevis Jr. *California Grizzly*. Berkeley and Los Angeles: University of California Press, 1955.

Wilkinson, Todd. *Science under Siege*. Boulder, Colo.: Johnson Books, 1998.

Willcox, Louisa. "Bear Necessities: Grizzlies, Wilderness, and the Science of Extinction." In *Wild Earth: Wild Ideas for a World Out of Balance,* edited by Tom Butler. Minneapolis, Minn.: Milkweed Press, 2002.

Wright, William H. *The Grizzly Bear: The Narrative of a Hunter-Naturalist.* New York: Charles Scribner's Sons, 1909.

Periodicals and Newspapers

Albert, Gene. "Glacier: Beleaguered Park of 1975." *National Parks & Conservation* (November 1975).

Arbour, Vince. "Bears and The Man." *Earth* (November 1971).

Auchly, Bruce. "On the Front Lines." *Montana Outdoors* (November/December 2002).

Bass, Rick. "Grizzly's Last Stand." *Time,* 5 September 2002.

Chadwick, Douglas. "Dreams of the Great Bear." *Defenders* (February 1976).

Clark, Frank. "The Killing of Old Ephraim." *Utah Fish and Game Bulletin* (September 1952).

Cole, Glen F. "Management Involving Grizzly Bears and Humans in Yellowstone National Park, 1970-73." *BioScience* (June 1974).

Craighead, Frank, Jr. "They're Killing Yellowstone's Grizzlies." *National Wildlife* (October/November 1973).

Fischer, Hank. "New Home for the Griz." *Defenders* (winter 1993).

———. "Bears and the Bitterroot." *Defenders* (winter 1996).

Franke, Mary Ann. "A Grand Experiment: 100 Years of Fisheries Management in Yellowstone." *Yellowstone Science* (fall 1996).

Frome, Michael. "Do Grizzlies Face a Grisly Future?" *Field & Stream* (January 1974).

———. "The Grizzly's Needs Should Come Before Man's." *Defenders* (February 1976).

Gilbert, Bil. "The Great Grizzly Controversy." *Audubon* (January 1976).

Herrero, Stephen. "Man and the Grizzly Bear (present, past, but future?)." *BioScience* (1 November 1970).

———. "Human Injury Inflicted by Grizzly Bears." *Science* (6 November 1970).

Housholder, Bob "The Grizzly Bear in Arizona." *Arizona Wildlife Sportsman* (July 1961).

Johnson, A. Stephen. "Man, Grizzly & National Parks." *National Parks & Conservation* (February 1972).

———. "Yellowstone's Grizzlies: Endangered or Prospering?" *Defenders of Wildlife News* (October 1973).

Jonkel, Charles. "Media Coverage Threatens Grizzlies." *Montana Kaimin* (University of Montana), 17 October 1975.

———. "Of Men and Bears." *Western Wildlands* (University of Montana) (winter 1975).

Lachenmeier, Rudy R. "The Endangered Species Act of 1973: Preservation of Pandemonium?" *Environmental Law* (Northwestern School of Law, Portland, Oregon) (fall 1974).

Long, Ben. "A Hunter, an Elk, and a Grizzly." *Bugle* (March/April 2002).

Moment, Gairdner B. "Bears: The Need for a New Sanity in Wildlife Conservation." *BioScience* (December 1968).

———. "Bears and Conservation: Realities and Recommendations." *BioScience* (November 1969).

Rearden, Jim. "The Status of Alaska's Big Bears." *Outdoor Life* (May 1976).

"Report on Yellowstone Grizzly study rejects 'facing extinction' charge." *National Park Service Newsletter* (September 1974).

Russell, Andy. "Are Grizzlies Man Killers?" *BC* (British Columbia) *Outdoors* (December 1968).

———. "Grizzly Country . . . a vanishing heritage." *BC* (British Columbia) *Outdoors* (February 1976).

Schneider, Bill. "The Mighty Grizzly . . . What Does the Future Hold?" *Western Outdoors* (October 1975).

———. "The Story Behind the Grizzly Bear Controversy." *Denver Post Empire Magazine*, 16 November 1975.

———. "The Grizzly: Is He Villain or Victim?" *Outdoor Life* (November 1975).

———. "Will the Grizzly Attack?" *National Wildlife* (February/March 1977).

Stringham, Stephan F. "Smokey and Mirrors: The War Between Science and Pseudoscience in Conserving the Grizzly Bear." *Wild Earth Magazine* (fall 2002).

Taylor, Ted M. "Vanished Monarch of the Sierra." *The American West* (May/June 1976).

Walcheck, Ken. "Lewis and Clark Meet the Awesome White Bear." *Montana Outdoors* (September/October 1976).

Wilkinson, Todd. "Gambling With Grizzlies." *Wildlife Conservation* (November/December 2001).

Wondrak, Alice K. "Yellowstone Wildlife Watching." *Yellowstone Science* (summer 2002).

Zaccagnini, Ronald. "Is the Grizzly Gone?" *Colorado Outdoors* (July/August 1975).

Zochert, Donald. "Grizzly Attacks Remain a Mystery." *Chicago Daily News,* 10 October 1976.

Brochures, Technical Reports and Government Documents

Blackfeet Indian Reservation. *Bear Management Plan and Guidelines for Bear Management.* December 1, 1998.

Craighead Wildlife-Wildlands Institute. *Status of the Yellowstone Grizzly Bear Population: Has It Recovered, Should It Be Delisted?* by John J. Craighead. October 1998.

The Endangered Species Act of 1973. 1973.

Flathead National Forest and Montana Department of Fish, Wildlife & Parks. *Living with Grizzlies,* n.d.

Fremont, Wyoming, County Commission. *Grizzly Bear Deemed Unacceptable Species.* Resolution 2002-04. March 12, 2002.

Herrero, Stephen. "Conflicts between Man and Grizzly Bears in the National Parks of North America." In *Bears—Their Biology and Management,* a selection of papers presented at the Third International Conference on Bear Research and Management, International Union for Conservation of Nature and Natural Resources, Morges, Switzerland, June 1974.

Interagency Conservation Strategy Team. *Draft Conservation Strategy for the Grizzly Bear in the Yellowstone Area.* March 2000.

Kempthorne, Dirk, governor of Idaho. *State of the State Address.* January 8, 2001.

Montana Department of Fish, Wildlife & Parks. *Investigative Team Report: Grizzly Bear Attack at the Blackfoot-Clearwater Wildlife Management Area.* October 30, 2001.

———. *Grizzly Bear Management Plan for Southwestern Montana.* April 2002.

———. *Montana Regulations: Black Bear.* 2002

———. *Montana Regulations: Deer and Elk.* 2002.

———. *How to Hunt Safely in Grizzly Country,* n.d.

National Park Service, Glacier National Park. *Bear Management Plan and Guidelines.* March 2001.

National Park Service, Yellowstone National Park. *Yellowstone Resources and Issues.* 2001.

Rock Creek Alliance. *Rock Creek Mine: What's at Stake and Why We Must Act Now,* n.d.

Sierra Club Grizzly Bear Ecosystems Project. *The Bear Essentials for Recovery,* by Louisa Willcox and David Ellenberger. May 2000.

Sierra Club Grizzly Bear Ecosystems Project. *The American West: Big Enough for All of Us?,* n.d.

———. *The Bear Truth: Once the Habitat Is Gone, So Is the Grizzly,* n.d.

———. *Guard the Grizzly Campaign.* N.d.

USDA Forest Service. *A Population Analysis of the Grizzly Bear,* by John J. Craighead, Joel R. Varney, and Frank Craighead, Jr. September 1974.

U.S. Fish and Wildlife Service. *Proposed Rules.* February 12, 1993.

———. *Grizzly Bear Recovery Plan (Revised),* by Christopher Servheen. September 1993.

———. *Analysis of the Current and Future Availability and Distribution of Suitable Habitat for Grizzly Bears in the Transboundary Selkirk and Cabinet-Yaak Ecosystems,* by Troy Merrill. 1997.

———. *Grizzly Bear Recovery in the Bitterroot Ecosystem, Final Environmental Impact Statement.* March 2000.

————. *Identification and Management of Linkage Zones for Grizzly Bears between the Large Blocks of Public Land in the Northern Rocky Mountains,* by Christopher Servheen, et al. September 4, 2001.

————. *Record of Decision and Statement of Findings for the Environmental Impact Statement on Grizzly Bear Recovery in the Bitterroot Ecosystem, Final Rule.* November 2000.

U. S. Geological Survey, Biological Resources Division. *Monitoring Grizzly Bear Populations Using DNA,* by Katherine C. Kendall and Lisette Waits. August 1, 2001.

————. *Grizzly Bears,* by Katherine C. Kendall, et al. May 14, 2002.

U.S. Geological Survey, Media Advisory Committee. *The Hair of the Bear: USGS Releases Grizzly Bear Numbers in Glacier National Park.* May 18, 2000.

U.S. Geological Survey, NRMSC Research Division. *Grizzly Bear and Black Bear Ecology.* November 4, 2002.

Varley, John D. and Paul Schullery, ed. *The Yellowstone Lake Crisis: Controlling a Lake Trout Invasion.* A report prepared for the director of the National Park Service. 1995.

Wyoming Game and Fish Department. *Wyoming Grizzly Bear Management Plan.* February 2002.

Year of the Great Bear Steering Committee. *The Interpretive Manual for the Year of the Great Bear,* by R. W. Sandford. 2001.

Index

The Author

Bill Schneider is the author of seventeen books and numerous magazine articles on wildlife, outdoor recreation, and environmental issues. For more information about Bill Schneider's books visit www.billschneider. net.